Mantle Nance's study of the con... Trinitarians and Unitarians ... marked by careful scholarship ..., although committed to the supernaturalism of Trinitarian belief, seeks to be fair and judicious throughout. Far from being a good, but dusty, relic of past concerns, it touches on many of the most crucial issues facing human thought and destiny today (or at any time). It is very much alive; a penetrating word for our times. ... Dr. Nance is not a hagiographer, for he accurately shows the differences between some of the Columbia (South Carolina) theologians and Calvin himself (whom they wished to follow). He shows, for instance, that the Columbia men, unlike Charles Hodge of Princeton, and unlike Calvin, were hesitant to ascribe autotheos ('self-deity') to the Son and the Spirit. Nance's explication of Trinitarian worship is greatly needed by so many evangelical churches, which seem effectively not to be far from a basically Unitarian approach (with some emphasizing the Father, others the Son, and others the Holy Spirit). What he writes on pages 202 (and following) should be of immense encouragement to ministers and congregations who want to worship the Triune God in Spirit and in truth.

DOUGLAS KELLY

Professor of Theology Emeritus, Reformed Theological Seminary,
Charlotte, North Carolina

If questioned, many people would affirm that they believe in God. But the real question is, 'Who is your God?' Is He the God of the Unitarian or the God presented in the Scriptures—God the Father, God the Son, and God the Holy Spirit, the mysterious 'three in one'—the God of the Trinity? Dr Mantle Nance provides an engaging historical consideration of this century's long debate as he discusses how early Southern Presbyterians in America encountered the popular and growing Unitarian influence in the 19th century, with the Presbyterians prevailing in the bustling religious regions of Columbia, SC, Charleston, SC, and New Orleans. If you love church history and desire to know our Triune God in a more glorious fashion, then *The Adorable Trinity: Standing for Orthodoxy in Nineteenth Century America* is a must read. I highly recommend it solely for the benefit of worshipping our majestic God, who has existed forever—Father, Son and Spirit—in constant love, communion, and glorious unity of essence and purpose. The reader will be encouraged in his or her walk with God.

ROD A. CULBERTSON
Associate Professor of Pastoral Theology
Reformed Theological Seminary, Charlotte, North Carolina

This book is a fascinating look at a neglected chapter in the history of the old South. Nineteenth-century Presbyterians associated with Columbia Seminary, concerned about Unitarian influence in the South, ably defended Trinitarian theology as the only answer to man's deepest need for forgiveness before a holy God. The author offers an inspiring account of southern theologians' convincing arguments that the Trinity is foundational to every aspect of Christian faith and practice. The book will be a delight to anyone interested in this era of America history.

S. DONALD FORTSON
Professor of Church History and Pastoral Theology
Reformed Theological Seminary, Charlotte, North Carolina

A timely, careful, well-documented study of Southern Presbyterian orthodoxy on the doctrine of the Trinity. It is thoughtful, clear and occasionally bold where it needs to be. Nance's point is that we need to recover a robustly Trinitarian shape to ministry in all of its aspects. And he is correct. The contents of this fine book will do much to bring a much-needed reformation to the twenty-first century church.

DEREK W. H. THOMAS
Senior Minister, First Presbyterian Church, Columbia, South Carolina
Chancellor's Professor, Reformed Theological Seminary
Teaching Fellow, Ligonier Ministries

In modern evangelical scholarship, there is commendably an emphasis on Trinitarian issues. This emphasis is usually accompanied by a throw-away line that in the past two centuries

American evangelicals were close to functioning Unitarians. Nance's detailed historical scholarship concerning Southern American Presbyterians significantly engaging with Unitarians in the 1800's cries out for some nuances to that throw-away line.

This study is fascinating in several respects. (1) Most, including me until recently, do not even know that there were Unitarians in the American South in the 1800's that were being engaged by the Southern Presbyterians. (2) The Presbyterians were keen to emphasize that an orthodox understanding of the Trinity significantly affected both faith and practice. (3) There are a large number of non-published primary sources used in this study that add much 'local' color and stimulate the reader.

This book is fascinating as to the historical details and heart-warming as to the defense of the 'Adorable Trinity.'

ROBERT CARA
Provost and Chief Academic Officer
Hugh and Sallie Reaves Professor of New Testament,
Reformed Theological Seminary, Charlotte, North Carolina

There is a certain lineage of southern Presbyterian theologians who, whatever their defects, nurtured a doctrine and devotion so intensely, pervasively, and uniquely trinitarian that they have long stood in need of closer study. What can account for this revival of excitement about the doctrine of the Trinity at this particular time and place? This book unlocks at least one part of the secret: these theologians and pastors knew themselves to be contending against an organized unitarian movement. By establishing this polemical context for their work, and then reading them sympathetically against this background, Nance has shed much light on an often ignored phase of American theological history.

FRED SANDERS
Professor of Systematic Theology, Torrey Honors Institute,
Biola University, La Mirada, California

A wonderful story of the triumph of the gospel through three faithful servants, who were giants of the southern Presbyterian church in the 19th Century. This book combines history and theology in a clear, accessible and edifying way. It reminds us why the biblical doctrine of the Trinity is central to the Christian faith and vital for our salvation. Even more, this work speaks to the heart, drawing believers in Christ to greater adoration of the Triune God.

WILLIAM B. BARCLEY
Senior Pastor, Sovereign Grace Presbyterian Church,
Charlotte, North Carolina

With interest in the Trinity blossoming today broadly in both academia and practical ministry, Mantle Nance's contribution to the field is most welcome. He introduces us to the labors of a forgotten portion of Christendom on this provocative subject— the nineteenth-century theologians of Old Columbia Seminary— James Henley Thornwell, Thomas Smyth, and Benjamin Morgan Palmer. Tossed out with the bathwater of sectionalism, slavery, and Civil War, their almost disremembered struggles against the Unitarian rationalism of their day make the Columbians a fascinating read on so many levels. Nance does not spare them where they fall short of their own Trinitarian belief. But neither does he fail to grasp the creative core of their insight: that the Trinity is not an abstract doctrinal loci but rather an immense dynamus for both faith and life.

W. DUNCAN RANKIN
Adjunct Professor of Systematic Theology, Reformed Theological
Seminary, Houston, Texas

# THE
# ADORABLE
# TRINITY

Standing for Orthodoxy in
Nineteenth-Century America

## MANTLE NANCE

**ⅢENTOR**
*Encouraging Christians to Think*

Copyright © Mantle Nance 2020

paperback ISBN 978-1-5271-0518-8
epub ISBN 978-1-5271-0569-0
mobi ISBN 978-1-5271-0570-6

10 9 8 7 6 5 4 3 2 1

Published in 2020
in the
Mentor Imprint
by
Christian Focus Publications Ltd,
Geanies House, Fearn, Ross-shire,
IV20 1TW, Great Britain.

www.christianfocus.com

Cover design by
Pete Barnsley

Printed and bound by
Bell & Bain

# Contents

Acknowledgements................................................. 9

Abbreviations..................................................... 11

1 Introduction to the Contemporary Relevance and
  Historical Context of our Study..................................... 13

SECTION 1: Columbia: James Henley Thornwell and
           Thomas Cooper................................................25

2 The Columbia Theatre: Thornwell versus Cooper...............27

3 Thornwell's Trinitarian Counteroffensive......................... 41

4 Thornwell's Theological Emphases Viewed in Light of
  His Stand for Trinitarianism....................................... 61

SECTION 2: Charleston: Thomas Smyth and
           Samuel Gilman................................................95

5 The Charleston Theatre: Smyth versus Gilman ..................97

6 Gilman and Smyth Battle for the Soul of Charleston........ 109

7 Smyth's Articles on the Trinity................................... 127

SECTION 3: New Orleans: Benjamin Morgan Palmer and
           Theodore Clapp ............................................. 149

8 The Palmer Family and Unitarianism ........................... 151

9 Theodore Clapp and the History of First Presbyterian
  Church of New Orleans............................................ 167

10 Palmer's Stand for the Trinity in New Orleans ................ 177

11 Historical Significance and Contemporary Relevance
of the Columbians' Stand for the Trinity ..................... 203

Appendix 1 ............................................................. 209

Appendix 2 ............................................................. 211

Appendix 3 ............................................................. 215

Appendix 4 ............................................................. 219

Bibliography ........................................................... 223

# Acknowledgements

Many thanks to the family and friends who, in addition to their prayers and encouragement, gave financially to afford me the privilege of researching and writing *The Adorable Trinity*. Much gratitude is due to friends at Sovereign Grace Presbyterian Church (Charlotte, NC), Union Hill Baptist Church (Thurmond, NC), Newberry Associate Reformed Presbyterian Church (Newberry, SC), and Ballantyne Presbyterian Church (Charlotte, NC).

Thanks to Jim Atkins for being supportive throughout and praying it through; David and Marie Eglinton for your generous and humbling hospitality; Christie Kelley for your constant administrative assistance; and Brandon Giella for your editorial and technical support.

Thanks to Nick Needham and Rob Shillaker for your skillful guidance and wisdom; Martin Cameron, Wayne Sparkman, Nathan Saunders, Emily Corbin, Steve Martin, Brandon Smith, Jason Piland, and Duncan Rankin for your invaluable research advice and assistance; Bobby Roberts, Jacob Jastrzembski, Phoebe Pritchett, Michael Moon, Josh Duemler, Mark Ross, Bob Cara, Rod Culbertson, Blair Smith, Jim Curtis, Jamie Grant, John McIntosh, Bruce Ritchie, Caroline Kelly, Philip Ross, and Malcolm Maclean for your helpful feedback; Rosanna Burton for your editorial guidance; and Douglas Kelly, for introducing me to many of the topics this work explores through your teaching, writing, and personal influence, and for teaching me through your example the joy of knowing, depending on, and praying to the Triune God of grace.

Thanks to my sons, Jackson Nehemiah and Aaron Palmer Hays Nance, for your persevering, supportive, and cheerful attitudes while so much of your daddy's time was taken up with this project, and for your powerful intercessions for its completion, and to my beautiful wife, Sally, for your unwavering love, indefatigable support, and effectual prayers throughout this project and our life together. You truly are my steel magnolia.

Most of all, I give thanks to the Father, the Son, and the Holy Spirit, for loving me, saving me, and enabling me to complete this project. *Soli Trinitati Adorabili Gloria!*

# *Abbreviations*

BMP    Benjamin Morgan Palmer

CBK    C. Benton Kline, Jr. Special Collections and Archives, John Bulow Campbell Library, Columbia Theological Seminary

CLS    Charleston Library Society

CW    *Collected Writings* of James Henley Thornwell

JHT    James Henley Thornwell

JHTP    James Henley Thornwell Papers

LOC    Library of Congress

RWSL    Ralph W. Steen Library, Stephen F. Austin State University

SCHS    South Carolina Historical Society

SCL    South Caroliniana Library

SCSR    Scottish Common Sense Realism

SPR    *Southern Presbyterian Review*

TC    Thomas Cooper

TJ    Thomas Jefferson

TJP    Thomas Jefferson Papers, Library of Congress

TS    Thomas Smyth

WSM    William Smith Morton Library, Union Presbyterian Seminary

# 1

# *Introduction to the Contemporary Relevance and Historical Context of our Study*

I N recent decades, Trinitarian theologians have lamented a lack of emphasis on the doctrine of the Trinity in contemporary Christian theology and practice: 'In modern times it is unfortunately the case that the enormous importance of the doctrine of the Trinity, and its revolutionary implications, have tended to be lost from sight, and sometimes to be treated as rather irrelevant, or only of peripheral significance for Christian faith and living.'[1] Indeed, 'most Christian people, while remembering the term "Trinity," have forgotten the central place the doctrine is to hold in the Christian life. It is rarely the topic of sermons and Bible studies, rarely the object of adoration and worship .... [The Trinity] is ignored in such a way that even among those who correctly understand the doctrine, it does not hold the place it should in the proclamation of the Gospel message, nor in the life of the individual believer in prayer, worship, and service.'[2]

---

1. Thomas Torrance, *The Christian Doctrine of God, One Being Three Persons* (Edinburgh: T&T Clark, 1996), p. 8.

2. James White, *The Forgotten Trinity: Recovering the Heart of Christian Belief* (Minneapolis, MN: Bethany House Publishers, 1988), p. 16.

Sadly, 'when it comes to the doctrine of the Trinity, evangelicals have underachieved.'[3] As a result, 'the ordinary Christian in the Western world who hears or reads the word "God" does not immediately and inevitably think of the triune Being – Father, Son, and Spirit … [but rather] of a supreme monad.'[4] Many Christians suppose that 'the doctrine of the Trinity is a piece of abstract theorizing, perhaps necessary as a test of Christian belief, but of little further interest.'[5] The doctrine is often taught in a way that 'tends to leave us cold' and turns God into a 'mathematical conundrum'. It is time to turn from cold abstraction to the practical 'warmth' of thinking, worshipping, and living 'Trinitarianly'.[6]

Modern writers looking for historical examples of robust Trinitarianism have mainly turned to church fathers, medieval theologians, and John Calvin. However, a handful of recent studies

---

3. Robert Letham, *The Holy Trinity In Scripture, History, Theology, and Worship* (Phillipsburg, NJ: P&R Publishing, 2004), back cover.

4. Lesslie Newbigin, *The Open Secret* (Grand Rapids, MI: Eerdmans, 1995), p. 27.

5. Colin Gunton, *Father, Son and Holy Spirit: Essays Toward a Fully Trinitarian Theology*, edited by Colin E. Gunton (London: T&T Clark, 2003), p. 6.

6. Ibid., pp. 6-18. For similar analysis: Robert Letham, *Through Western Eyes, Eastern Orthodoxy: A Reformed Perspective* (Fearn, Scotland: Mentor, 2007), p. 238; Fred Sanders, 'The Trinity.' In *Mapping Modern Theology: A Thematic and Historical Introduction* (Edited by Kelly M. Kapic and Bruce L. McCormack. Grand Rapids, MI: Baker Academic, 2012), p. 21-45; Michael Horton, *Covenant and Salvation: Union with Christ* (Louisville: Westminster John Knox, 2007), p. 136; James Torrance, *Worship, Community & The Triune God of Grace* (Downers Grove, IL: InterVarsity Press, 1996), p. 20; Gerald Bray, 'Evangelicals Losing Their Way: The Doctrine of the Trinity.' In *The Compromised Church: The Present Evangelical Crisis*, pp. 53-65. Edited by John Armstrong (Wheaton, IL: Crossway, 1998), *The Doctrine of God* (Leicester: InterVarsity Press, 1993), pp. 139, 246; Donald Fairbairn, *Life in the Trinity: An Introduction to Theology with the Help of the Church Fathers* (Downers Grove, IL: IVP Academic, 2009), p. 11; Bruce Ware, *Father, Son, & Holy Spirit: Relationships, Roles & Relevance* (Wheaton, IL: Crossway Books, 2005), pp. 156-157; Alister McGrath, 'The Doctrine of the Trinity: An Evangelical Reflection.' In *God the Holy Trinity: Reflections on Christian Faith and Practice* (Edited by Timothy George. Grand Rapids, MI: Baker Academic, 2006), p. 27; Michael Reeves, *Delighting in the Trinity: An Introduction to the Christian Faith* (Downers Grove, IL: IVP Academic, 2012), pp. 9-18.

have highlighted the Trinitarianism of Christians after Calvin such as John Owen, Jonathan Edwards and Herman Bavinck.[7]

By exploring the lives, ministries and theological contributions of three nineteenth century pastor-scholars connected to Columbia Seminary, we will discover additional examples of Christians who championed the doctrine and implications of the Trinity. We will examine how they faced challenges to the Trinitarian faith and how those challenges shaped their theological emphases and ministries. We will detail the little-known conflict between Unitarianism and Trinitarianism in the nineteenth century American South, and we will consider what today's church can learn and apply from the Columbians' stand for 'the adorable Trinity'.[8]

---

7. Brian Kay, *Trinitarian Spirituality: John Owen and the Doctrine of God in Western Devotion* (Milton Keynes, UK: Paternoster, 2007); Amy Pauw, *The Supreme Harmony of All: The Trinitarian Theology of Jonathan Edwards* (Grand Rapids, MI: Eerdmans, 2002); Steven Studebaker, *Jonathan Edwards' Social Augustinian Trinitarianism in Historical and Contemporary Perspectives* (Piscataway, NJ: Gorgias Press, 2008); William Schweitzer, *God Is a Communicative Being: Divine Communicativeness and Harmony in the Theology of Jonathan Edwards* (London: T&T Clark, 2012); James Eglinton, *Trinity and Organism: Towards a New Reading of Herman Bavinck's Organic Motif* (London: T&T Clark International, 2012). For an excellent introduction to an array of evangelicals since Calvin who emphasised various elements of Trinitarian theology, see Fred Sanders, *The Deep Things of God: How the Trinity Changes Everything* (Wheaton, IL: Crossway, 2010).

8. 'The Adorable Trinity' was one of the Columbia theologians' favorite names for God. Today, 'adorable' usually means 'cute', but they used it to mean 'worthy of utmost adoration, love and devotion'. Columbia Seminary was founded in 1828. In 1927 it was moved from Columbia, South Carolina, to Decatur, Georgia. For histories of the seminary after its move to Decatur, see J. McDowell Richards, *As I Remember It: Columbia Seminary 1932–1971* (Decatur, GA: CTS Press, 1985) and J. Davison Philips, *Time of Blessing, Time of Hope: Columbia Theological Seminary, 1976–1986* (Decatur, GA: Columbia Theological Seminary, 1994). For the most recent comprehensive study of the seminary's history, see Erskine Clarke, *To Count Our Days: A History of Columbia Theological Seminary* (Columbia, SC: University of South Carolina Press, 2019). We are using terms such as 'Southern United States' and 'American South' to refer to the Southeastern states of America, which seceded to form the Confederate States of America in the early 1860s.

## Southern Unitarianism and Columbia's Trinitarianism

Before we begin our examinations of the individual theatres of the conflict, it will be helpful to set the stage by providing an overview of the Unitarianism found in the nineteenth-century South and the Trinitarianism of Columbia Seminary. The Unitarians that the Columbia theologians were chiefly seeking to counter were found in three Southern cities: Columbia and Charleston, South Carolina, and New Orleans, Louisiana. Although Unitarians were scattered in various parts of the South, these were the three locations where anti-Trinitarian forces gained the most Southern ground in the first half of the nineteenth century.

In Columbia, Thomas Cooper used his influence as president of South Carolina College to propagate Unitarian notions.[9] In Charleston and New Orleans, Samuel Gilman and Theodore Clapp used their pulpits to advance the Unitarian cause. Although seven Unitarian churches were started in the antebellum South, only the Charleston and New Orleans congregations were strong enough to remain intact through the Civil War.[10]

### The Influences and Characteristics of Southern Unitarianism

Two different strands of anti-Trinitarian thought influenced Southern Unitarianism: the Socinianism of England and the Arianism of New England. A major theological influence on the leadership of the Southern Unitarian movement was Joseph Priestley (1733–1804), who relocated from his native England to America in 1794. Priestley popularized the theology of the Italian reformer, Faustus Socinus (1539–1604), who represented the rationalist wing of the Protestant Reformation. Socinus and the rationalist reformers taught the supremacy of human reason and, consequently, that incomprehensible theological

---

For a discussion of the history and culture of the South that connects to our study, see Douglas Kelly, *Preachers with Power: Four Stalwarts of the South* (Edinburgh: Banner of Truth, 1992) pp. xi-xxvi.

9. South Carolina College is now the University of South Carolina.

10. John Macaulay, *Unitarianism in the Antebellum South* (Tuscaloosa, AL: University of Alabama, 2001), pp. 3, 65.

ideas such as the Trinity should be rejected. In addition to rejecting the divinity of Christ, Socinus rejected the doctrines of original sin, substitutionary atonement, and justification by faith alone.

The rationalistic theology of Socinianism flourished in places such as Transylvania and Poland, and Priestley was determined to see it flourish in England and the United States. Due to the influence of the Enlightenment in Britain and America, Priestley found audiences that were increasingly open to the religious rationalism he presented.

Though Priestley insisted that Socinianism was the only theology worthy of being called 'Unitarian', there was another movement afoot in New England laying claim to the title.[11] There, especially in and around Boston, Massachusetts, clerics were increasingly promoting a brand of theological liberalism that was, like the Unitarianism of Priestley, influenced by rationalism, but which espoused an Arian, rather than Socinian, Christology.

Arianism is based on the Christology of Arius of Alexandria (256–336), who taught that Christ is not God, but rather the first and greatest created being, more like God than any other creature, pre-existent to the rest of creation, and the one through whom everything else was made. Arianism was condemned in 325 at the Council of Nicaea, which declared Athanasian Christology— Trinitarianism—to be the Church's official teaching.[12]

Thus, unlike the Socinian Unitarians, who believed that Christ was a mere man who did not exist until the conception of Jesus, the Arian Unitarians believed that 'Christ, though less than God, was more than man.'[13] But the Arians were like the Socinians in that they too were 'rationalists at heart'.[14] The difference between

---

11. Joseph Priestley, *An History of Early Opinions Concerning Jesus Christ, Compiled from Original Writers Proving that the Christian Church Was at First Unitarian*, vol. 1 (Birmingham: Person and Rollason, 1786), pp. 80-81.

12. Athanasianism is named for Athanasius of Alexandria (296–373).

13. Sydney Ahlstrom, *A Religious History of the American People* (New Haven, CT: Yale University Press, 1972), p. 392.

14. J. Kelly, *Early Christian Doctrines: Revised Edition* (New York: Harper Collins Publishers, 1978), p. 243.

Arianism and Trinitarianism is fundamentally epistemological: 'Arianism proceeded from human reason, Athanasianism from divine revelation; and each used the other source of knowledge as a subordinate and tributary factor. The former was deistic and rationalistic, the latter theistic and supernaturalistic, in spirit and effect. The one made reasonableness, the other agreement with Scripture, the criterion of truth.'[15]

If Priestley was the representative of Socinian Unitarianism in America, the representative of the more Arian-leaning stripe was William Ellery Channing (1780–1842). Channing was a graduate of Harvard College, America's oldest institution of higher learning. Although the Puritans established Harvard to train clergy in the orthodox faith, it had essentially become a Unitarian institution by the early nineteenth century. Leaders in every sphere of American life were being educated by Harvard's popular Unitarian faculty, including divinity professor, Henry Ware; professor of rhetoric, John Quincy Adams, who became the country's sixth president; and professor of sacred literature, Andrews Norton, who wrote influential works such as *A Statement of Reasons for Not Believing the Doctrines of the Trinitarians*.

For forty years Channing pastored Boston's Federal Street Church, which, after Harvard, was the leading Unitarian institution in the nation, and he became known as 'the Luther of the Boston reformation'. As a founder of the American Unitarian Association, he sought to ensure that American Unitarianism was more Arian than Socinian by denouncing Priestley's doctrine. Although the clergy of New England embraced Channing's theology, they eventually welcomed Priestley's adherents into their increasingly popular movement.[16]

What emerged in the South by the mid-1820s was a brand of Unitarianism that was not dogmatic about Arian-Socinian

---

15. Philip Schaff, *History of the Christian Church*, vol. 3, 3rd edition (Peabody, MA: Hendrickson Publishers, 2006), p. 123.

16. J. Bowers, *Joseph Priestley and English Unitarianism in America* (University Park, PA: The Pennsylvania State University Press, 2007), pp. 1-13.

Christological distinctions, but rather more broadly rationalistic and anti-Trinitarian. Uniformity regarding the precise nature of Christ and the Holy Spirit, the meaning of the atonement, the reality of future punishment, and other doctrines traditionally considered to be litmus tests of orthodoxy was not required. Some of the Southern Unitarians leaned towards Priestley's Socinianism and others towards Channing's Arianism, but they found unity in their common aim.

## The Aim of the Southern Unitarians

We have already noted the common epistemological ground of the Southern Unitarians: they were rationalists. In addition to this, we can summarise what unified them by saying that they had a common *aim*: overturning historic Trinitarian orthodoxy in general and the Calvinistic heritage of Britain and America in particular.

Most of the Unitarians in our study grew up in Calvinistic homes, learned the *Westminster Shorter Catechism* as children, and attended Calvinistic churches and historically Calvinistic schools. They came to see Calvinism as the enemy of intellectual enlightenment, spiritual freedom, and moral improvement. Having been emancipated from what they viewed as an oppressive theological system, they wanted to help others experience the same emancipation. They sought to cultivate what they understood to be the simplicity of primitive Christianity, disencumbered from human creeds and confessions.

In order to win converts to their cause, they made much of the apparent failures of John Calvin himself, especially his culpability in the execution of Spanish anti-Trinitarian Michael Servetus. In order to present Calvinism as bigoted and Unitarianism as liberating, they routinely vilified Calvin as a murderer and extolled Servetus as a martyr for enlightened, liberated Christianity.

The Southern Unitarians were optimistic about the spread of Unitarianism, believing that within a generation Unitarianism would be the dominant religion in Europe and America. They developed a Unitarian millennialism, believing that Unitarianism would finally unify Christians, Jews, and Muslims, along with the rest of humanity, in a common monotheistic religion based on the ethical teachings of Jesus. As we will see, they labored vigorously to accomplish that aim.

## The Aim of the Columbians

The Unitarians of the South and the theologians of Columbia were well suited to be theological opponents: the Unitarians were adamantly anti-Calvinistic and optimistic about the future of Unitarianism; the Columbians were thoroughly Calvinistic and, in no small measure due to their postmillennial eschatology, optimistic about the future of Trinitarianism. Whereas the Unitarians' optimism was rooted in their positive view of human nature working in concert with Enlightenment rationalism, the Columbians' optimism was rooted in their confidence in the reviving power of the Holy Spirit working in concert with the Gospel, which alone can transform sinful hearts.

To apply Schaff's language to the conflict, the Southern Unitarians elevated human reason, the Columbians elevated divine revelation; the former was rationalistic, the latter was supernaturalistic, in spirit and effect; the one made reasonableness, the other agreement with Scripture the criterion of truth. It was a classic contest of liberal versus conservative, with the Unitarians trying to change and the Columbians trying to conserve the South's religion and culture. The Columbians had observed Unitarianism's influence in formerly Puritan New England, and they were determined to protect the South from its encroachments.

It is important to remember that the Columbia men were part of a class of Southern clergy who have been described as 'gentlemen theologians'. They were well educated, relatively affluent, well connected, and highly esteemed by the majority of Southerners as guides and guardians of their culture, which they viewed as their 'Southern Zion'. Their role was to maintain Christian orthodoxy and cultivate evangelical piety so that their Southern Zion would flourish.[17]

---

17. E. Brooks Holifield, *The Gentlemen Theologians: American Theology in South-*

Thus, because Unitarianism took aim at the Trinitarian view of God, the Columbians laboured to promote the doctrine of the Trinity, which they believed to be the *sine qua non* of Christianity and, consequently, the Christian South. In their view, Unitarianism presented a false gospel devoid of saving power, and it was their duty to defeat it, for the welfare of the South and the salvation of the world. There was a 'serpent in their garden', and they believed it was their duty to crush it under their feet.[18]

## *The Influences and Characteristics of Columbia's Trinitarianism*

As we have already noted, the Columbians believed their Trinitarianism was based on divine revelation; they believed the Scriptures of the Old and New Testaments reveal one God in three distinct and co-equal persons. In addition, they were the conscientious inheritors of the Trinitarian theology of the Church. In their writing and preaching on the Trinity they referenced Church Fathers from the West, such as Augustine, and from the East, such as Gregory of Nazianzus. They promoted the Church's historic Trinitarian creeds and choruses, and their theology reflected the *Westminster Standards*, though they were not afraid to point out places where the *Standards* could be more robustly Trinitarian.

They especially looked to John Calvin to deal with the rationalism of their day, and their theology bears significant resemblance to his, though they did not follow him on every point. In addition,

---

*ern Culture* (Durham, NC: Duke University Press, 1978), pp. 12, 36-49, 85, 154; James Farmer, Jr. *The Metaphysical Confederacy: James Henley Thornwell and the Synthesis of Southern Values* (Macon, GA: Mercer University Press, 1986), pp. 117, 121, 126, 286-287; Erskine Clarke, *Our Southern Zion: A History of Calvinism in the South Carolina Low Country, 1690–1990* (Tuscaloosa, AL: University of Alabama Press, 1996), p. 119; David Calhoun, *Our Southern Zion: Old Columbia Seminary (1828–1927)* (Edinburgh: Banner of Truth, 2012), p. xv.

18. Elizabeth Fox-Genovese and Eugene D. Genovese. *The Mind of the Master Class: History and Faith in the Southern Slaveholders' Worldview* (New York: Cambridge University Press, 2005), p. 587.

they looked to other forebears such as John Owen, who, like Calvin, had sought to counteract Unitarian threats to orthodoxy.

Just as we have identified two types of Unitarianism, theologians often identify two ways that Trinitarians have understood the doctrine of the Trinity. These two ways of describing the Trinity have been referred to as the Latin (or Western) Trinity model and the Social (or Eastern, or Greek) Trinity model. The Latin model, without denying the threeness of God, begins with and emphasizes the *oneness* of God; the Social model, without denying the oneness of God, begins with and emphasizes the *threeness* of God. The Latin model understands each person of the Trinity to be more like a way of being, while the Social view emphasizes the distinct personhood of each member of the Trinity. Thus, the Latin model does not picture God as a kind of society of distinct persons, whereas the Social model, as the name implies, pictures God as a perfectly cooperative, loving society of persons, united in their divinity and purpose through *perichoresis*, or mutual indwelling.[19]

Pressing the Latin view too far could lead to modalism (the view that God is only one person who appears to us in three modes or manifestations of being), while pressing the Social view too far could lead to tritheism (the view that there are three gods united in some way). Having an appreciation of both the Latin and Social approaches can help prevent these errors and assist the Trinitarian theologian in maintaining orthodoxy.[20]

---

19. Stephen T. Davis, *Christian Philosophical Theology* (Oxford: Oxford University Press, 2006), pp. 60-78; N. Needham, *2000 Years of Christ's Power, Part Three: Renaissance and Reformation* (London: Grace Publications Trust, 2004), pp. 104-05.

20. For the Latin view, see Brian Leftow, 'Modes without Modalism.' In *Persons: Human and Divine* (Edited by Peter van Inwagen and Dean Zimmerman. Oxford: Oxford University Press, 2007), pp. 357-75. For the Social view, see Cornelius Plantinga, 'Social Trinity and Tritheism.' In *Trinity, Incarnation, and Atonement: Philosophical and Theological Essays* (Edited by Ronald J. Feenstra and Cornelius Plantinga. Notre Dame, IN: University of Notre Dame Press, 1990), pp. 21-47. For critiques of the Latin versus Social Trinity paradigm, see Michel René Barnes, 'De Régnon Reconsidered,'

Unlike some modern theologians, the Columbians were not polemicists for either the Latin or Social Trinity view. However, as we will see throughout our study, they did emphasize certain elements of Trinitarianism that are more characteristic of the Social Trinity model: they tended to emphasize the *threeness* of God, which should not come as a surprise, given the fact that they were responding to Unitarianism; they made much of the idea that God is a society of loving, benevolent persons united perichoretically; and they espoused another notion typically associated with the Social view, a belief in God the Father as the 'fount of divinity'.

With these brief introductions to the Unitarianism of the South and the Trinitarianism of the Columbians behind us, let us turn to the first theatre of the conflict between them, Columbia, South Carolina, where James Henley Thornwell sought to counteract the Unitarianism advanced there by his one-time idol, Thomas Cooper.

---

*Augustinian Studies* 26 (1995), pp. 51-79; Lewis Ayres, *Nicea and Its Legacy: An Introduction* (Oxford: Oxford University Press, 2004), pp. 141-44.

# SECTION 1
# Columbia

## James Henley Thornwell
## and Thomas Cooper

## 2

# *The Columbia Theatre: Thornwell versus Cooper*

J AMES Henley Thornwell was born on 9th December 1812 near Cheraw, South Carolina. His father, a plantation overseer, died when he was eight years old, leaving his mother, a devout Calvinistic Baptist, to raise him and his siblings in relative poverty. From an early age Thornwell demonstrated a tremendous intellectual prowess coupled with remarkable ambition, which drew the attention of many.

James Gillespie, a wealthy planter, and William Robbins, a prominent attorney, especially took an interest in Thornwell. During his teenage years, he lived first with Gillespie and then with Robbins. The two men worked together to mentor him, finance his education, and provide him fatherly direction. However, they offered him two different theological perspectives. Gillespie, a lifelong Episcopalian, was an orthodox Trinitarian. Robbins, who was even more of a moulding influence on Thornwell, was a Unitarian. Originally from Massachusetts, Robbins was reared in the Unitarianism of that region and continued to espouse it during the time Thornwell lived with him. Thus, during his late teens, Thornwell's most influential mentor was an adherent to Channing's Unitarianism.[1]

---

1.  JHT to Gillespie, 4 March 1837, JHTP, SCL; Michael O'Brien, *Conjectures of*

A few years later, Robbins converted to Trinitarianism through the preaching of evangelist Daniel Baker. He publicly professed his faith in the Trinity and joined Saint David's Episcopal Church in Cheraw. But before his conversion, he sent Thornwell to study under another Unitarian who had likewise relocated to South Carolina: Thomas Cooper, the president of South Carolina College.[2]

## Thomas Cooper's Unitarian Encroachments

Cooper was born in Westminster, London, on 22 October 1759, into a family of significant wealth. He attended Oxford University, but he did not receive a degree because he refused to sign *The Thirty-Nine Articles*, article one of which affirms 'Faith in the Holy Trinity'. He became a barrister, but his wealth enabled him to spend time pursuing his favorite interests: philosophy, theology, science, and, especially, the advancement of political freedoms for those outside the Anglican faith, Unitarians in particular.[3]

Whereas Robbins represented the more Arian-leaning form of Unitarianism, Cooper was a Socinian. He was a close friend and disciple of Joseph Priestley and even named one of his sons Thomas Priestley Cooper after himself and his mentor. Priestley had been raised as a Calvinist and could recite the *Westminster Shorter Catechism* in its entirety at the age of four, but, as we already noted, he became the leading champion for Socinianism in his generation.[4]

Cooper and Priestley worked together to extend the privileges that England's Toleration Act afforded Dissenters, including the

---

Order: Intellectual Life and the American South, 1810–1860, 2 vols. (Chapel Hill, NC: University of North Carolina Press, 2004), p. 1115.

2. Robbins to JHT, 23 August 1834, JHTP, SCL; Benjamin Palmer, Jr., *The Life and Letters of James Henley Thornwell D.D., LL.D: Ex-President of the South Carolina College, Late Professor of Theology in the Theological Seminary at Columbia, South Carolina* (Richmond, VA: Whittet & Shepperson, 1875), pp. 2-82.

3. Dumas Malone, *The Public Life of Thomas Cooper* (New Haven, CT: Yale University Press, 1926), pp. 4-5.

4. Charles Himes, *Life and Times of Judge Thomas Cooper* (Carlisle, PA: Himes Estate, 1918), p. 35; Steven Johnson, *The Invention of Air: A Story of Science, Faith, Revolution, and the Birth of America* (New York: Riverhead Books, 2008), p. 70.

right to hold public office, to those who disbelieved the Trinity. The pair became attached to revolution societies in England, formed associations with the Jacobins of France, and published tracts advocating political revolution. Edmund Burke accused Cooper of treason in the House of Commons. In his *Reply to Burke's Invective*, Cooper offered unqualified endorsement of revolutionaries such as Thomas Paine, and the public viewed his pamphlet as a call to revolution.[5]

Cooper and Priestley eventually became disillusioned by the persistent conservatism of England and the turbulent radicalism of France, believing that 'in neither land could one be truly free'.[6] Thus, they immigrated to America in 1794, when Cooper was thirty-four, settling in Northumberland, Pennsylvania, which was a sort of haven for 'fugitives of English persecution'.[7] Priestley conducted Unitarian services each Sunday, which Cooper attended, first at his home and then, as the congregation grew, at a neighboring school.[8]

Cooper remained quiet for a time, but ever the controversialist, he began publishing a newspaper in which he criticized President John Adams. In 1800, Cooper was charged with violating the Sedition Act, which banned the publication of scandalous or malicious writings against the federal government. He was found guilty, sentenced to six months in prison, and fined one hundred dollars. The judge in the case declared, 'Take this publication in all its parts, and it is the boldest attempt I have known to poison the minds of the people.'[9]

---

5. Malone, *Cooper*, pp. 20-26; Thomas Cooper, *Reply to Burke's Invective in the House of Commons, on the 30th of April 1792* (London: J. Johnson, 1792), p. 67.

6. Malone, *Cooper*, p. 68.

7. Ibid., p. 83.

8. Thomas Cooper, 'A Review of Dr Priestley's Theological Works.' In Joseph Priestley, *Memoirs of Dr Joseph Priestley*, 2 vols. (London: J. Johnson, 1806), p. 824.

9. Thomas Cooper, *An Account of the Trial of Thomas Cooper, of Northumberland: on a charge of libel against the President of the United States, 1800* (Philadelphia: John Bioren, 1800), pp. 6-7, 42.

Some Americans viewed Cooper as a demagogue deserving deportation; others venerated him as a champion for free speech. Priestley wrote his friend Theophilus Lindsey, who had founded Essex Street Chapel, the first Unitarian congregation in England, saying, 'Mr Cooper has been convicted of a libel, on the Sedition Act, and is now in prison; but he has gained great credit by it, and he will, I doubt not, be a rising man in the country.'[10] Priestley's prediction proved to be correct. Overall, the trial raised public opinion of Cooper and, after serving his prison sentence and lying low for a few years, he became a judge in Northumberland in 1804.[11]

One of Cooper's greatest admirers became President Thomas Jefferson, an Anti-federalist and champion of the First Amendment. Jefferson soon became Cooper's closest American friend, and the two corresponded frequently. Like Cooper, Jefferson was a friend and follower of Priestley.

Once, when Jefferson's daughter Martha wrote him asking about his views on theology, he replied, 'I have written to Philadelphia for Doctor Priestley's History of the Corruptions of Christianity, which I will send you, and recommend an attentive perusal, because it establishes the groundwork of my view of this subject.'[12] Jefferson commended the same to his friend Henry Fry:

> The work of Dr Priestley which I sent you has always been a favourite of mine. I consider the doctrines of Jesus as delivered by himself to contain the outlines of the sublimest system of morality that has ever been taught but I hold in the most profound detestation and execration the corruptions of it which have been invented by priestcraft and established by kingcraft constituting a conspiracy of church and state against the civil and religious liberties of mankind.[13]

---

10. John Rutt, *Life and Correspondence of Joseph Priestley* (London: R. Hunter, 1832), p. 436.
11. Malone, *Cooper*, pp. 145-50.
12. TJ to Martha Jefferson Randolph, 25 April 1803, TJP.
13. TJ to Henry Fry, 17 June 1804, TJP.

A decade later he wrote to John Adams that he had read Priestley's *Corruptions of Christianity* many times and rested on it as the basis of his own faith:

> I remember to have heard Dr Priestley say that if all England would candidly examine themselves, and confess, they would find that Unitarianism was really the religion of all: and I observe a bill is now pending in parliament for the relief of Anti-Trinitarians. It is too late in the day for men of sincerity to pretend they believe in the Platonic mysticisms that three are one, and one is three; and yet the one is not three, and the three are not one: to divide mankind by a single letter into ὁμοούσιανς and ὁμοιούσιανς, but this constitutes the power and the profit of the priests. Sweep away their gossamer fabrics of factitious religion, and they would catch no more flies. We would all then, like the Quakers, live without an order of priests, moralise for ourselves, follow the oracle of conscience, and say nothing about what no man can understand, nor therefore believe; for I suppose belief to be the assent of the mind to an intelligible proposition.[14]

Similarly, echoing the teachings of Priestley, Jefferson declared,

> No one sees with greater pleasure than myself the progress of reason in its advance toward rational Christianity. When we shall have done away with the incomprehensible jargon of the Trinitarian arithmetic, that three are one, and one are three; when we shall have knocked down the artificial scaffolding reared to mask from view the simple structure of Jesus; when, in short, we shall have unlearned everything taught since his day, and got back to the pure and simple doctrines he inculcated – we shall then be truly and worthily his disciples; and my opinion is that, if nothing had ever been added to what flowed purely from his lips, the whole world would at this day have been Christian.[15]

Cooper and Jefferson believed that the best way to influence America in a more Unitarian direction was through higher education. In

---

14. TJ to John Adams, 22 August 1813, TJP.

15. Quoted in George Cooke, *Unitarianism in America: A History of Its Origin and Development* (Boston: American Unitarian Association, 1902), p. 125.

1811, Cooper became the chair of chemistry at Dickinson College, a position he held until 1817, when he became chair of chemistry and mineralogy at the University of Pennsylvania. Meanwhile, Jefferson was working diligently towards his dream of establishing a world-class university near Monticello, his plantation in Charlottesville, Virginia. The Commonwealth of Virginia incorporated Jefferson's dream—the University of Virginia—in 1819, though classes did not commence until 1825.[16]

Jefferson believed that an integral part of the university's success would be having Cooper join the faculty. Other members of the board, who more accurately represented the religious sentiments of Virginians (who were predominantly Presbyterians and Episcopalians), were averse to Cooper's appointment. The majority perceived that in his push for Cooper's appointment as diversified chair of science, philosophy, and law, Jefferson was showing his hand: he wanted the state's university to be a Unitarian school like Harvard. Joseph Cabell, a friend of Jefferson in the state legislature and a member of the board, warned him that the Presbyterians believed 'the Socinians are to be installed at the University for the purpose of overthrowing the prevailing religious sentiments of the country'.[17]

Undaunted, Jefferson continued to push for Cooper's appointment. He told members of the board: 'Cooper is acknowledged by every enlightened man who knows him to be the greatest man in America in the powers of his mind, and in acquired information, and that without a single exception.'[18] Ultimately, the Presbyterians of the state, not wanting their tax dollars to fund an anti-Trinitarian institution, pressured the board to thwart Cooper's appointment. As William Cabell wrote to his brother Joseph, 'I fear that Cooper's appointment will do the University infinite injury. His religious views are damnable, as exhibited in

16. Malone, *Cooper*, pp. 211, 230; Philip Bruce, *History of the University of Virginia, 1819–1919: The Lengthened Shadow of One Man*, 5 vols. (New York: The Macmillan Company, 1920), p. 2.59.

17. Vincent Munoz, *God and the Founders: Madison, Washington, and Jefferson* (Cambridge: Cambridge University Press, 2009), p. 107.

18. Bruce, *Virginia*, p. 1.202.

a book published by him shortly after the death of Priestley. You will have every religious man in Virginia against you.'[19] Leading the opposition to Cooper was Presbyterian clergyman John Holt Rice, who wrote a widely disseminated article expressing strong disapproval of Cooper.[20] Lamenting evangelical efforts to block Cooper's appointment, Jefferson wrote his friend William Short:

> Their pulpits are now resounding with denunciations against the appointment of Dr Cooper, whom they charge as a monotheist in opposition to their Tritheism. Hostile as these sects are in every other point to one another they unite in maintaining their mystical theogony against those who believe there is one God only. The Presbyterian clergy are the loudest, the most intolerant of all sects, the most tyrannical, and ambitious, ready at the word of the lawgiver, if such a word could be now obtained, to put the torch to the pile, and to rekindle in this virgin hemisphere the flames in which their oracle Calvin consumed the poor Servetus, because he could not find in his Euclid the proposition which has demonstrated that three are one, and one is three, nor subscribe to that of Calvin, that magistrates have a right to exterminate all heretics to Calvinistic creed.[21]

Jefferson was devastated by the board's decision to acquiesce to the Presbyterians. He wrote two of the board members who had been absent from the decisive meeting:

> Another subject on this, as on former occasions, gave us embarrassment. You may have heard of the hue and cry raised from the different pulpits on our appointment of Dr Cooper, whom they charge with Unitarianism as boldly as if they knew the fact, and as presumptuously as if it were a crime and one for which, like Servetus, he should be burned. And perhaps you may have seen the particular attack made on him in the

19. Ibid., p. 1.204.

20. John Rice, 'A Review of "Memoirs of Dr Joseph Priestley and Observations of His Writings," by Thomas Cooper,' *The Virginia Evangelical and Literary Magazine* (February 1820): pp. 63-74.

21. TJ to William Short, 13 April 1820, TJP.

Evangelical magazine. For myself I was not disposed to regard the denunciations of these satellites of religious inquisition, but our colleagues, better judges of popular feeling, thought that they were not to be altogether neglected, and that it might be better to relieve Dr Cooper, ourselves and the institution from this crusade .... I do sincerely lament that untoward circumstances have brought on us the irreparable loss of this professor, whom I have looked to as the corner-stone of our edifice. I know of no one who could have aided us so much in forming the future regulations of our infant institution, and although we may hereafter procure from Europe equivalents in the sciences, they can never replace the advantages of his experience, his knowledge of the character, the habits, and the manners of our country, his identification with its sentiments and principles, and the high reputation he has obtained in it generally.[22]

Having been prevented from an appointment at Virginia, Cooper accepted an offer to become professor of chemistry at South Carolina College in Columbia. Many South Carolinians were enamoured with Cooper's state's rights politics and his intellectual acumen, and were, at least at the outset, willing to overlook his theological liberalism. In June of 1820, after the death of Jonathan Maxcy, the first president of the college, the trustees appointed Cooper president *pro tempore*. In December of 1821, by a vote of ten to nine, the board elected him as president.[23]

As suggested in Cooper's narrow election, it did not take long for tensions to rise within the college and throughout the state over his Unitarian views. Cooper and Jefferson exchanged correspondences lamenting the opposition they were receiving from the Presbyterians in their respective states. Their hopes had been high for the South Carolina legislature, which oversaw the college, that 'priestcraft has not in that body the baleful ascendancy it has elsewhere'.[24]

22. TJ to Robert Taylor and Chapman Johnson, 16 May 1820, TJP.
23. Malone, *Cooper*, p. 343; Erwin Green, *A History of the University of South Carolina* (Columbia, SC: The State Company, 1916), p. 33.
24. TJ to TC, 12 April 1823, TJP.

However, Cooper informed Jefferson that, although he believed Unitarianism would ultimately prevail in Columbia, the Presbyterians presently maintained control of the city:

> Our town here is crowded with Presbyterian parsons; they are a systematic and persevering sect, and while they have the address to cajole the people out of their money, their power will increase. He who has any regard for the peace of himself and his family can venture to stem this tide of fanaticism? About 20 Years hence the prevailing sect among the better informed people, will be the Unitarian.[25]

By 1823, Presbyterians and other orthodox Christians represented a majority in the legislature and had gained a majority on the college's board. Jefferson wrote to Cooper, 'I am sorry to learn by your letter of the 6th that the *genus irritabile vatum* revive their persecutions against you in a state on whose liberal opinions I had believed that fanaticism had no hold.'[26] Fearing his removal, Cooper asked Jefferson if there were any chance he could move to Virginia with the prospect of joining the faculty at Virginia. Jefferson had disappointing news. Virginia's opposition to Cooper remained, 'excited by the clamors of the same tritheistical hierophants, and listened to by some from fears respecting the success of our college.'[27]

In Columbia, Cooper survived the initial wave of Presbyterian efforts to remove him, but, unlike Jefferson, he was not a skilled politician, willing to downplay his unpopular Unitarian views. In private correspondence with his friend John Adams, Jefferson freely shared,

> The wishes expressed in your last favor, that I may continue in life and health until I become a Calvinist, at least in his exclamation of 'mon Dieu! jusque a quand!' would make me immortal. I can never join Calvin in addressing his god. He was indeed an atheist,

---

25. TC to TJ, 20 November 1822, TJP.
26. TJ to TC, 30 May 1823, TJP. *Genus irritabile vatum* is Latin for 'irritable race of poets'.
27. TJ to TC, 30 May 1823, TJP.

which I can never be; or rather his religion was Daemonism. If ever man worshipped a false god, he did. The being described in his 5 points is not the God whom you and I acknolege [sic] and adore, the Creator and benevolent governor of the world; but a daemon of malignant spirit. It would be more pardonable to believe in no god at all, than to blaspheme him by the atrocious attributes of Calvin.[28]

Cooper declared such sentiments publicly. At least twice during his presidency he published a tract titled 'An Exposition of the Doctrines of Calvinism,' in which he sought to prove that one who *really believes* those doctrines, and *makes them the guide of his conduct* cannot be 'a good citizen or a good man'.[29] He wrote, 'I challenge any reader to produce me, from ancient or modern times, a set of tenets so absolutely, so unprovokedly, cruel, blasphemous, and devilish.'[30] Speaking of the tenets of the *Westminster Confession of Faith*, he announced,

> Where a deliberate adoption of these tenets induces holders to act in conformity to them, it cannot but be that his temper is sored, that he becomes malignant, intolerant and full of deep rooted hatred toward those who, as he thinks, in opposing him, oppose God. Undoubtedly, as a class of preachers and teachers, the most rancorous, the most obstinate, the most intolerant and persecuting, the most avaricious, ambitious and dangerous are the Presbyterian clergy of the United States. Their designs however are more than suspected: their view of establishing a compulsory national religion, an unholy alliance between church and state, and a regular system of TYTHES, are now pretty well understood.[31]

Of the *Confession*'s doctrine of God, he believed,

---

28. TJ to John Adams, 11 April 1823, TJP. '<u>mon Dieu</u>! Jusque a quand!' means '<u>My God</u>! How long!'

29. Thomas Cooper, 'Exposition of the Doctrines of Calvinism' (New York: 1834), p. 4.

30. Ibid., p. 7.

31. Ibid., p. 16.

This is horrible blasphemy against the character of God Almighty, who by this doctrine is transformed into a tyrant, furious, revengeful, capricious, cruel, and wicked, far beyond our worst conception of any earthly despot, inasmuch as omnipotence is added to these attributes, and eternal duration to his vindictive punishment …. Is this religion? Can such a being be a fit object of worship? Is it possible not to contemplate with horror and strong disgust a tyrant so detestable? Is it from such an example we are to take our lessons of benevolence, and to learn peace on earth and good will toward men?[32]

Suffice it to say, the Presbyterians of South Carolina grew weary of having their tax dollars support Cooper's salary and watching him mold the future leadership of the state. A college president in nineteenth-century America was 'the greatest single educative force encountered by the students' and his 'opportunities for shaping opinions and moulding character were almost unlimited, and many a president utilized them to the utmost.'[33] Moreover, the presidency of South Carolina College was 'one of the most prominent and sought-after positions in the State. In prestige it ranked just behind the United States Senatorships and the governorship.'[34] As South Carolina's Presbyterians increasingly sent their sons to other colleges to keep them from 'Old Coot', enrollment at South Carolina College steadily declined.[35]

---

32. Ibid., p. 17.

33. George Schmidt, *The Old Time College President* (New York: Columbia University Press, 1930), p. 11.

34. Daniel Hollis, 'Thornwell and the Status Quo,' in *University of South Carolina*, 2 vols. (Columbia, SC: University of South Carolina Press, 1951–1956), p. 1.142. The abiding importance of the college and its presidency was communicated years later in President Thornwell's letter of resignation when he accepted the call to train ministers at Columbia Seminary: 'The College, in itself, may be the most important, and yet not the most important for me' ('Thornwell Resignation,' 29 November 1854, JHTP, SCL).

35. 'Coot' was short for 'cooter', a type of turtle. To many, Cooper resembled a cooter because he was less than five feet in stature, but with a large head. In the words of one student, 'He was a perfect taper from the side of his head down to his feet; he looked like a wedge with a head on it' (Marion Sims, *The Story of My Life* (New York: D. Appleton and Company, 1884), p. 82).

With pressures for his removal mounting once again, 'the old controversialist had had enough of it; at seventy-four even he was weary of strife. On 27 November 1833, he resigned the presidency.'[36] For the state's Presbyterians, his departure came none too soon. Famed Presbyterian evangelist to the slaves, Charles Colcock Jones, who was a Columbia Seminary graduate and professor, represented the general sentiment in his appraisal of Cooper: 'That old man has done this state more evil than fifty years can remove. He has a world of iniquity to answer for in poisoning the State with his infidel principles.'[37]

According to many of his contemporaries, the most promising student to sit at Cooper's feet was a young man named James Henley Thornwell. Already tending towards a Unitarian direction because of Robbins, Thornwell was attracted to Cooper's teaching and 'fell at first under the charm of his influence'.[38]

During his first year under Cooper's mentorship, he viewed Cooper as his idol.[39] He did not maintain his idolatry of Cooper throughout his college career, however. Another member of the faculty, professor of philosophy Robert Henry, had also noted Thornwell's rare abilities and invested in the collegian. After Henry's death, Thornwell would write that, in contrast to Cooper, Henry was 'a thoroughgoing advocate of the Nicene creed'.[40] Through Henry's influence, Thornwell began to question more deeply the Unitarian doctrines he had imbibed from Robbins and Cooper. He entered a prolonged mental conflict, comparing and contrasting Unitarianism with historic Trinitarianism. In the end, he confessed that he found Unitarianism to be 'a system

---

36. Malone, *Cooper*, p. 362.

37. Erskine Clarke, *Dwelling Place: A Plantation Epic* (New Haven: Yale University Press, 2005), p. 172.

38. Palmer, *Thornwell*, p. 61.

39. Ibid.

40. James Thornwell, 'Memoir of Dr Henry' *Southern Quarterly Review 3*, no. 1 (April 1856), p. 202.

that would not hold water'.[41] He would later share with one of his divinity students, 'When I went to College, I was under Dr Cooper; but read the Bible through, and became convinced as to the nature of God's plan of salvation.'[42] After they had converted to Trinitarianism, Robbins wrote Thornwell, 'I do not fear for your principles in religion – they withstood the insidious approaches of Dr Cooper.'[43]

As we will discuss in more detail, Thornwell would eventually join the faculty at South Carolina College and become the president of his alma mater. The young man who idolized South Carolina's most famous anti-Trinitarian would become the state's leading champion for Trinitarianism and be tasked by his fellow Presbyterians to reverse the Unitarian advancements his former idol had made at the state's college. The irony that Cooper trained the very one who would reverse his efforts was not lost on Palmer:

> Who could have dreamed, when this ribald infidelity was in the zenith of its power, that it was even then nourishing in its bosom a champion for the truth, who would soon enter the lists, and take up the gage of battle, and bear it off upon its triumphant lance! Who that, eight years before, saw a half-grown youth sitting at the feet of the great apostle of Deism, and drinking in his counsels as the inspiration of an oracle, could foresee the advocate for Christianity, standing for its defence upon the platform of its evidences, and undoing the work of his own oracle and guide! Who could then have foretold that an infidel philosophy was whetting the dialectics which should unravel its own sophisms, and feathering the arrow by which its own life should be pierced; that Deism itself should be made to train the giant strength by which its own castle should be demolished, and the spell of its foul enchantment be dissolved! Who can understand the ways of God? It was the young Saxon monk, climbing Pilate's staircase upon his knees, who shook the gates of Papal Rome. It was the young man

---

41. Palmer, *Thornwell*, p. 79.

42. Ibid., p. 96.

43. Robbins to JHT, 23 August 1834, JHTP, SCL.

bearing the garments of those who stoned the first martyr, who filled the world with the faith which once he destroyed.[44]

Indeed, Thornwell's chief objective became 'persuading others to duplicate his own personal history of conversion' and 'this was to repudiate Thomas Cooper'.[45] It is to this chief objective and repudiation that we now turn our attention.

---

44. *Thornwell*, p. 146. That Palmer referred to Cooper as 'the apostle of Deism' is understandable; there is much overlap between Deism and Unitarianism. Deism has been thought of as religion-less or church-less Unitarianism. O'Brien referred to Cooper as both a Deist and a Unitarian. *Conjectures*, pp. 866, 1020. Singer called him a 'noted Deist and Unitarian.' C. Gregg Singer, *A Theological Interpretation of American History* (Nutley, NJ: Craig Press, 1964), p. 83. Thornwell understood Cooper to have been 'a Socinian, and afterwards a Deist.' 'Memoir of Dr Henry,' p. 201. Cooper, as a disciple of Priestley, consistently identified himself as a Unitarian. 'A Review of Dr Priestley's Theological Works,' p. 708; Thomas Cooper, 'A Summary of Unitarian Arguments,' in *Tracts: Ethical, Theological, and Political* (Warrington, PA: W. Eyres, 1789), p. 501; TC to TJ, 6 May 1823, TJP. For this reason, his principal biographer, Malone, also viewed him as a Unitarian. *Cooper*, pp. 16, 273. See also, Mark Beliles and Jerry Newcombe, *Doubting Thomas? The Religious Life and Legacy of Thomas Jefferson* (New York: Morgan James, 2014), passim. Like most Unitarians who immigrated to the South, Cooper was without a Unitarian church to attend. Ironically, when he lived in Columbia, he was a member of *Trinity* Episcopal Cathedral. Green, *South Carolina*, p. 43. Evidently, Cooper remained resolute in his rejection of Trinitarianism throughout his life. See Appendix 1, 'Cooper's Dying Letter to His Physician.'

45. O'Brien, *Conjectures*, p. 1117.

# 3

# *Thornwell's Trinitarian Counteroffensive*

**D**URING his senior year of college, Thornwell embraced Trinitarianism as 'God's plan of salvation'.[1] However, he did not immediately join a church, as he was unsure of what sort of church to join. Of course, he eventually settled on Presbyterianism, but there are at least two different versions of how that came about.

Palmer's account is that on an evening stroll in downtown Columbia, Thornwell wandered into a bookshop and happened upon a volume titled *Confession of Faith*. He had never heard of it, but he saw that it contained a system of Christian doctrine. He purchased it for twenty-five cents, read through it that night, and embraced its contents.[2]

---

1. Palmer, *Thornwell*, p. 96.

2. It was common for Thornwell, even in his more mature years, to study through the night: 'This peculiarity ... marked his whole career. His studies were prosecuted chiefly at night, and he was habitually a late sleeper. He claimed this, indeed, as an idiosyncrasy; and many were the ingenious arguments he would invent, in playful banter, to prove that the day was intended for rest, and the night for work; and that man, in his perverseness, had wrongfully changed the original and proper arrangement of Providence' (Ibid., p. 23). In a letter to a friend, Professor Thornwell described his routine: 'I sit up all night, reading, musing, and smoking; and just before

J. Marion Sims told a different story. Originally from Lancaster, South Carolina, Sims became friends with Thornwell while both were collegians. Sims would later become a leading physician and is considered by many to be the father of modern gynecology.[3] According to Sims, Thornwell became a Presbyterian not because he stumbled into a bookshop, but rather because he fell in love.

According to Sims' version of the story, shortly after graduating from college, Thornwell became enamored with a beautiful and accomplished sister of a fellow classmate. He desired to marry her, but she was an uncompromising Presbyterian who would not think of marrying outside the Presbyterian faith. After a number of conversations with her, Thornwell remained unconvinced of her position. 'Then,' according to Sims, 'this beautiful woman told him if he would take the ordinary Confession of Faith, and study that, she thought he would see the truth. He did so, and he rose from its perusal a converted man; and from that time he determined to give himself to the Church.'[4]

Though Thornwell became an uncompromising Presbyterian, his Presbyterian love interest did not consent to marry him. Sims did not blame her. Although Thornwell was a 'giant in intellect' who made everyone else 'seem to be a mere [intellectual] pygmy in his grasp', he was 'a poor, dirty-looking, malarial-looking boy ... very small, very thin, very pale and looked as if he had never had enough to eat.'[5]

Though the precise nature of Thornwell's first exposure to Presbyterianism may be up for debate, his subsequent attachment

---

the sun, with its orient beams, dispels ghosts, goblins, and infernal spirits to their respective jails, I stretch my limbs upon an ample couch, continue my cogitations till my soul is locked in the silent embrace of slumber sweet; and I abide in the land of dreams until it becomes a man to refresh nature in a more active way' (Ibid., p. 310).

3. Sara Spettel and Mark Donald White, 'The Portrayal of J. Marion Sims' Controversial Surgical Legacy,' *The Journal of Urology* 185 (June 2011), pp. 2424-27.

4. Sims, *Story of My Life*, p. 107.

5. Ibid., p. 108.

to it is not. In April of 1832, he settled in Sumterville, South Carolina, where he worked as a schoolmaster. On 13 May 1832, he publicly professed faith in Christ and joined the Concord Presbyterian Church. Any doubts regarding the Triunity of God had vanished. On that momentous day, he wrote out a prayer of celebration and consecration in which he 'ascribed all the praise' to 'the glorious Three-in-one'.[6] During this same period of time, he concluded that the Triune God was calling him to be a minister of the gospel.[7]

By November of 1832, he was back in Cheraw, and, beginning in January of 1833, he served as the principal of the academy where he had excelled as a student. He and many others in the community experienced a spiritual revival, with many professing conversion to Christ. This would prove to be formative for Thornwell's understanding of the Christian life and ministry, in which he would pray and preach for such times of refreshing.[8]

In the spring of 1834, Ebenezer Porter, a professor at Andover Seminary, paid a visit to his former pupil, Urias Powers, who was Thornwell's pastor at the Presbyterian Church of Cheraw. After meeting Thornwell and discerning his giftedness, Powers offered him the opportunity to attend Andover for free. Thornwell accepted, and shortly thereafter he moved to Andover.[9]

Free tuition was not the only factor motivating Thornwell to attend Andover rather than the newly established seminary in Columbia; he believed that Andover would afford him a better opportunity to learn German, Syriac, Chaldee and Arabic. However, the professor who taught these languages left the institution around the time of Thornwell's arrival. In addition to this disappointment, Thornwell, who was now a decidedly 'Old School' Presbyterian, found Andover to be 'awfully New

---

6. Palmer, *Thornwell*, p. 95.

7. Thornwell had sensed God might be calling him into ministry even before his conversion to the Trinitarian faith. Ibid., pp. 46-50, 100-01.

8. Ibid., pp. 106-107; JHT Journal, JHTP, CBK.

9. See Palmer, *Thornwell*, pp. 115-16.

School'.[10] He also turned up his nose at the culture of the institution. He wrote Gillespie, 'It is peopled with a sad mixture of gentlemen and ploughboys. I use the term gentleman in its vulgar sense, having reference merely to manners and not to the heart.'[11]

Dissatisfied with Andover, Thornwell headed twenty-five miles south to Cambridge, Massachusetts, and enrolled at Harvard Divinity School because of its reputation for language training. He was determined to master the oriental languages and, in this pursuit, his mantra became, 'What man has done, man can do.'[12] In Gillespie he also confided, 'I feel anxious to accomplish much while I do live, for I am apprehensive that the seeds of early death are implanted within me.'[13]

Correspondences written at this time reveal that Thornwell went to Harvard with the intention of studying ancient languages before transferring to Columbia Seminary, and that he had aspirations to teach theology at Columbia.[14] But, at Harvard, he encountered in full force the Unitarianism he had come to reject. One of his future protégés, John L. Girardeau, described what Thornwell encountered when he wrote, 'Unitarianism has been organized in a denominational form and has been enthroned in the Athens of America and at Harvard University.'[15] Only a couple of years after he himself

---

10. Ibid., pp. 115-16. We will discuss the Old School-New School debate shortly.

11. JHT to Gillespie, 13 August 1834, JHTP, SCL.

12. JHT to Gillespie, 4 March 1837, JHTP, SCL.

13. Ibid. Thornwell did die at the relatively young age of forty-nine on 1 August 1862 at the home of his friend William White in Charlotte, North Carolina. Palmer, *Thornwell*, pp. 521-25.

14. JHT to Gillespie, 13 August 1834; JHT to Alexander Pegues, 14 August 1834; JHT to Gillespie, 27 August 1834, JHTP, SCL.

15. Girardeau, *Sermons*, edited by George A. Blackburn (Columbia, SC: The State Company, 1907), p. 127. In the nineteenth century, Boston was known as 'the Athens of America'. 'When conservative Presbyterian minister Lyman Beecher moved to Boston in 1816, he expressed disappointment at what had taken place: "All the literary men of Massachusetts were Unitarian; all the trustees and professors at Harvard College

had been intensely wrestling with the claims of Unitarianism, Thornwell wrote a childhood friend:

> I am now comfortably settled in this venerable abode of science, literature, and learning. The Library contains thirty-nine thousand volumes, and the Athenaeum Library of Boston, sixty thousand; to both of which I have access, besides the privilege of attending all the Lectures of the College. You see, therefore, that the advantages I enjoy, and the facilities for study, are liberal and encouraging. I room in Divinity Hall, among the Unitarian students of Theology; for there are no others here. I shall expect to meet and give blows in defence of my own peculiar doctrines; and God forbid that I should falter in maintaining the faith once delivered to the saints. I look upon the tenets of modern Unitarians as little better than downright infidelity. Their system, as they call it, is a crude compound of negative articles, admirably fitted to land the soul in eternal misery. The peculiarity of their belief consists in *not believing*. Read over their tracts and pamphlets, and you will find that they all consist, not in establishing a better system, but simply in *not believing* the system of the Orthodox. Ask them to tell you what they *do* believe, and they will begin to recount certain doctrines of the Orthodox, and tell you very politely that they do *not* believe these. The truth is, they have nothing positive; their faith is all negative; and I do not know that the Bible holds out a solitary promise to a man for *not believing*. And yet these *not-believers* talk about Christian charity with a great deal of pompousness, and take it hugely amiss that they are not regarded by pious men as disciples of Jesus. Have you seen 'Norton's statement of reasons for *not believing* the doctrine of Trinitarians?' It is a queer book, and should be read just for the curiosity of seeing its absurdity and nonsense. When a difficult passage stares him in the face, he

---

were Unitarian; all the elite of wealth and fashion crowded Unitarian churches'" (Thomas O'Connor, *The Athens of America: Boston 1825–1845* (Boston, MA: University of Massachusetts Press, 2006), p. 11). 'By the time the American Unitarian Association was formed in 1826, there were already 120 churches of the new denomination in Massachusetts, including twenty of the twenty-five oldest Calvinist churches in the United States' (Ibid).

turns it off very nicely, by saying Paul was mistaken here; that he did not understand the real nature of Christianity, and therefore blundered. Sometimes he makes even Jesus Christ go wrong; because He happened to be busy about something else, and did not have time to correct Himself. Now, a man who can swallow such stuff as this, can swallow anything. It is an open defiance of all the established laws of exegesis; and the doctrines, which need such miserable subterfuges to support them, cannot come from God. No, my friend, we are never safe in departing from the simple declarations of the Bible.[16]

With words that indicate that his friend was undergoing the kind of struggle he had gone through a couple of years before, he continued:

Let me entreat you to read Shuttleworth on the consistency of Revelation with reason. It is the ablest work which has issued from the British press since Butler's Analogy. Read it carefully, and you will find philosophy bowing at the altar of religion; read it prayerfully, and you must become a Christian.

The Unitarian will tell you that experimental religion is all an idle dream; but, my friend, believe not the tale. It is no such thing. The truly pious man walks with God; he is under the influence of the Holy Spirit; the consolations of the Gospel support him in affliction, and cheer him in distress. There is such a thing as holy communion with the blessed Trinity; as a peace of mind which passeth all understanding; as joy in the Holy Ghost, and consolation in believing. There is no fanaticism, no enthusiasm here; it is all sober truth; and those who laugh at these things now, will weep bitterly in a coming day. May God be with us both! May He take us under the shadow of His wing and save us in the hour of final retribution![17]

---

16. JHT to A. H. Pegues, 14 August 1834, JHTP, SCL. See Norton, *Statement of Reasons for Not Believing the Doctrines of the Trinitarians.*

17. JHT to A. H. Pegues, 14 August 1834, JHTP, SCL. See Shuttleworth, *The Consistency of The Whole Scheme of Revelation with itself and with Human Reason*; Joseph Butler, *Analogy of Religion, Natural and Revealed* (New York: Harper & Brothers Publishers, 1860).

These words provide a glimpse into what would become the core of Thornwell's ministerial labors. In coming years, he would 'give blows' to Unitarianism and promote 'holy communion with the blessed Trinity'. As we will see, this twofold way of dealing with Unitarianism's encroachments would become a hallmark of Columbia's mission.

Disappointed by what he found at Andover and Harvard, he returned to South Carolina in October of 1834. He planned to enter the senior class at Columbia in January to round out his seminary studies, but the churches of South Carolina were in urgent need of pastors. On 28 November 1834, Harmony Presbytery examined him for licensure, and he easily demonstrated his proficiency. During his examination, Columbia professor Thomas Goulding said, 'Brethren, I feel like sitting at this young man's feet as a learner.'[18]

On 12 June 1835, Thornwell was ordained and installed as the pastor of the newly established Presbyterian Church of Lancaster. He wrote Gillespie regarding the day of his first sermon:

> On that day – a day never to be forgotten, I actually trembled in the sanctuary of God and breathed forth a deep earnest and heartfelt prayer to the Holy Ghost to baptize me with divine influence and to make my labours, humble though they be, effective means for the salvation of sinners. It requires but little experience to convince a minister that all his help must come from the Lord. We actually preach to dead men. There is a deep and settled carnality in the heart of man which the whole artillery of pulpit eloquence is utterly unable to shake unless accompanied with the mighty influence of the Holy Spirit.[19]

In April he took charge of two other churches, Waxhaw and Six-Mile Creek. To say the least, pastoring three churches kept the young man busy: 'From one of these charges to another he was in the habit of driving through the country at a very high

---

18. Henry White, *Southern Presbyterian Leaders* (New York: The Neale Publishing Company, 1911), p. 312; Palmer, *Thornwell*, p. 127.

19. JHT to Gillespie, June 13, 1835, JHTP, SCL.

rate of speed behind a mettlesome horse named "Red Rover".[20] He soon became known not only for his high-speed travels, but also for his Christ-centered, practical preaching that aimed for conversion. One who heard him often during this time described his preaching as 'intensely practical, and plain; nothing abstract. The impression in my mind, now, is that of earnest expostulation with sinners. Now, to-day, is the day of salvation. He was very earnest; his eye kindled with intense excitement; his whole frame quivered. His sermons created great enthusiasm among the people of all denominations, who crowded into the little church until it overflowed.'[21] The young minister was marked by gravity in the pulpit and levity without: 'Men stopped to wonder at him as he passed along the streets, striving to put together the solemnity of his pulpit utterances and the exuberant pleasantry of the private companion.'[22]

On 3rd December 1835, the poor preacher 'married up' to Nancy Witherspoon of Lancaster. Her father had served as South Carolina's Lieutenant-Governor and her great-uncle was the famous Rev. John Knox Witherspoon (1723–1794).[23] Thornwell enjoyed the transition from the difficulties of poverty and singleness to the comforts of increasing financial prosperity and marital bliss. He wrote Gillespie, 'I have one of the best wives in the world, for she manages every thing and just leaves me to my books and study.'[24]

Thornwell's time in Lancaster was short-lived. In the fall of 1837, he was elected as a professor at South Carolina College. Since his graduation six years earlier, the Presbyterians of the state had managed to affect significant change at the college.

---

20. White, *Leaders*, p. 312.

21. Palmer, *Thornwell*, p. 130.

22. Ibid., p. 136.

23. Originally from Scotland, John Witherspoon became the president of the College of New Jersey (now Princeton University) and was a signer of the Declaration of Independence.

24. JHT to Gillespie, 4 March 1837, JHTP, SCL.

Other denominations in South Carolina, largely in reaction to the Unitarian views being propagated by Cooper, had established or were exploring the establishment of their own colleges. In 1826, South Carolina's Baptists established Furman University, named for Baptist preacher and colonial patriot Richard Furman (1755–1825). In 1838, the Associate Reformed Presbyterians established Erskine College, named for Scottish Seceder Ebenezer Erskine (1680–1754). The Methodists founded Wofford College, named for Methodist minister Benjamin Wofford (1780–1850) in 1854, and the Lutherans followed suit, establishing Newberry College in 1856. Meanwhile, the mainline Presbyterians were focusing on the reformation of the state college.[25]

The college's board was familiar with Thornwell's transformation from a disciple of the apostle of Unitarianism to a budding stalwart for the Trinitarian faith. They also knew something of his intellectual abilities. They were hoping that he would employ both his convictions and his intellect for the reformation and success of the college.

They were not disappointed. Thornwell served briefly as Professor of Belles Lettres and Logic, and then, after two years pastoring a few blocks away at First Presbyterian Church, he was tasked with leading spiritual reformation as Chair of Sacred Literature and the Evidences of Christianity and college chaplain, positions that were established to counteract Cooper's influence. Thornwell became president of the college in 1851 and served in that capacity until becoming professor of theology at Columbia in 1856. Well before he assumed the presidency, 'he had achieved actual, if unofficial,

---

25. It would not be until 1880 that Presbyterians would establish Presbyterian College in Clinton, South Carolina. We pointed out the influence of Virginia's Presbyterians at the University of Virginia, to the chagrin of Jefferson and Cooper. In addition, North Carolina's Presbyterians exercised significant influence at the University of North Carolina from its founding in 1789 until the late 1800s. In Georgia, Presbyterians enjoyed seasons of influence at the University of Georgia, which was opened in 1801. Ernest Thompson, *Presbyterians in the South*, 3 vols. (Richmond: John Knox Press, 1963–1973), pp. 1.261-63.

hegemony over the institution.'[26] Thomas Law summarised the Presbyterians' appraisal of Thornwell's tenure:

> At the time when young Thornwell entered South Carolina College its president was Dr Thomas Cooper, a man captivating in many respects, but a blatant infidel, who was using his high office to poison the minds of the choicest young men of the State attending upon its chief institution of learning, and in disseminating infidel influences from which our people did not recover for a generation or more. But Dr Thornwell seems to have been the man whom God raised up, qualified and sent to this very fountain of baleful influence to correct and purify it, and redeem the State from its pernicious power.[27]

During his time at the college, Thornwell was the anti-Cooper. For over a decade, Cooper had sought to influence future culture-shapers—lawyers, doctors, entrepreneurs, politicians, and clergy —in a Unitarian direction. Under mounting pressure from the state's Trinitarian voices and only months after the establishment of Columbia Seminary a few blocks away, Cooper delivered the commencement address to the class of 1830. In that speech, which young Thornwell very likely heard first-hand, Cooper mentioned God only in passing: 'Thank God, old men are not destined to live forever in this world' and 'I pray God you may all anxiously aspire to that highest and best of characters.'[28] With Presbyterian pressures for his resignation and the recent establishment of the seminary no doubt in mind, Cooper declared:

> This is not a theological institution and I rejoice that it is not. We are freed from the quarrelsome questions of orthodoxy and heterodoxy, and are wisely left to bestow our attention on objects

26. James Farmer, Jr., *The Metaphysical Confederacy: James Henley Thornwell and the Synthesis of Southern Values* (Macon, GA: Mercer University Press, 1986), p. 80.

27. Thomas Law, 'Dr Thornwell as a Preacher and a Teacher,' *Thornwell Centennial Addresses* (Spartanburg, SC: Band and White Printers, 1913), pp. 11-12.

28. Thomas Cooper, 'Address to the Graduates of South Carolina College, 1830' (Columbia: 1830),' pp. 10, 12.

of more direct and practical utility. By the Constitution of South Carolina, our legislators are prohibited from intermeddling with religious subjects, or legislating on religious considerations: and so of course are all those who derive their authority under them. 'The free exercises and enjoyment of religious profession and worship,' (says our Constitution,) shall forever hereafter be allowed in this State to all mankind, *without discrimination or preference.*

About religion, therefore, I have little to urge. While you remained members of this institution, I have always said to you, what I have always said to the Students who preceded you – that while you are under the control of your parents, it is right and it is wise in you to adopt and profess their religious tenets as your own. They may be in error; but you are quite sure that they are incapable of willfully misleading you. Moreover, while you were here, the College duties were abundantly sufficient, if faithfully attended to, to occupy the whole of your time. But now, that you have arrived at an age when the laws of nature, and the laws of the land, set you free from parental control, and permit you to think for yourselves, take care that your religion is your own; the honest result of your own diligent and impartial inquiry. Whatever you may decide upon in this respect, let your faith be known and judged of by its fruits; by the moral worth of your character, and the habitual uprightness of your conduct. This is all that society has a right to look to. Whoever takes the liberty of inquiring beyond this, inquires impertinently. To our fellow-men we are accountable for our conduct, to no human being are we accountable for our opinions. If I tolerate what I deem the errors and heresies of my neighbor, he has no right to quarrel with me for mine.[29]

Thornwell's chapel sermons and commencement addresses, which he delivered as chaplain and then as president, could not have been more different. In blinding contrast to the messages he heard from Cooper, Thornwell's chapel sermons and presidential addresses were marked by nothing less than *Trinitarian evangelism*. With

---

29. Ibid., p. 7.

Cooper-repudiating language, President Thornwell urged 'the chosen young men of the state' to 'lay their laurels at the feet of Jesus' and take the salvation of their souls seriously because 'God is serious, who exerciseth such patience towards us. Christ is serious, who shed his blood for us. The Holy Ghost is serious, who striveth against the obstinacy of our hearts.'[30] With language clearly meant to counteract the teaching and legacy of his old idol, he declared to the collegians,

> The mysteries of the cross have ever been the stone of stumbling and the rock of offence to philosophic pride, and yet I am firmly persuaded that the essence of Christianity lies precisely in the scheme of redemption. It is a religion for sinners, and whatever illustrations it gives of Natural Theology and the precepts of Moral Philosophy are subsidiary to the end of persuading men to be reconciled to God through the blood of the Redeemer. It is a dispensation of pardon to the guilty and of sanctifying grace to the unholy and depraved. If you are disposed to contemplate Christianity in any other light than as a revelation of God's mercy and grace to [the] fallen in the mediation of His Son, if you are disposed to treat it simply as a development of the doctrine of Natural Religion and to believe that its blessings can be secured by a punctual observance of what are called the duties of morality, I shall have to regret that my labour has been lost among you. You have not so been instructed in the Gospel of Christ. I call these walls to witness that I have not shunned to declare unto you. And the God who searches the hearts and tries the reins of the children of men, knows the intensity of that solicitude with which in season and out of season I have testified to you repentance towards God and faith in the Lord Jesus Christ.[31]

He regularly used this kind of anti-Cooper Trinitarian exhortation, seeking to convince the young men of the college that 'the man who denies the atoning death of the Son, the regenerating

---

30. 'God's Covenant Promise,' 10 October 1852, JHTP, SCL.
31. 'Commencement Sermon,' 6 December 1852, JHTP, SCL.

grace of the Spirit and the eternal love of the Father denies the Gospel. He has denied the faith and is worse than an infidel.'[32] And he summoned them to follow in his footsteps by withstanding what Robbins had called the 'insidious approaches' of Unitarians such as Cooper:

> Never, never be ashamed of the Gospel. Never be ashamed of a crucified Saviour and an indwelling Spirit. Let not an atheist's laugh or a skeptick's sneer deprive you of the richest honour that God can confer on man, the honour of sharing with His own Son the glory of His Heavenly kingdom. My young friends may I hope to meet you at the right hand of the Judge in the day of final accounts? Shall I be permitted to rejoice that I have not labored in vain, nor spent my strength for nought?[33]

In the same address, Thornwell appealed to the collegians:

> My young friends I tell you plainly that none can act well their parts unless they are imbued with the great principles of the Gospel. Christianity is the moral lever of the world. That you may have prejudices against the scheme of salvation by grace, and that the Devil may tempt you with the sanctimonious objections of hypocrites, pharisees and formalists is nothing strange. There are divers forms of infidelity. One attacks the external evidences of religion and endeavors to prove that there are no sufficient credentials of its Divine origin. That form, once buried, has arisen from the dead, but it has not yet revived upon our shores. Your training here has enabled you to grapple with this aspect of skepticism whenever it may assail you. There is another form in which it is more dangerous because more insidious, a form in which the Divine origin of Christianity is acknowledged, but every thing which makes it precious as a system of salvation for sinners is expunged from it. The world in its charity and politeness may apply to these wretched sophisters the name of Christian, but in the eye of God they are infidels of the deepest dye. They acknowledge the seal of Heaven but

---

32. 'Address to the Graduates of South Carolina College,' n.d., JHTP, SCL.
33. Ibid.

deface the handwriting within. The man who denies the atoning death of the Son, the regenerating grace of the Spirit and the eternal love of the Father denies the Gospel. He has denied the faith and is worse than an infidel. These are the doctrines of salvation, and you are saved just in proportion as their truth is accomplished in your own experience. These are the ennobling truths of the Gospel. They introduce you to a noble fellowship and fill you with noble aspirations. It is a strange perverseness that should recoil from a system which makes them God's son and [Christ's] brethren. Remember then I beseech you that it is only in this world of mortal solecisms, where language is often studiously contrived to veil a lie, it is only in this world of sin and death that the arch hypocrisy is honoured by which a man passes for a disciple of Christ when he is not only not led by Christ's Spirit, but absolutely sneers at the thought of any such influences. Depend upon it my young friends that if you have not the Spirit of Christ, you are none of His. If you have never been baptized into His death, if you have never felt the fellowship of His resurrection, if you have never longed for the glory of His presence, if you have never been renewed by the power of His grace, you are infidels in as damning a sense of the term as if you sneered with Gibbon, railed with Voltaire, or prevaricated with Hume. You must be in Christ or you cannot be saved. I shall feel that I have accomplished much if I have disarmed you or your prejudices against the evangelical scheme. But a mightier work remains to be done. Let me beg you not to leave these walls without seeking that union with Christ which is the source of evangelical power. You would be shocked at the imputation that moral excellence is not your highest aim, but this cannot be compassed without the Gospel. You must die with Christ, if you would live with Him above, if you would accomplish your part on earth so as to gain God's approbation and render death a blessing.[34]

Clearly, Thornwell took seriously the board's directive to counteract the teaching of his one-time idol at South Carolina

---

34. Ibid. For candid impressions of Thornwell's preaching by one of his colleagues, see Appendix 2.

College. As seen in their dismissal of Cooper and their appointment of Thornwell, the Presbyterians of the state were determined to retake the college. They were also determined to establish a seminary that would help counteract Cooper's Unitarianism.

## Columbia Seminary Established to Counteract Unitarian Advances

In December of 1828 the Synod of South Carolina and Georgia established the unimaginatively named Theological Seminary of the Synod of South Carolina and Georgia. Its five original students met for one year in Lexington, Georgia, under the direction of Pastor Thomas Goulding, who often boasted that he was 'the first native of Georgia that became a Presbyterian minister since the foundation of the world!'[35] Though Goulding had received a private education in Connecticut, as well as training for the legal profession, which he pursued before becoming a minister, he had no formal seminary training. In spite of his lack of formal training, Goulding, 'a thorough Calvinist of the Genevan school,' was respected as a 'well-read and polished scholar' who had 'gathered rich harvests from the fields of literature'.[36]

In January of 1830, with Goulding continuing as professor, the seminary relocated to Columbia. The school became popularly known as Columbia Theological Seminary, though the name was not formally accepted until 1925. Ironically, just two years later, the seminary relocated to Decatur, Georgia, where it remains today, still bearing the name Columbia Theological Seminary.

---

35. George Howe, 'History of Columbia Theological Seminary,' in *Memorial Volume of the Semi-Centennial of the Theological Seminary at Columbia, South Carolina* (Columbia, SC: Presbyterian Publishing House, 1884), p. 132.

36. F. Goulding, 'Memorial of Thomas Goulding, D. D.' in *Memorial Volume of the Semi-centennial of the Theological Seminary at Columbia, South Carolina* (Columbia, SC: Presbyterian Publishing House, 1884), pp. 184, 185.

The Synod's motivations for establishing Columbia were 'to raise up a qualified and native ministry to supply the destitute places, and to preside over the extant churches; and to provide an institution free from the *skeptical influences which then pervaded the College of the State.*'[37] Rather than retreating to a remote location, the founders situated the seminary just a few blocks from the college. Their strategy was ambitious but straightforward: retake the state, beginning with the capital city, for the Trinitarian faith.[38]

The young seminary's constitution also announced its commitment to Reformed theology: 'The design of this institution is, and ever shall be, to educate young men for the gospel ministry, who shall believe, love and preach the doctrines of the Bible, as set forth in the Confession of Faith of the Presbyterian Church.'[39] At his inauguration, each professor was required to pledge, 'In the presence of God and these witnesses, I do solemnly subscribe the Confession of Faith, Catechisms, and other standards of government, discipline, and worship of the Presbyterian Church in the United States as a just summary of the doctrines contained in the Bible, and promise and engage not to teach, directly or indirectly, any doctrine contrary to this belief, while I continue a Professor in this Seminary.'[40]

The Old School-New School division in American Presbyterianism required Columbia to make its theological identity crystal clear:

---

37. William Robinson, *Columbia Theological Seminary and the Southern Presbyterian Church, 1831–1931: A Study in Church History, Presbyterian Polity, Missionary Enterprise, and Religious Thought* (Decatur, GA: Dennis Lindsey Printing Company, 1931), pp. 12-16, emphasis added.

38. Louis LaMotte, *Colored Light: The Story of the Influence of Columbia Theological Seminary 1828–1936* (Richmond, VA: Presbyterian Committee of Publication, 1937), pp. 35-36; Benjamin Palmer, Jr., 'Opening Address' in *Memorial Volume of the Semi-Centennial of the Theological Seminary at Columbia, South Carolina* (Columbia, SC: Presbyterian Publishing House, 1884), pp. 3-8.

39. Robinson, *Columbia*, p. 209.

40. Ibid.

New School Presbyterianism largely—though not entirely—in the North, was more open to the spirit of the age, and accommodated itself theologically to some aspects of Arminianism and other elements of post-Enlightenment thought. The Old School, which comprised a slight majority in the North and a vast majority in the South, cordially and strictly held to the robust Calvinism of the Westminster standards, and consciously saw itself as challenging the errors of the age. The Presbyterian Church in America ... split over this very issue in 1837.[41]

By the 1830s, Princeton Seminary, which was founded in 1812, had clarified itself as a bastion of Old School Presbyterianism, as had Union Seminary in Virginia, which was also founded in 1812, as the department of theology at Hampden-Sydney College. However, as Thornwell had discovered first-hand, the other leading institution where Reformed ministers were trained had embraced a New School identity. Though established in 1807 as an alternative to the Unitarianism at Harvard, Andover Seminary was, nonetheless, 'founded by a union of the old Calvinists with the Hopkinsians on a platform of avowed toleration.'[42] Thus, with existing Reformed seminaries aligned with different sides of the Old School-New School debate, the question of Columbia's theological identity was on the minds of many.

In 1830, a graduate of Andover, George Howe, joined Goulding as the second member of the faculty. As the more formally educated of the two, Howe became the chief architect of the curriculum, which he based largely on that of his alma mater. Howe's perceived sympathies with New School theology created a crisis at Columbia. At the time, accusations of Unitarianism were often levelled at those who espoused New School theology. As Columbia alumnus Louis LaMotte put it, 'Charges that the

---

41. Douglas Kelly, 'Robert Lewis Dabney,' in *Reformed Theology in America: A History of Its Modern Development*, edited by David F. Wells (Grand Rapids, MI: Baker Books, 1997), p. 214.

42. Robinson, *Columbia*, p. 20. Hopkinsians adhered to New School theology.

faculty sympathized with New School theology, which shaded off into Unitarianism in New England, began to be whispered.'[43] Many feared that, if New School sympathies were tolerated, the seminary would become the very thing it was established to defeat.

Aaron Leland, who, like Howe, was a native of Massachusetts, joined the faculty in 1833. In August of 1834, Leland wrote to his friend Thomas Smyth, an influential member of the board, 'The state of the seminary is bad: we talk of peace but there is no kinship or cordiality. The efforts of Dr G[oulding] ... against Br. H[owe] are secret but untiring. The accusation now is heresy.'[44] Feeling that his voice was not being heard, Goulding, who was never known 'to relax, in public or in private, one jot or tittle of his creed,' left the seminary and returned to the pastorate.[45] Shortly thereafter, charges of heresy against the other professors appeared in print, and local churches produced resolutions regarding the direction of the seminary.[46]

Thus, the new seminary became a microcosm of the Old School-New School tensions, which were dire: 'As the 1830s unfolded, trust eroded, charity dissipated, and the exercise of raw ecclesiastical power for party advantage created a chasm that was impassable.'[47] To many, the future of Columbia Seminary seemed just this bleak.

However, Columbia survived once it clarified its Old School commitments. At the Synod of 1838, Howe and Leland admitted that in earlier days they had leaned towards New Schoolism, but they had eventually embraced the Old School position. The Synod appointed a committee led by Thornwell to write a letter to the churches clarifying the Old School orthodoxy of the seminary. Thornwell's leadership at this crucial juncture laid the foundation

43. LaMotte, *Colored Light*, p. 55.

44. Holifield, *Gentlemen Theologians*, p. 195.

45. Goulding, 'Memorial,' p. 185.

46. Robinson, *Columbia*, pp. 20, 161.

47. Fortson, *Presbyterian Creed*, p. 126.

for his reputation as the 'Calvin', 'Knox' and 'Calhoun' of the Southern Presbyterian Church, and helped establish Columbia as a bulwark from which a Trinitarian counteroffensive could be launched against Unitarian encroachments in South.[48]

---

48. Calhoun, *Our Southern Zion*, pp. 48-49; Robinson, *Columbia*, pp. 211-12. As the 1838 Synod revealed, Thornwell took his role as a presbyter seriously. As a professor at the college, he received criticism for missing some of his classes. He responded to the college president: 'I have been absent, since October, three times – once in attendance upon the sessions of the Synod of South Carolina at Camden, which were held in November, and twice in attendance upon the sessions of the Presbytery of Charleston. I am a member of these ecclesiastical bodies; and according to a distinct understanding betwixt the Board of Trustees and myself, at the time of my election, my connection with the College was to be no hindrance to my full discharge of all my duties as a member of the Courts of my Church. It was only upon the condition, that I should be at liberty to attend the meetings of any and of all the judicatories, with which I was connected, that I consented to accept the appointment which I hold. If the Board have forgotten this understanding I regret it, or if they think it injurious to the College, I hope they will say so frankly and at once; but you and they will see that a man ceases to be effectively a Presbyterian minister when he relinquishes this right' (JHT to Preston, 9 May 1850, JHTP, SCL). For Thornwell as 'Calvin', see Palmer, *Thornwell*, p. 558; as 'Knox', see Paul Garber, 'A Centennial Appraisal of James Henley Thornwell,' in *A Miscellany of American Christianity*, edited by Stuart C. Henry. Durham (NC: Duke University Press, 1963), pp. 7, 24; as 'Calhoun,' see Eugene Genovese, *The Southern Front: History and Politics in the Cultural War* (Columbia, MO: University of Missouri Press, 1995), pp. 12, 34. South Carolinian John C. Calhoun was a US senator, vice president, and the leading politician in the South at the time.

*4*

# Thornwell's Theological Emphases Viewed in Light of His Stand for Trinitarianism

AS many scholars have noted, Scottish Common Sense Realism (SCSR) influenced Thornwell's epistemology.[1] SCSR was a reaction to the epistemology of the Scottish philosopher David Hume, which was marked by *scepticism* about what the human mind can know outside itself. In contrast, the epistemology of SCSR was marked by *certainty* about what the mind can know outside itself. The Scottish Realists maintained that there are 'certain primary intuitions, or fundamental laws of belief, implicitly contained in the constitution of the mind, which, brought into contact with the materials derived from the external world, enable us to know.'[2]

---

1. Theodore Bozeman, 'James Henley Thornwell: Ancient and Modern,' *Affirmation* 6, no. 2 (1993), pp. 50-71; David Garth, 'The Influence of Scottish Common Sense Philosophy on the Theology of James Henley Thornwell and Robert Lewis Dabney,' PhD diss. (Union Theological Seminary, 1979), passim; Holifield, *Gentlemen Theologians*, p. 111; Farmer, *Metaphysical Confederacy*, p. 92; J. Ligon Duncan, III, 'Common Sense and American Presbyterianism: An Evaluation of the Impact of Scottish Realism on Princeton and the South,' MTh thesis (Covenant Theological Seminary, 1987), pp. 45-74.

2. Girardeau, quoted in Palmer, *Thornwell*, p. 541.

Scottish philosophers Thomas Reid and Dugald Stewart developed the philosophy, and moderates in the Church of Scotland made it popular, but it was the conservative great-uncle of Nancy Witherspoon Thornwell who brought it to America when he became president at Princeton.[3] Influenced by Witherspoon, American Presbyterians found in SCSR 'both the epistemological and ontological basis of their natural theology and their philosophical ethics', and they espoused it 'virtually en bloc'.[4] In fact, a wide variety of American thinkers embraced the philosophy, from Unitarian Thomas Jefferson to Old School Princetonian Charles Hodge. SCSR 'was not so much a set of conclusions as it was a way of thinking that could commend itself to a variety of thinkers.'[5]

Gillespie, Robbins, and Cooper taught Thornwell the philosophy, and he eventually used it as a 'handmaiden' for his theology.[6] Macaulay has argued that 'Southern liberals like Samuel Gilman and Southern conservatives like James Henley Thornwell and Robert Lewis Dabney were indebted to Scottish Common Sense Realism for offering a broad foundation on which to reconcile some of their differences and in essence share a common Southern Christian rationalism.'[7] According to Macaulay, through their commitment to SCSR, Gilman and Thornwell possessed many 'shared theological assumptions and positions'.[8]

---

3. Sydney Ahlstrom, 'Scottish Philosophy and American Theology,' *American Society of Church History* 24 (September 1955): pp. 257-72; John Macleod, *Scottish Theology in Relation to Church History* (Edinburgh: Publication Committee of the Free Church of Scotland, 1943), p. 213.

4. 'Common-sense,' in *New Dictionary of Theology* (Downers Grove, IL: InterVarsity Press, 1988); Theodore Bozeman, *Protestants in an Age of Science: The Baconian Ideal and Antebellum Religious Thought* (Chapel Hill: The University of North Carolina Press, 1977), p. 38.

5. George Marsden, 'Scotland and Philadelphia: Common Sense Philosophy from Jefferson to Westminster,' *Reformed Theological Journal* 29 (1979), pp. 8-12; Holifield, *Gentlemen Theologians*, p. 111.

6. Palmer, *Thornwell*, pp. 39, 45; Holifield, *Gentlemen Theologians*, p. 111.

7. Macaulay, *Unitarianism in the Antebellum South*, p. 8.

8. Ibid.

Though it is important to recognize that Thornwell shared certain epistemological assumptions with the Unitarians, it is also important to note that he rejected others and sought to provide alternatives to them. In contrast to the Unitarians, who believed that whatever is incomprehensible is unacceptable, he followed the Church Fathers, who stressed divine incomprehensibility. He embraced the attitudes of Cyril of Jerusalem, who said, 'Our highest knowledge is to confess our ignorance,' and Gregory of Nazianzus, who said, 'I love God because I know Him. I adore Him because I cannot comprehend Him.'[9]

Thornwell especially looked to Calvin to deal with what he called the 'rationalistic infidelity' of the Unitarian movement.[10] While Princeton and Union continued to use Turretin's *Institutes* as their primary textbook, Thornwell replaced it with Calvin's *Institutes* when he became professor of theology at Columbia. Reflecting Calvin, Thornwell disavowed theological systems that assume man's ability to comprehend the divine:

> A theology which has no mysteries; in which everything is level to human thought, and capable of being reduced to exact symmetry in a human system, which has no facts that commend assent while transcending the province of human speculation, and contains no features which stagger the wisdom of human conceit; – a system thus thoroughly human is a system which is self-condemned. It has no marks of God upon it. For His footsteps are on the sea, and His paths in the great waters, and His ways past finding out. There is no searching of His understanding. Such a system would be out of harmony with that finite world in which we have our place. For there mystery encompasses us behind and before – in the earth, the air, the sea and all deep places, and especially in the secrets of our own souls. Man lives and breathes and walks amid mystery in this scene of phenomena and shadows, and yet he would expect no

---

9. James Thornwell, *Collected Writings*, edited by John B. Adger and John L. Girardeau, 4 vols. (Richmond, VA: Presbyterian Committee of Publication, 1871), pp. 1.125, 158.

10. Palmer, *Thornwell*, p. 534.

mystery in that grand and real world of which this is only a dim reflection![11]

In other words, Thornwell believed he could trace heresy to hubris: 'Most heresies have risen from believing the serpent's lie, that our faculties were a competent measure of universal truth. We reason about God as if we possessed an absolute knowledge. The consequence is, we are lost in confusion and error.'[12]

More specifically, he believed that a hubristic epistemology lies behind Unitarianism: 'There is in Theology a region which must be left to the dominion of faith; it can never be entered with the torch of Logic; and most fundamental errors proceed from a disregard of this significant fact, and are only abortive efforts to define the indefinable. The Socinian hopes by searching to find out God, and because he cannot think the Trinity according to the laws of Logic, he denies its existence.'[13]

Perhaps with Cooper's 'A Summary of Unitarian Arguments' in mind, Thornwell summarized the Unitarian's foundational problem:

> The Unitarian professes to understand the Infinite Personality of God, and rejects the doctrine of the Holy Trinity with a smile of contempt. He forgets meanwhile that his argument has only proved that there cannot be three human persons in the same numerical essence. He has quietly eliminated the very element which, for aught he knows or can show, redeems the doctrine from all reasonable objection. Until he can tell us *what* the Infinite is, we need not listen to him while he undertakes to inform us *how* the Infinite is. It is so easy to slide into the habit of regarding the infinite and finite as only different degrees of the same thing, and to reason from one to the other with the same confidence with which, in other cases we reason from the less to the greater, that the caution cannot be too much insisted on that God's thoughts are not our thoughts, nor God's

---

11. Thornwell, *CW*, p. 1.140. See John Calvin, *Institutes of the Christian Religion*, edited by John T. McNeill, translated by Ford L. Battles, 2 vols. (Louisville: Westminster John Knox, 2006), pp. 1.5.9; 1.13.1, 21.

12. Thornwell, *CW*, p. 1.141.

13. Ibid., p. 1.471.

ways our ways. To treat the power which creates and the human power which moves a foreign body as the same thing; to apply to creation the laws and conditions which limit the mechanisms of man; to represent the infinite as only a higher degree of human knowledge; and to restrict each to the same essential conditions and modifications, is to make man God, or God man – a fundamental falsehood, which must draw a fruitful progeny in its train.[14]

According to Thornwell, the only remedy for the 'presumption of the Socinian' is the 'mysterious operations of that Spirit whose office it is to take of the things of Christ and show them unto men.'[15] That was Thornwell's own testimony: he had once been guilty of the 'presumption of the Socinian' but the Spirit of God, working through the Scriptures, had lovingly united him to God's beloved Son by his 'mysterious operations'. This pneumatological emphasis, in addition to SCSR, must be acknowledged in order to have an accurate understanding of Thornwell's theological epistemology.

Palmer summarized it this way:

> Penetrated with the conviction that God can be known only so far as He has been pleased to reveal Himself, [Thornwell] bowed with perfect docility before the dogmatic authority of the Scriptures. The writer has heard him say a dozen times, 'I have been cogitating upon such and such a subject, and can see no flaw in my reasoning, but I am gravelled with one verse in the Bible;' and then he would add, with inexpressible simplicity, 'You know, P., that if there is but one passage of Scripture against us, our speculations must go to the winds.' In this were signalized at once the modesty of the philosopher and the humility of the Christian. He brought all his conclusions to this touch-stone; and wherever he found a 'thus saith the Lord,' he ceased to reason, and began to worship. He first sought, by careful exegesis, to ascertain the meaning of God's word; then to collate and classify, until he built up a systematic theology. As the inductive philosopher ranges through nature, collects his facts, and builds up his science, so

---

14. Ibid., pp. 1.141, 163; Cooper, 'Summary of Unitarian Arguments,' pp. 472-88.
15. Thornwell, *CW*, p. 2.342.

the theologian ranges up and down the inspired record, collects its doctrines as they are strewn in magnificent profusion through the histories, poems, epistles and prophecies of the Bible; and in the same spirit of caution, constructs his scheme of divinity.[16]

And, in a letter to a colleague, Thornwell explained,

> The longer I live, and the more I think, the more profound is my conviction of human ignorance. I can say, too, that I have a growing attachment to the great truths of Christianity. I feel that I am rooted and grounded in the gospel; that its doctrines are incorporated into my whole life, and are the necessary food of my soul. I have looked at the matter on all sides; and I can say, from the heart, that I desire to glory in nothing but the cross of the Lord Jesus Christ. The distinction of being a Christian is the highest honour I would court; and the shallow metaphysics that would take from me the promises of God's Word, I do most heartily despise.[17]

As Thornwell's journal shows, his pneumatological epistemology was not theoretical but rather pastoral. Journal entries demonstrate his desire for Spiritual revival for himself and his parishioners and show his belief that revival came in answer to private and congregational prayer. Entries include sentiments such as the following:

> My mind this day has been much concerned for the welfare of my little flock. Some of them manifest the Spirit of the gospel; but others are cold and lifeless, and seem to take no sort of interest in eternal things. O Lord, revive Thy work .... One fact diminishes the interest of the social prayer meeting – Our male members are so few and diffident that we have never more than three, and often, but <u>one</u> prayer. May the Lord give our few members the Spirit of prayer .... One of the boys bids fair for a desperado. May the Lord arrest him by his Spirit! Great God, give them all hearing ears and understanding hearts .... Was engaged in private prayer for a revival of God's work among the people of Waxhaw .... I am

---

16. Palmer, *Thornwell*, pp. 545-46.
17. JHT to Williams, 26 August 1850, JHT Papers, SCL.

wretched and blind and naked – But the blood of Christ can cleanse me and the Spirit of Christ can purify .... Save me from a legal spirit .... May my heart be the temple of the Holy Ghost .... Reveal to me thy glory in the person of Jesus Christ. May I see the Saviour's loveliness and surrender myself unreservedly to him .... Attended camp meetings at Bethesda. Seasons of refreshing. Oh Lord revive thy work. Stir up Christians and awaken and convict the careless and unconcerned.[18]

Thornwell's epistemology should not only be understood by what it had in common with Unitarians such as Cooper and Gilman through SCSR, it should also be understood in light of Thornwell's effort to stand for Trinitarian supernaturalism against Unitarian rationalism. For Thornwell, there was a complimentary relationship between SCSR and pneumatology: the mind is furnished with the capacity to know reality outside itself, but, in order to know *divine* reality, a gracious illuminating work of the third person of the Trinity is required.

## Thornwell's Trinitarian Hermeneutic

In keeping with his conviction that theology is fundamentally receptive rather than speculative, Thornwell based his Trinitarianism on the Bible. Believing that the God of both the Old and New Testaments is the *Triune* God, he had a Trinitarian hermeneutic of both Testaments. He believed that the doctrine of the Trinity was communicated in the first verse of the Bible through the name *Elohim*. Rather than interpreting the plurality expressed in this title for God as a *pluralis majestatis*, he believed that 'This word by its very form is intended to express the triune Personality of God. It is the name of the Trinity – the Father, the Son and the Holy Ghost.'[19]

---

18. JHT Journal, passim, JHTP, CBK. Beginning in 1802, Bethesda Presbyterian Church in York, South Carolina, held large camp meetings, such as the one Thornwell attended, and became a focal point of the Second Great Awakening. See Lacy Ford, Jr., *Origins of Southern Radicalism: The South Carolina Upcountry 1800–1860* (Oxford: Oxford University Press, 1988), p. 26.

19. Thornwell, *CW*, p. 1.150.

He also believed that the words 'Let us make man in our image,' in Genesis 1:26, communicated the Triune nature of God.[20]

This put him at odds with Calvin and most of his Reformed contemporaries.[21] His Trinitarian hermeneutic was less like Calvin and his own generation, whose wariness of eisegesis controlled their hermeneutic, and more like the church fathers, who 'had no qualms whatsoever about reading preconceived theological ideas into a given passage, as long as they got those ideas from elsewhere in the Bible.'[22]

In 'A Summary of Unitarian Arguments', Cooper pointed out that the Council of Sirmium (351) 'anathematized all who denied that God the Father spake to God the Son, when he said, "Let us make man."'[23] But, noted Cooper, 'the attempts that have been made by Trinitarian expositors formerly, to deduce the doctrine

---

20. Ibid.

21. John Calvin, *Genesis,* vol. 1, *Commentaries* (Grand Rapids, MI: Baker Books, 2003), p. 1.1; Charles Hodge, Systematic Theology, 3 vols. (Peabody, MA: Hendrickson Publishers, 2003), pp. 1.442-82; Robert Dabney, *Systematic Theology* (Edinburgh: Banner of Truth, 1996), p. 182; William Shedd, *Dogmatic Theology* (Phillipsburg, NJ: P&R Publishing, 2003), p. 227. Thornwell was familiar with Calvin's commentaries, including his commentary on Genesis (*CW*, pp. 1.111, 564). Although Thornwell parted ways with Calvin regarding the interpretation of *Elohim*, he was in agreement with Calvin's contemporary, Heinrich Bullinger, who held that '*Bara Elohim*' in Genesis 1:1 reveals 'the mystery of the reverend Trinity; for Moses seemeth to have said in effect, In the beginning that God in the Trinity created heaven and earth' (Quoted in Douglas Kelly, *Systematic Theology*, vol. 1, *Grounded in Holy Scripture and Understood in the Light of the Church; The God Who Is: The Holy Trinity* (Fearn, Scotland: Mentor, 2008), p. 1.292).

22. Fairbairn, *Life in the Trinity*, p. 110. For analysis of the church fathers' Trinitarian hermeneutic, see ibid., pp. 108-29. 'In interpreting the Bible, we start with the immediate context of the passage in question, and we generally refuse to allow any interpretation of that passage that cannot be drawn from the passage itself. In sharp contrast, the church fathers started with the whole Bible, with its entire message, and they read each passage in light of that entire message. We start from the narrow and work to the broad. They started from the broad and read each narrow passage in light of their understanding of the Bible's broad, overall message' (Ibid., p. 111).

23. Cooper, 'Summary of Unitarian Arguments,' p. 516.

of the Trinity from the Old Testament, have been so inconceivably absurd, that even Trinitarians, of *modern* times, reject them entirely.'[24] Thornwell was willing to be out of step with 'modern' Trinitarians in this regard, and, as we will see, other Columbians were willing to do the same.

## Thornwell's Trinitarian Soteriology

### *The Trinitarian Nature of Natural Religion*

Thornwell believed in the Trinitarian nature of both 'natural religion' and 'supernatural religion'. He preferred to use the terms 'natural religion' and 'supernatural religion' rather than the more common terms of 'natural religion' and 'revealed religion' because he believed that 'we are as much indebted to revelation for any adequate knowledge of natural religion as for the mysteries of the Gospel'.[25] By 'natural religion', Thornwell meant the religion of Adam and Eve before the fall; by 'supernatural religion' he meant the religion of grace after the fall. According to Thornwell, because natural religion is based on God's self-disclosure, it does not consist of a vague, Unitarian conception of God: 'The doctrine of the Trinity is a doctrine of natural religion.'[26]

Thornwell noted his disagreement in this regard with Joseph Butler, author of the highly influential *Analogy of Religion, Natural and Revealed.* Butler asserted that natural religion is directed exclusively to God the Father who, in natural religion, is experienced as a Unitarian God, and that revealed religion is directed to all three Persons of the Godhead.[27] Thornwell, on the other hand, posited that the difference between natural and supernatural religion is 'not in the *objects* to which they are respectively directed, but in the *relations* under which those objects are contemplated.'[28] Natural religion contemplates God as

---

24. Ibid.
25. Thornwell, *CW*, p. 2.61fn.
26. Ibid., p. 2.64.
27. Butler, *Analogy of Religion*, pp. 208-09.
28. Thornwell, *CW*, p. 3.210.

Creator and Governor; supernatural religion contemplates God as Redeemer and Savior, but,

> The Trinity is alike the object of both. It was the Father, Son, and Holy Ghost who created Adam, and he was bound to worship the Trinity—for there is no other God—under the pain of idolatry. Natural religion is as much revealed as supernatural. If its object be the Trinity, nature never could discover the personality of the Deity. Adam was dependent upon the Author of his being for the knowledge of His name. And though, when the object of worship was once made known, and the relations in which man stood to the Deity discovered, the duties were a matter of obvious deduction, yet, as the same holds in supernatural religion, revelation is equally important to both. By natural religion we understand the religion of man in his state of nature as he came from the hands of his Maker; by supernatural religion, the religion of sinners redeemed by grace and restored to the favour of God. The covenant of works is natural, the covenant of grace supernatural, religion; and both are equally revealed.[29]

By emphasizing the Trinitarianism of natural religion, Thornwell was distinguishing himself from the nineteenth-century norm, which gave pre-eminence to natural theology. He believed that natural theology alone would never lead one to know the Triune God, but rather to merely assent to a vague Unitarian deity. He wanted to present a clear alternative to the general drift towards Unitarianism, which he believed was nothing more than theological nominalism: 'If we do not believe *one God* in *three Persons*, we embrace only a name without the reality.'[30]

Thornwell loved the *Westminster Standards*, to which he subscribed as a presbyter and professor.[31] Yet, so strong was his desire to rid the church of any confusion or compromise with Unitarianism,

---

29. Ibid.

30. Ibid., p. 1.607.

31. Ibid., pp. 1.575-576; Palmer, *Thornwell*, pp. 162, 165, 172; W. Rankin, *James Henley Thornwell and the Westminster Confession of Faith* (Greenville, SC: A Press, 1986); *Constitution of the Theological Seminary of the Synod of South Carolina and Georgia* (Columbia, SC: 1844).

Thornwell was willing to critique the *Standards* when he felt they fell short of adequately articulating God's Triunity. Specifically, he criticised question four of the *Shorter Catechism*, which asks, 'What is God?' and answers, 'God is a Spirit, infinite, eternal and unchangeable in his being, wisdom, power, holiness, justice, goodness and truth.' Thornwell found that definition to be defective: 'It seems to me that the peculiar personality of God should have been distinctly and prominently announced. He is not only Spirit, but Personal Spirit, and not Personal barely, but Tri-personal – the Father, the Son and the Holy Ghost.'[32] Thornwell was well aware that subsequent questions in the *Catechism* teach the tri-personal nature of God, but he wanted it to be conveyed at the outset.

On the other hand, nineteenth century Unitarians enthusiastically affirmed the definition provided in question four. George Burnap declared, 'No better definition can be given than the answer ... "God is a spirit, infinite, eternal, unchangeable in his being, wisdom, power, holiness, justice, goodness, and truth." As long as we keep to this definition, our conception of God is clear, distinct, and unembarrassed.'[33] Of course, he went on to condemn question six, which asserts the Triunity of God: 'But the moment you introduce three persons into his essence, all becomes to us darkness and confusion, inconsistency and contradiction.'[34] According to Burnap, question six contains 'one of the most marvellous fallacies ever imposed upon the human mind'.[35]

In his critique of the *Catechism*, as in other instances, Thornwell's Trinitarian emphasis placed him out of step with his Old

---

32. Thornwell, *CW*, p. 1.161; James Thornwell, 'A Student's Notes on Theological Lectures delivered by JHT,' Part 4 (Columbia Seminary Notebooks, Reformed Theological Seminary Library Archives, Jackson, MS), p. 4.47.

33. George Burnap, 'Unitarian Christianity Expounded and Defended,' in *The Old and the New: Or, Discourses and Proceedings at the Dedication of the Re-Modeled Unitarian Church in Charleston, S.C. on Sunday, April 2, 1854. Preceded by The Farewell Discourse Delivered in the Old Church, on Sunday, April 4, 1852* (Charleston, SC: Samuel G. Courtenay, 1854), p. 128.

34. Ibid.

35. Ibid.

School compatriots. Hodge of Princeton believed, 'Probably the best definition of God ever penned by man, is that given in the Westminster Catechism: "God is a Spirit, infinite, eternal, and unchangeable, in his being, wisdom, power, holiness, justice, goodness, and truth."'[36] Thornwell's willingness to critique the Standards should also be viewed in contrast to Dabney of Union, who maintained that 'The Confession will need no amendment until the Bible needs to be amended'.[37] Against such a notion, Thornwell argued, 'A Protestant Church, with an unchangeable creed, is an anomaly. Its very name is a confession of its liability to err; and that no provision should be made for correcting its errors seems not a little extravagant …. What we insist on is, that our Standards should not be rendered absolutely unalterable.'[38] His theological priority reflected his own conversion experience: he was first a Trinitarian and then a Westminsterian.

### The Trinitarian Nature of Supernatural Religion

In July of 1852, representing South Carolina College, Thornwell visited Harvard once again. He wrote his wife regarding his impression of the commencement activities:

> They concluded the dinner by singing the seventy-eighth Psalm. This has been an old custom, handed down from the Puritan fathers. It was really an imposing ceremony; and I should have enjoyed it very much, if I had not remembered that they were all Unitarians, witnessing, in this very service, to their own condemnation…. You cannot imagine how attractive this place is to me. There is but one draw-back, and that is the *religion*; it makes me sad to see such men, so accomplished, so elegant, at once such finished gentlemen and such admirable scholars, sunk into so vile a faith. I have really had scruples about associating with them as I have done.[39]

---

36. Hodge, *Systematic Theology*, p. 1.367.

37. Robert Dabney, 'The Doctrinal Contents of the Confession,' in *Memorial Volume of the Westminster Assembly, 1647–1897* (Richmond, VA: The Presbyterian Committee of Publication, 1897), p. 95.

38. Thornwell, *CW*, pp. 4.442-43.

39. Palmer, *Thornwell*, p. 361.

Thornwell viewed Unitarianism as 'vile' not only because it denies the Trinity, but also because to deny the Trinity is to deny any hope of salvation. For Thornwell, saving grace is necessarily Triune grace. Thus, as we will now consider, every aspect of his soteriology was remarkably Trinitarian.

## The Trinity and the Plan of Redemption

If one were only to read the characterization of Thornwell's theology proffered by Cambridge historian Michael O'Brien, one might believe that Thornwell had very little to say about redemption. According to O'Brien, 'As was the norm in the Calvinist tradition, Thornwell's was a God-centered Christianity, in which Christ was a marginal figure. He was thus very far from the twentieth-century tradition of Southern evangelicalism, whose every second word was to become "Jesus." Thornwell's "Lectures on Theology" of the late 1850s barely mention Christ.'[40] In addition, 'Thornwell's language about God was often ecstatic, almost sensually masochistic, and centered more on God's power and will than on his love.'[41]

Although it is beyond our scope to address O'Brien's claim that the marginalization of Christ is 'the norm in the Calvinist tradition', we will address his claim that Christ and the love of God were marginalized in Thornwell's theology. Regarding his claim that Thornwell's 'Lectures on Theology' 'barely mention Christ', several points should be made. 'Lectures on Theology' are the sixteen lectures included in volume one of Thornwell's *Collected Writings*. The 'Lectures' should be read in light of the prefatory comments of the editor of volume one, John Adger, who stressed that these lectures only covered Thornwell's teaching on theology proper, creation, the covenant of works, and hamartiology. Thornwell had planned to publish lectures covering Christology and soteriology, but 'death cut short the full execution of his plan'.[42]

---

40. O'Brien, *Conjectures*, p. 1119.

41. Ibid.

42. Adger in Thornwell, *CW*, p. 1.23.

In volume two of Thornwell's *Collected Writings*, Adger incorporated a number of Thornwell's discourses that focused on Christological and soteriological themes. Yet, contrary to O'Brien's claims, even in 'Lectures on Theology', Thornwell stressed the Triunity of God and consistently declared his belief that true theology is founded only on the revelation and knowledge of God *in Christ*.[43]

As we broaden the scope from 'Lectures on Theology' to the rest of his writings, we find even more evidence that O'Brien's assertion that Thornwell's Christianity was one in which 'Christ was a marginal figure' is simply a mischaracterisation. We will not attempt to amass all the evidence to disprove O'Brien's assertion; a sampling must suffice.

The following excerpts chosen from various 'genres' of Thornwell's writings reveal the true character of his Christianity: When his first fiancée broke off their engagement, a young, heartbroken Thornwell wrote a friend about his reliance on the 'Spirit of Christ'.[44] During his first pastorate, Thornwell wrote Gillespie: 'Whenever the Lord calls, I trust, I shall be ready to go. I belong to him and not to myself. The gospel of the Son of God can support me abundantly. Jesus is all-sufficient and I have no doubts of his willingness to save me. I have much vileness. I am less than the least of all his mercies, but, blessed be his name, they are free and he assures me that I am welcome to Christ and full and complete redemption in him. I believe his assurance and in the name of Christ can often give the challenge to all my spiritual enemies, "who shall separate me from the love of Christ?"'[45] To a ministerial colleague he wrote, 'I desire to glory in nothing but the cross of the Lord Jesus Christ.'[46]

---

43. For his emphasis on the Triunity of God, see *CW*, pp. 1.23, 26, 28, 141, 150-152, 161, 163, 189, 205, 440. For his Christ-centredness, see *CW*, pp. 1.29-32, 39, 71, 76, 80, 98-99, 133, 138-139, 150-151, 155-156, 161, 197, 200, 201, 261, 287-300, 310, 423, 426, 428, 436-441.

44. JHT to Alexander Pegues, 8 July 1835, JHTP, SCL.

45. JHT to Gillespie, 4 March 1837, JHTP, SCL.

46. Palmer, *Thornwell*, p. 344.

In his journal, he prayed, 'I am wretched and blind and naked – But the blood of Christ can cleanse me and the Spirit of Christ can purify …. May my heart be the temple of the Holy Ghost …. Reveal to me thy glory in the person of Jesus Christ.'[47]

To his young children he wrote, 'You must pray to God every night when you go to bed, and every morning when you get up. You must ask Him, for the sake of Jesus Christ, to give you His Spirit. The Spirit will make you feel that you are sinners, that you need a Saviour; and will enable you to believe in Jesus Christ …. Jesus Christ saves children, as well as grown people.'[48]

Representative of the focus of his pulpit ministry, as chaplain at South Carolina College, he declared to the collegians:

> The glory of Christianity is its Saviour, and His power to save is in the blood by which He extinguished the fires of the curse, and the righteousness by which He bought life for all his followers. Jesus made our curse, Jesus made our righteousness, this, this is the Gospel! All else is philosophy and vain deceit. This it is which gives Christianity its power. By this, and this alone, it subdues the ferocity of passion, disarms temptations of its violence, disrobes the world of its charms, changes the tiger into the lamb, and makes the lion eat straw like the ox. This constitutes the grand difference between the religion of Mohammed and the religion of Jesus, between the Koran and the Bible.[49]

Again, to the collegians he explained the nature of Christianity: 'The nature of religion: It is just friendship with God through X. It is a personal intercourse with the Father of our spirits, a real living communion with Him that made us. What can be more sublime, what more ennobling, what more purifying? In his word, his ordinances and our duties, we know Him to be present as we know the presence of a friend.'[50]

---

47. JHT Journal, JHTP, CBK, 19 June 1836, 5 September 1836.
48. Palmer, *Thornwell*, p. 295.
49. Thornwell, 'The Necessity and Nature of Christianity,' *CW*, p. 2.97.
50. 'God's Covenant Promise,' 10 October 1852, JHTP, SCL.

He asked the graduates of the class of 1852: 'Have I succeeded in impressing upon any of you the importance of religion and particularly of that work of the Holy Ghost by which you are brought into union with Christ?'[51] And as he was delivering the address, he cried out in prayer, 'Blessed Jesus I commend these young men to thee and fervently beseech thee to draw them to thyself.'[52]

In a baccalaureate address he told the students, 'No religion can ever solve for a sinner the problem of life or quicken him who is dead in trespasses and sins but the Gospel of Jesus Christ.... In the spirit of Paul, we should count all things but loss for the excellency of the knowledge of Jesus Christ our Lord.'[53]

At the General Assembly of 1856, he declared, 'The charity for man which sacrifice obviously expresses was conspicuous in the whole career of Jesus. His bosom glowed with love.'[54] In another sermon he spoke of that 'supreme love, that wonderful love of God which spared not His own Son, but delivered Him up for His enemies .... Here is the magic of the Cross; it presents a scene of love such as the world had never seen before and will never see again .... Here was love, unspeakable love, "When God the mighty Maker died for man the creature's sin."'[55] One wonders why O'Brien would say that Thornwell's Christianity was one in which 'Christ was a marginal figure', when Thornwell himself constantly reiterated his belief that 'the cross of Christ is the centre of the Christian system'.[56]

Thornwell's Christ-centred redemptive preaching should be understood in contradistinction to what he called the 'Christless Christianity'—the moralism—of Cooper, who insisted that atonement for sin and regeneration by the Spirit were superfluous

---

51. 'Commencement Sermon,' 6 December 1852, JHTP, SCL.

52. Ibid.

53. 'Baccalaureate Address,' 4 December 1854, JHTP, SCL.

54. 'The Sacrifice of Christ,' CW, p. 2.422.

55. 'The Nature of Salvation,' CW, p. 2.379.

56. 'The Necessity of the Atonement,' CW, p. 2.57.

and even dangerous doctrines, and that 'the Unitarian opinion contains every thing necessary to influence the dispositions and the practice of men on the side of morality.'[57] Thornwell believed that it was no coincidence that Unitarians such as Cooper rejected both the orthodox plan of redemption and the doctrine of the Trinity, for he believed the two doctrines are inextricably related. As chaplain, Thornwell asserted to the students under his care,

> The doctrine of the Trinity is so evidently involved in the scheme of redemption that it is morally impossible to deny the one without denying the other. The most satisfactory proof of the essential unity and personal distinctions of the Father, the Son and the Holy Ghost is to be found in the offices which each discharges in the economy of grace. If not a single passage existed in the Scriptures directly establishing this mysterious truth of revelation, it might be collected as a necessary inference from the moral appearances which we are called to contemplate in the plan of salvation. The same principle of ratiocination by which we establish the Being of God from the operation of His hands, the natural disposition to ascend from effects to the causes which produce them—to follow a stream until we reach the fountain by which it is supplied—will also lead us from the phenomena of grace to acknowledge three agents of unlimited perfections, essentially the *same* and yet *distinct*. As the heavens declare the glory of God, and the firmament showeth His handiwork, as the invisible things of Him are clearly seen, being understood by the things that are made, so the purpose, execution and accomplishment of that wonderful method by which the guilty are accepted, the dead are quickened and the ruined saved, reveal, clearly as any effect can disclose its cause, the separate, distinct and harmonious operations of the Triune God.[58]

Moreover, Thornwell sought to explain how Christians, from uneducated laity to learned clergy, could so readily believe a

---

57. Palmer, *Thornwell*, p. 79; Cooper, 'A Summary of Unitarian Arguments,' p. 501.

58. 'The Personality of the Holy Ghost,' *CW*, p. 2.343.

doctrine so incomprehensible as the Trinity. He emphasized to the undergraduates:

> The evidence, perhaps, upon which the large majority of Christians receive this article of faith is the spiritual experience of their own hearts. They have not studied isolated texts nor collected together the names, titles and achievements which are promiscuously ascribed to each of the Persons of the Godhead; but they have been conscious of their own moral necessities – they have admired the beauty and rejoiced in the fitness of those exquisite arrangements by which their need has been relieved. They know, because they have felt, the love of the Father, the grace of the Son, and the communion of the Holy Spirit …. That scheme stands like a temple of majestic proportions, and bears visibly engraved upon its portals, not only the name of God, like the ancient temple of Isis, but also the sublime mystery of His personal distinctions. In walking about Zion, telling her towers and marking well her bulwarks, we perceive the hand of the Father, the hand of the Son and the hand of the Holy Ghost. There are palaces adorned for the great King which we are exhorted to consider, for there the Trinity reigns, there God displays his mysterious personality, and the whole house is filled with His glory.[59]

Thus, argued Thornwell to the future culture shapers of South Carolina, the Unitarian rejects the Trinity, of which he cannot fully conceive, while concurrently rejecting grace, of which he feels no need. The Trinitarian accepts the Trinity, of which he likewise cannot fully conceive, because he accepts grace, of which he desperately feels his need. The more one appreciates grace, the more one adores the persons of the 'adorable Trinity' for their distinct roles in the plan of grace.[60]

Scholars have noted that Thornwell differed from Charles Hodge regarding the validity of Roman Catholic baptism, with Thornwell denying and Hodge affirming it. We raise the issue here not to engage in a lengthy discussion of it, but rather to

59. Ibid., pp. 2.343-45.
60. Ibid., pp. 2.323, 341, 345-46.

highlight one of the primary reasons *why* Thornwell held that position.

Hodge and Thornwell agreed that Unitarian baptism should be rejected because Unitarians affirm neither the ontological Trinity (who the Triune God is) nor the economic Trinity (what the Triune God does in redemption). Hodge, however, argued that Roman Catholic baptism is valid because the Roman Catholic Church affirms the ontological Trinity. In response, Thornwell argued that the ontological Trinity cannot be divorced from the economic Trinity. He reasoned that, because the Trinity revealed in the plan of free grace is the only Trinity there is, the Trinity of Roman Catholicism is a false Trinity. To his fellow presbyters, he announced that 'the Trinity of Rome is officially a different Trinity than ours …. To baptize in the name of the Father, Son and Spirit is not to pronounce these words as an idle form or a mystical charm, but to acknowledge that solemn compact into which these glorious Agents entered, from eternity, for the redemption of the Church.'[61]

In order to prevent a scenario in which only Old School Presbyterian baptisms would be accepted, Thornwell emphasized his belief that the fundamental doctrines of salvation by grace alone are what must be maintained in order for baptism to be valid. Thus, while denying the validity of Roman Catholic baptism, Thornwell sought to maintain a spirit of evangelical catholicity: 'To be immersed or sprinkled—a formal invocation of the names of the Trinity accompanying the deed—is not necessarily to be baptized. There must be reference to the economy of grace, a distinct recognition of that precious scheme of redemption *in its essential features and fundamental doctrines*, without which ordinances are worthless and duties are bondage.'[62]

---

61. Thornwell, 'Baptism of the Church of Rome,' *CW*, pp. 3.295-97; Charles Hodge, 'Romish Baptism,' *The Biblical Repertory and Princeton Review* 17, no. 3 (July 1845), pp. 446-68. Neither Thornwell nor Hodge used the terms ontological Trinity or economic Trinity. We are using the terms to summarise their arguments.

62. Thornwell, 'Baptism of the Church of Rome,' *CW*, p. 3.295.

## The Trinity and the Atonement

Scholars have also noted that Thornwell viewed the atonement through a strong Trinitarian lens.[63] However, exploration as to *why* Thornwell would have theologized about the atonement in such a robustly Trinitarian way has been lacking. The only scholar who has thoroughly explored this question is literary scholar Thomas Jenkins.

According to Jenkins, Thornwell emphasized the Trinitarian nature of the atonement because of the influence of romanticism on his theology. When it comes to character development, the literary styles of neoclassicism and sentimentalism 'emphasise a certain emotional singularity', but in romanticism, 'there is a fascination with emotional ambivalence.'[64] Whereas characters within neoclassical and sentimental literature only exhibit one predominant feeling, 'romantic characters typically struggle with contradictory feelings.'[65]

Jenkins posited that the influence of these literary movements on nineteenth-century American Protestantism was as follows: Neoclassicism characterized God as exclusively serene; sentimentalism characterized Him as exclusively sympathetic; but romanticism characterized Him as ambivalent. Neoclassical and sentimental notions about God more naturally led to Unitarian theologies in which God was defined by a single emotion, which, for nineteenth-century Unitarians, was sympathetic love. On the other hand, theologians influenced by romanticism were 'lucky to have the Trinity', because through the interpersonal relationships of the Trinity, God's emotional life is not one-dimensional but rather complex.[66]

One of those lucky theologians was Thornwell, who, as Jenkins observed, was particularly concerned with the 'social relations of the Trinity'.[67] Jenkins also noted the way Thornwell

---

63. Kelly, *Systematic Theology*, pp. 2.435-36; O'Brien, *Conjectures*, pp. 397, 1142-43.
64. Thomas Jenkins, *The Character of God: Recovering the Lost Literary Power of American Protestantism* (Oxford: Oxford University Press, 1997), pp. 7, 8.
65. Ibid., p. 8.
66. Ibid., p. 100.
67. Ibid., p. 104.

presented the emotional complexity of the atonement, with the Son demonstrating love to the Father while the Father poured out His wrath on His beloved sin-bearing Son. Based on these observations, Jenkins surmised that romanticism is what led Thornwell to develop his doctrine of Trinitarian atonement.

However, the closest Jenkins came to providing evidence for his thesis was when he pointed out that Thornwell had been a professor of 'belles lettres' (literature valued for its aesthetic quality). But to argue that Thornwell's Trinitarian doctrine of the atonement was the result of his interest in literature is a stretch, especially since there is no evidence that he had a particular proclivity for *romantic* literature.[68]

A more tenable answer to why Thornwell emphasized the Trinitarian nature of the atonement is because of his overall Trinitarian response to Cooper's Unitarianism. The sermon that Jenkins analyzed—'The Necessity of the Atonement'—was one that Thornwell preached to the graduates of South Carolina College. For over a decade Cooper had delivered the annual address to graduates, including Thornwell himself. Needless to say, he did not speak to the students about their need for atonement.[69] In fact, Cooper believed that the evangelical doctrine of redemption leads to immorality and social decay: 'That a life of crime may be fully expiated by a few minutes of repentance, may be Calvin's religion, but it is not a tenet that society ought to encourage.'[70]

To collegians and anyone else who would listen, Cooper had portrayed 'the idolatrous worship of Jesus Christ as God equal to the Father, the doctrine of the Trinity connected with it, and that of atonement, as the chief and most signal corruptions of Christianity, and the most obstinately retained.'[71] He taught that the Cross was not a substitutionary atonement for sin and that

---

68. Ibid.

69. For examples, see 'Address to the Graduates of South Carolina College, 1821' (Columbia: 1821) and 'Address to Graduates, 1830.'

70. Cooper, 'The Scripture Doctrine of Materialism,' p. 8.

71. Cooper, 'A Review of Dr Priestley's Theological Works,' p. 766.

the doctrine of penal substitution was monstrous.[72] For Cooper, the Cross was merely an example of human devotion to God, which should inspire others to devote themselves to God as well.[73]

In his chapel sermons and addresses on the atonement, Thornwell sought to counter the teaching of his one-time idol, though he never mentioned him by name. Speaking unfavourably in public about one's predecessor would be out of step with the rules of Southern gentility. So, instead of mentioning Cooper directly, he spoke of 'sophists', 'skeptics' and 'Socinians' who viewed the necessity of atonement as 'inexplicable jargon'.[74] According to Thornwell, Unitarians view atonement as unnecessary because the Unitarian God is neither a God of justice nor a God of love. Justice and love require relationship, which a Unitarian deity does not inherently possess.[75] Only the Triune God is inherently just and loving, and thus only the Triune God is able and willing to provide full atonement for sin:

> God cannot absolutely pardon. He can only transfer the punishment. He cannot set aside the sanction of His law, but only can give it a different direction. Who, then, can save from going down to the pit? It was reserved for the wisdom of the Eternal to answer this question. The sublime idea of the incarnation and death of the Son could only have originated in the mind of Him who is wonderful in counsel and unsearchable in His judgments. In Jesus, the Mediator of the new covenant, we behold a kinsman, who, through the eternal Spirit, is able to endure the wrath of God—a man who can satisfy justice and yet recover from the stroke—a Being who could die and in dying conquer death.[76]

---

72. Cooper, 'An Exposition of the Doctrines of Calvinism,' p. 15.

73. Cooper, 'A Review of Dr Priestley's Theological Works,' p. 576.

74. Thornwell, 'The Necessity of the Atonement,' *CW*, p. 2.208.

75. Ibid., pp. 2.234-48.

76. Ibid., p. 2.255. As this quote demonstrates, Hebrews 9:14 was foundational for Thornwell's doctrine of Trinitarian atonement. See also 'The Sacrifice of Christ,' *CW*, p. 2.416.

To Thornwell and his classmates, President Cooper had declared, 'It is the habit of mental exertion, the facility of studying, arising from constant practice, the acquired power of commanding and fixing your attention, upon which you must rely for your future reputation and success.'[77] To the graduates who had been under his tutelage, President Thornwell offered a different recipe for success:

> Let me impress it upon you that the first, the indispensable element of success in your future career must be sought in the favour of God.... No doubt, my brethren, your bosoms are bounding with hope, the future seems full of promise, and you are eager to enter upon the scenes of manly life. But be assured that the first care which should demand your attention is the salvation of the soul. What you first need, most pressingly need, is to have your conscience purged from dead works by the blood of Him who, through the Eternal Spirit, offered Himself without spot unto God.[78]

## The Trinity and the Doctrine of Adoption

Several scholars have discussed the fact that Columbia emphasized adoption more than Princeton and Union.[79] They have argued that the reason for that was because, while Princeton and Union used Turretin's *Institutes* and followed him in subsuming adoption under justification, Columbia used Calvin's *Institutes* and followed him in giving a prominent place to adoption.[80]

---

77. Cooper, 'Address to the Graduates, 1830,' p. 5.

78. Thornwell, 'Necessity of the Atonement,' *CW*, p. 2.259.

79. Robinson, *Columbia*, pp. 209-19; Sinclair Ferguson, 'Reformed Doctrine of Sonship,' in *Pulpit and People: Essays in Honour of William Still*, edited by Nigel M. De S. Cameron and Sinclair B. Ferguson (Edinburgh: Rutherford House, 1986), pp. 81-88; Douglas Kelly, 'Adoption: An Underdeveloped Heritage of the Westminster Standards,' *The Reformed Theological Review* 52, no. 3 (Sept.–Dec. 1993), pp. 110-20; Stephen Berry, *Sons of God, An Examination of the Doctrine of Adoption in the Thought of John Lafayette Girardeau* (St. Louis, MO: PCA Historical Center, 1997); Tim Trumper, 'An Historical Study of Adoption in the Calvinistic Tradition.' PhD diss. (University of Edinburgh, 2001), pp. 398-455.

80. R. Webb, *Christian Salvation: Its Doctrine and Experience* (Richmond, VA: Presbyterian Committee of Publication, 1921), p. 399; Kelly, 'Adoption,'

O'Brien offered a different theory, suggesting that Thornwell emphasized adoption because of his own personal journey of living in servants' quarters as the son of an overseer, experiencing the death of his father, and then being adopted into 'the warmth of the household' of patrons Gillespie and Robbins.[81] The same sort of theory might be applied to Columbia theologian John L. Girardeau, who also emphasized adoption. Girardeau's mother died when he was very young and his father was a rather distant figure in his life.[82] In addition to these theories, it is important to view the Columbians' doctrine of adoption in light of their stand for the Trinity. Unitarian theology presented a doctrine of the universal fatherhood of God. A popular joke was that Unitarians believed in the fatherhood of God, the brotherhood of man, and the neighborhood of Boston![83]

We will discuss adoption at later points in our study, but for now we will simply note that Thornwell and the other Columbians made much of adoption because they wanted to present the biblical doctrine in contrast to the Unitarian's doctrine of universal fatherhood. The Columbians insisted that the only way sinners

---

p. 112; Francis Turretin, *Institutes of Elenctic Theology*, edited by James T. Dennison, Jr., translated by George Musgrave Giger, 2 vols. (Phillipsburg, NJ: P&R Publishing, 1992), pp. 2.256-68.

81. O'Brien, *Conjectures*, pp. 1114, 1145.

82. George Blackburn, ed., *The Life Work of John L. Girardeau, D.D., LL.D.* (Columbia, SC: The State Company, 1916), p. 19. Girardeau was converted as a student at Charleston College while under Smyth's ministry. As a student at Columbia, he heard the sermons of Thornwell at the college chapel and Palmer at First Presbyterian. After graduating from Columbia, he pastored Zion Presbyterian Church, an outreach to the slaves. In 1876, Girardeau became a professor at Columbia Seminary, from which he retired in 1895. Kelly, *Preachers with Power*, pp. 121-29; Calhoun, *Our Southern Zion*, pp. 221-40. For a thorough examination of Girardeau, see C. Willborn, 'John L. Girardeau (1825–98), Pastor to Slaves and Theologian of Causes: A Historical Account of the Life and Contributions of an Often Neglected Southern Presbyterian Minister and Theologian.' PhD diss. (Westminster Theological Seminary, 2003).

83. George Tindall, and David E. Shi., *America: A Narrative History*, 4th ed. (New York: W. W. Norton & Company, 1996), p. 513.

can know and enjoy the fatherhood of God is through faith in His eternal Son and by the ministry of His eternal Spirit.[84]

## The Trinity and the Lord's Supper

Scholars have also pointed out that Thornwell and Columbia espoused Calvin's view of the Lord's supper, which emphasizes mystical communion with the incarnate, ascended Christ through the supper, while Hodge and Princeton, as well as Dabney and Union, espoused the Zwinglian view of the supper, which is sometimes called the mere memorial view. Scholars have traced this difference to Princeton and Union's use of Turretin's *Institutes* and Columbia's use of Calvin's.[85]

However, this does not fully explain why the Columbians *championed* the Calvinian view of the supper to the extent they did. As we have already noted, there were facets of Calvin's theology that the Columbians did not champion. Something more was at play in their strong advocacy of a Calvinian view of the supper.

According to Holifield, the difference between Columbia and the other Old School seminaries was because of 'two distinctive patterns' in nineteenth-century American Reformed theology, 'the first approximating a Catholic accent on the category of continuity, the second approaching a radical Protestant emphasis on discontinuity.'[86] Holifield suggested that the Columbia theologians were among those who were willing to accept 'categories of continuity that at times approximated the Roman Catholic tradition', while the theologians at Princeton and Union represented 'another pattern present within the Reformed tradition: the

---

84. John Girardeau, *Discussions of Theological Questions*, edited by George A. Blackburn (Richmond, VA: Presbyterian Committee of Publication, 1905), pp. 432-33, 472; *Sermons*, edited by George A. Blackburn (Columbia, SC: The State Company, 1907), pp. 1.421-31; Palmer, 'Invocation,' BMP Papers, CBK.

85. See Robinson, *Columbia*, pp. 97-101; Calhoun, *Our Southern Zion*, pp. xiii, 141-42.

86. E. Holifield, 'Mercersburg, Princeton, and the South: The Sacramental Controversy in the Nineteenth Century,' *Journal of Presbyterian History* 54 (1976), p. 238.

impulse to accent discontinuity, in various ways, as the prevailing theological category.'[87]

However, if the pattern of Thornwell's theology were 'a Catholic accent on the category of continuity', would this not have led him to accept the validity of Roman Catholic baptism? And if Hodge's prevailing theological approach were 'to accent discontinuity' with the Roman Catholic tradition, would he not have likely rejected the validity of Roman Catholic baptism? Simply put, Holifield's thesis does not adequately answer the question *why* Columbia embraced and championed the Calvinian view of the supper when the other leading Reformed seminaries did not.

Columbia's advocacy of Calvin's doctrine of the supper is most helpfully viewed not as part of an overriding accent on 'continuity', but rather as part of Columbia's overriding accent on Trinitarian supernaturalism in response to the inroads of Unitarian rationalism. Previous scholars are right to point out Thornwell's use of Calvin's *Institutes* at Columbia and the way that shaped Columbia's eucharistology, but it should be stressed first and foremost that Thornwell's implementation of Calvin's *Institutes* was in and of itself part of his overall effort to 'deal hard blows' to Unitarian rationalism and equip his students to do the same.[88] Thornwell believed that Calvin provided an anti-rationalistic Trinitarianism that would help him counteract the influence of Cooper, and he urged his seminary students to look to Calvin in order to deal with 'the emergencies of the conflict with Rationalistic infidelity'.[89]

Surviving student notes demonstrate that Thornwell walked his classes through the first three books of Calvin's *Institutes*, with analysis and study questions.[90] He squeezed so much out of the *Institutes* that one student declared, 'That man, Jimmie

---

87. Ibid.

88. Palmer, *Thornwell*, p. 344.

89. Ibid., p. 534.

90. James Thornwell, 'A Student's Notes on Theological Lectures delivered by JHT,' part 3 (Columbia Seminary Notebooks, Reformed Theological Seminary Library Archives, Jackson, MS). Thornwell, *CW*, pp. 1.597-650.

Thornwell, finds in Calvin's *Institutes* what John Calvin himself never thought of!'[91] It is worth noting that Thornwell's lengthiest classroom analysis of the *Institutes* was Calvin's treatment of the Trinity. He urged his students to receive the doctrine of the Trinity with humility and defend it with tenacity. He provided them with Calvin's Scripture proofs for the Trinity and equipped them with his refutations of the 'evasive interpretations' of the Unitarians.[92]

When John Adger became chair of church history and polity at Columbia, Thornwell took him aside and said, 'I hope you will make the Fourth Book of Calvin's Institutes your text-book in church government, for I, in my department, carry our students through the first three books so that they learn Calvin's theology, and it would be well for them to go with you over the Fourth Book that they may get his views of church government; *besides, I do believe in Calvin's doctrine of the Lord's Supper.*'[93]

Adger, who had studied under Hodge at Princeton, but who joined Thornwell in his advocacy of Calvin's view of the supper, believed that the Presbyterians' increasing tendency to espouse the Zwinglian view was because of the increasing influence of rationalism in the nineteenth century.[94] In fact, nineteenth century *Unitarians* essentially adopted Zwingli's view on the basis of their rationalistic assumptions. Cooper followed Priestley in condemning Calvin's view because it contained 'superstitious

---

91. James S. Cozby, quoted in Thomas Law, 'Dr Thornwell as a Preacher and a Teacher,' *Thornwell Centennial Addresses* (Spartanburg, SC: Band and White Printers, 1913), pp. 5-21.

92. Thornwell, *CW*, p. 1.609; 'A Student's Notes,' p. 3.28-36.

93. John Adger, 'Calvin Defended Against Drs Cunningham and Hodge,' *The Southern Presbyterian Review* 27, no. 1 (January 1876), p. 134. Adger grew up in Charleston, where his father, who was originally from Ulster, became a wealthy merchant. He attended Princeton Seminary and became a missionary to the Armenians. He then established a ministry to the slaves of Charleston. From 1857 until 1874 he taught church history, polity, and sacraments at Columbia (*My Life and Times*, pp. 9-40, 78, 137-45, 164-202; Calhoun, *Our Southern Zion*, pp. 137-40; Clarke, *Our Southern Zion*, pp. 142-55).

94. John Adger, *My Life and Times, 1810–1899* (Richmond, VA: The Presbyterian Committee of Publication, 1899), pp. 72-78, 134.

and unwarrantable' notions 'that will not bear the test of reason, scripture, or experience.'[95] On the other hand, 'Zuinglius, and a few others, appear, from the account given of their tenets, to have come pretty near the truth; and Faustus Socinus, with that penetration and sagacity which generally accompanied him in theological disquisitions, has in his tract *De usu et fine caenae domini*, in a great measure explained this institution, according to the simplicity in which it is found in scripture.'[96] For Cooper, the supper was simply 'a solemn, but cheerful rite, in remembrance of Christ' to be observed in a 'devout, serious, and *rational* manner'.[97]

To counteract this Unitarian rationalistic view of the supper, Columbia articulated a Trinitarian supernaturalistic eucharistology. Thornwell emphasized the way in which the supper is not an end in itself, but rather a means of grace by which the soul of the communicant directly communes with the incarnate Christ by the Spirit. Those who administer and partake of the sacraments must 'look beyond the visible symbols to the personal agency of the Holy Ghost to render them effectual ... and they cannot be used with any just conception of their *real nature* without leading the soul directly to [Christ]. Any theory of their office which even proposes the temptation to stop at themselves is utterly destructive of their true design.'[98] For Thornwell, the supper is a channel through which the believer experiences and is nourished by his 'mystical union' with the incarnate Son.[99]

Following Calvin, Adger rooted his theology of the supper in John 1:1-4, 6:22-59, and 1 Corinthians 10:16, and he articulated a doctrine of the supper that emphasizes the Trinitarian nature of God, the hypostatic union of the Son, and the efficacious ministry of the Spirit. For Adger, the mystery of the supper is based on the mystery of the incarnation. Christ is the Word, and in Him is life. The only hope for humanity, being dead in sin, is to be restored

---

95. Cooper, 'A Review of Dr Priestley's Theological Works,' p. 486.

96. Ibid., p. 497.

97. Ibid., p. 493.

98. Thornwell, *CW*, p. 3.302.

99. Ibid., pp. 3.395-96.

to life through communion with the Word. In our sin, we remain separated from the Word, but 'if he comes nigh, and takes our flesh, and makes it vivifying for us—that is, joins himself to our flesh and joins us to him by his Spirit—we may then hope.'[100]

The reality of this mystical union is signified and sealed to the communicant as, by faith, he partakes of the body and blood of Christ. Representative of Columbia's Trinitarian supernaturalism over against Unitarian rationalistic presuppositions, Adger quoted with affirmation the words of the one he called 'the great, because humble, Genevese':

> I will not be ashamed that it is too high a mystery either for my mind to comprehend, or my words to express; and, to speak more plainly, I rather feel than understand it. The truth of God therefore, in which I can safely rest, I here embrace without controversy. He declares that his flesh is the meat, his blood the drink, of my soul; I give my soul to him to be fed with such food. In his sacred supper he bids me take, eat and drink his body and blood, under the symbols of bread and wine. I have no doubt that he will truly give and I receive.[101]

Adger declared Columbia's unapologetic confidence in Calvin's doctrine of the supper:

> Let transubstantiators and consubstantiators, and all other who exaggerate the sacraments on the one side, and let Socinians and Rationalists, and all other depreciators of them on the other, say what they will, we admire more than we can express the consummate skill and masterly power with which, with the Word for his rule and the Spirit his guide, Calvin steered betwixt Scylla and Charybdis, and framed for us a statement of revealed truth on this difficult subject, which makes it not level to our comprehension, of course, but yet not confused or self-contradictory.[102]

Adger insisted that the reason Presbyterians were increasingly rejecting Calvin's doctrine of the supper was the same reason

---

100. Adger, *My Life and Times*, pp. 312-13.

101. Ibid., p. 314; Calvin, *Institutes*, p. 4.17.32.

102. Adger, *My Life and Times*, p. 314.

Unitarians rejected the Trinity: although it is Scriptural, it is incomprehensible. He explained the danger of this approach to theology: 'If we were to abandon all the mysterious doctrines which are unintelligible to our weak comprehension, we should just abandon our whole faith. The whole of Christianity moves in the sphere of the supernatural.'[103] Adger believed that previous generations of Christians had accepted Calvin's view because, in contrast to many nineteenth-century Presbyterians, 'they were not tinctured in the slightest degree with the rationalism of this age, and they accepted it, as they perceived it in the word.'[104] However, 'the tendencies of the age, especially in New England, are rationalistic, and even Presbyterians are often too much inclined to suffer a disparagement of the supernatural.'[105]

Adger knew he was critiquing the views of mentors such as Hodge and friends such as Dabney, who taught his students at Union that Calvin's view was 'not only incomprehensible, but impossible.'[106] Adger also knew his position conflicted with that of Cunningham who taught his students at New College in Edinburgh that Calvin's view was 'unsuccessful', 'unintelligible' and 'the greatest blot in the history of Calvin's labours as a public instructor'.[107] Adger responded with intramural banter: 'Now I have great respect for William Cunningham, but more for John Calvin. I hardly know any modern writer whom I esteem more highly than Cunningham, and this is perhaps the only blot I ever discovered upon any of his writings.'[108]

---

103. Ibid., p. 316.

104. Ibid., p. 326.

105. Ibid., p. 325.

106. Ibid., p. 314; Charles Hodge, 'Doctrine of the Reformed Church on the Lord's Supper,' The Biblical Repertory and the Princeton Review 20 (April 1848), pp. 227-77; Dabney, Systematic Theology, p. 811.

107. William Cunningham, The Reformers and the Theology of the Reformation (Edinburgh: T&T Clark, 1862), p. 240.

108. Adger, My Life and Times, p. 315. According to Holifield, Adger was following the teaching of John Williamson Nevin, who, like Adger, had studied under Hodge but embraced Calvin's view (Holifield, 'Mercersburg,

## Thornwell's Doctrine of the Trinity as the Archetype of Human Society

In 'The Necessity of the Atonement', Thornwell explained to the students of South Carolina College, 'Absolute solitude of Being is wholly incompatible with the actual exercise of moral qualities. Society is the element of virtue, and hence I turn with delight to those representations of the Scriptures in which it is implied that God is necessarily social as well as holy—that such is the nature of His essence that while absolutely one it exists eternally in the threefold distinction of Persons.' Because they are intrinsically relational, God's affections, such as His eternal love, require a society of persons: 'If the unity of God implied unity of Person,' then there would be 'no object but Himself on which His affections might be placed.'[109] Thus, 'the Trinity is a glorious society,' marked by an 'unutterable blessedness which accrues to the Persons of the Trinity from their mysterious communion with each other.'[110]

O'Brien suggested that Thornwell's Trinitarianism was representative of nineteenth-century Southerners in general, who prized social interaction, feared loneliness, and disparaged solitude. According to O'Brien, 'Thornwell once hazarded that God himself did not like to be alone, and this explained the existence of the Trinity, which was a sort of society.'[111] Seeking to summarize Thornwell's theology as representative of the Southern society, O'Brien explained, 'If God feared loneliness, how much more did humans?'[112]

---

Princeton, and the South,' pp. 240, 245). Although Adger was certainly familiar with Nevin, there is no evidence in Adger's writings that he was persuaded to adopt Calvin's position because of Nevin. In all his writings on the topic, Adger only mentioned Nevin once, with reference to his chronicle of various churches' historic affirmation of Calvin's position. It is more accurate to say that Adger, like Nevin, followed Calvin (See Adger, *My Life and Times*, p. 322; John Nevin, *The Mystical Presence: A Vindication of the Reformed or Calvinistic Doctrine of the Holy Eucharist* (Philadelphia: S. R. Fisher & Co., 1867)).

109. Thornwell, *CW*, pp. 2.234-35.

110. Ibid., p. 2.243.

111. O'Brien, *Conjectures*, p. 397.

112. Ibid.

Thornwell clearly viewed the Trinity as 'a sort of society', but he just as clearly did not believe the Trinity could be explained because 'God himself did not like to be alone'. Thornwell made it abundantly clear that he believed there was never 'a period when God was a solitary Being in the depths of eternity'.[113] Contrary to O'Brien's characterization, Thornwell believed that human society is the ectype of a completely satisfied, uncreated divine society.

Other Columbians followed Thornwell by portraying the benevolence, fellowship, and love of the divine society as the archetype for human society. Their writings on this theme are beautiful.[114] But we would be remiss if we did not point out the Columbians' failure to apply this beautiful doctrine in their *own* society.

If the Trinity is the archetype of human society, then surely the honor that the co-equal divine persons show one another provides a model for human society that precludes the system of race-based chattel slavery that the Columbians defended.[115] It should be pointed out that the Unitarians on whom our study focuses likewise defended slavery; the Columbians were not unique in their support of it.[116] But, with their doctrine of the Trinity as the

---

113. Thornwell, *CW*, p. 2.234. For a response to the idea that God was a monad who later became a trinity, see Shedd, *Dogmatic Theology*, pp. 220-24.

114. Thornwell, *CW*, pp. 2.234-35; Girardeau, *Sermons*, pp. 78, 319-23; *Discussions*, p. 422.

115. See John Adger, 'The Christian Doctrine of Human Rights and Slavery,' *Southern Presbyterian Review* 2, no. 4 (March 1849): pp. 569-87; Thomas Smyth, *The Unity of the Human Races* (New York: George P. Putnam, 1850); James Thornwell, 'Slavery and the Religious Instruction of the Coloured Population,' *Southern Presbyterian Review* 4, no. 1 (July 1850): pp. 105-41; 'Report on Slavery,' *Southern Presbyterian Review* 5, no. 3 (January 1852): pp. 379-94; Benjamin Palmer, 'Slavery A Divine Trust: The Duty of the South to Preserve and Perpetuate the Institution as it Now Exists' (New York: George P. Nesbitt & Co., 1861).

116. See Malone, *Cooper*, pp. 284-85, 288-89; Daniel Howe, 'A Massachusetts Yankee in Senator Calhoun's Court: Samuel Gilman in South Carolina,' *The New England Quarterly* 44, no. 2 (1975), pp. 202, 205; 'Samuel Gilman,' and '"Parson" Theodore Clapp' in *Encyclopedia of Religion in the South*, pp. 305, 177; Theodore Clapp, 'Slavery: A Sermon Delivered in the First Congregational Church in New Orleans, 15 April 1838' (New Orleans:

archetype of human society, were they not even more without excuse for their defense of it? The Columbians criticized non-Trinitarian theologies for their inability to provide a theological framework for understanding human social relations, but their own Trinitarianism presented a model of social relations that was surely at odds with the system of slavery they condoned.[117]

As difficult as it is for the twenty-first century mind to imagine, the Columbia divines were in many ways *progressive* within their society. They labored for the conversion of the black population and stressed that they were fully the *imago dei*. They sought to encourage the Southern Church to love and nurture the blacks in their midst. Columbia professor Charles Jones, Girardeau's cousin and mentor in his ministry to the slaves, applied Jesus' admonition, 'You shall love your neighbor as yourself,' to the white Christian's relationship to Southern blacks. He declared, 'And who are our neighbors if the Negroes are not? They are members of the same great family of men; and members of our own communities and parts of our very households; and spend their days in our service. If we see them stripped of necessary religious privileges, and lying in their depravity, helpless, and exposed to eternal death, shall we be neighbors unto them if we look upon them and see their misery and pass by without affording them what relief may be in our power?'[118]

The Columbians deserve commendation for ministering the Gospel to the slaves in the face of frequent, sometimes life-threating, opposition from hostile forces within their culture.[119] However, their doctrine of the Trinity as the archetype of human society provided

---

John Gibson, 1838); *Autobiographical Sketches and Recollections, During A Thirty-Five Years' Residence in New Orleans* (Boston: Phillips, Sampson & Company, 1858), pp. 93, 403; Macaulay, *Unitarianism*, pp. 158-70.

117. Thornwell, *CW*, pp. 2.234-35; Girardeau, *Theological Questions*, pp. 8-12, 403-04.

118. Charles Jones, *The Religious Instruction of the Negroes in the United States* (Savannah, GA: Thomas Purse and Co., 1842), pp. 160-161.

119. Adger, *My Life and Times*, p. 173; Blackburn, *Girardeau*, pp. 101-103; Willborn, 'Girardeau,' p. 121.

a foundation for going much further in showing love and honour to their co-equal divine image-bearers.

## Summary

In his first year as president of South Carolina College, Cooper confidently promised Jefferson that in twenty years Unitarianism would become the prevailing denomination in Columbia.[120] That was not to be the case. The Presbyterians of the state were determined to thwart Cooper's designs. They accomplished their goal by establishing Columbia Seminary only blocks away from the seat of Cooper's regnancy and gaining control of South Carolina College. For the shaping of the seminary and the college as robustly anti-Unitarian, pro-Trinitarian institutions, they looked to Thornwell, who had been 'under the charm of Cooper's influence', but had become a stalwart for 'the adorable Trinity'.[121]

Thornwell accomplished what he had been tasked to do by 'breaking down the spirit of infidelity, which had largely taken possession of the State.'[122] In his tenth year at the college, he wrote, 'Under God's blessing, I have succeeded beyond what I could hope, in changing the whole current of association upon the speculative question of the truth of Christianity.'[123] Contrary to Cooper's prediction, Presbyterianism grew rapidly and Unitarianism all but died out in Columbia by the end of the nineteenth century. By the early decades of the twentieth century, First Presbyterian Church had planted six more churches in Columbia, while the Unitarians were not able to establish a single church there until 1950.[124]

---

120. TC to TJ, 20 November 1822, TJP.

121. Palmer, *Thornwell*, p. 61; Thornwell, *CW*, pp. 2.195, 323.

122. Palmer, *Thornwell*, p. 300.

123. Ibid.

124. David Calhoun, *The Glory of the Lord Risen Upon It: First Presbyterian Church Columbia, South Carolina 1795–1995* (Columbia, SC: R. L. Bryan, 1994), p. 194; 'Our UUCC History' accessed 21 May 2016: http://www.uucolumbia.dreamhosters.com/about-us/our-story/history/.

## Section 2

# Charleston

## Thomas Smyth and Samuel Gilman

## 5

# *The Charleston Theatre: Smyth versus Gilman*

WE now travel southeast through the Palmetto State from Columbia to Charleston in order to examine the conflict as it was embodied by Columbia pastor-scholar Thomas Smyth (1808–1873) and renowned Unitarian minister Samuel Gilman (1791–1858).

## Overview of Smyth's Life, Ministry, and Relationship to Columbia Seminary

Smyth was born in Belfast on the 14th June 1808 to Samuel and Ann Magee Smith.[1] His father was a successful businessman and an elder in the Presbyterian Church. Smyth was so weak as an infant that he was not expected to live. He grew up 'sickly and dwarfed', but, through the influence of his persevering mother, he became an avid reader and bibliophile.[2] He distinguished himself

---

1. The ancient spelling of the surname was 'Smyth', but Samuel Smyth changed it to 'Smith' because of 'the trouble of the letter y.' Thomas changed the spelling back to 'Smyth' at the General Assembly of 1837 in order to avoid being confused with another presbyter named Thomas Smith. Smyth's son, Augustine Smythe, added an 'e', which the family has retained. Smyth Family Papers, SCHS.

2. Thomas Smyth, *Autobiographical Notes, Letters, and Reflections of Thomas Smyth, D. D,* edited by Louisa Cheves Stoney (Charleston, SC: Walker, Evans & Cogswell Co., 1914), pp. 11, 113.

as a student at the Institute of Belfast and graduated from Belfast College with honors. He made his public profession of faith at the age of twenty-one.

Believing that God was calling him into ministry, Smyth began pursuing a divinity degree at Highbury College in London. His studies were interrupted in 1830 when he and his family immigrated to America. He became a student at Princeton Seminary, and two of his professors, Archibald Alexander and Samuel Miller, encouraged him to become the supply pastor at Second Presbyterian Church in Charleston. Around the same time, he also received a call from First Presbyterian Church of Columbia. After much deliberation, he chose to serve the Charleston congregation and became their pastor in 1832.[3]

Smyth married Margaret Adger, the sister of John Adger. Their father, James, was reportedly the fourth richest man in the United States. He and his new son-in-law had much in common: both were Ulster men who had immigrated to America with a vision for success. Smyth immediately made a favorable impression on James, and he made his profession of faith and joined Second Presbyterian shortly after Smyth started his ministry there.[4] Thus, like Thornwell, the young minister 'married up', and he enjoyed living in the wealthiest part of one of the most affluent cities in America.[5]

Smyth's ministry was known for its evangelistic focus: 'He could not preach without pleading with sinners,' and he often reminded his congregants that they were 'Christ's representatives and agents for the conversion of the world'.[6] He desired to be an overseas missionary, but chronic illness prevented him. He served as the chairman of the missions committee in the Synod of South Carolina for twenty-six years and 'doubtless exerted a more direct

---

3. Ibid., pp. 11-21; 80-82.

4. Ibid., pp. 61-62; Adger, *My Life and Times*, p. 39.

5. Clarke, 'Thomas Smyth,' 1. Smyth's home was at 12 Meeting Street (now 18 Meeting Street).

6. Thomas Smyth, *The Complete Works of Thomas Smyth*, edited by J. W. Flinn. 10 vols. (Columbia, SC: R. L. Bryan Company, 1905–1912), pp. 10.766, 767; 7.371-408.

and extensive influence in awakening and diffusing a missionary spirit than any other minister in [the Presbyterian Church].'[7] He focused much of his ministerial energy on the black people of Charleston, and, with Adger and Girardeau, he established churches for the slaves.[8]

In addition, 'the training of a godly ministry enlisted the most eager zeal of Dr Smyth. To this end he gave loyal support to the Columbia Seminary. With voice, pen and purse he aided in upbuilding this school of the prophets. Numerous gifts in money and books came from himself and his people.'[9] At around twenty thousand volumes, Smyth's personal library was one of the largest in the country. Though other seminaries vied for it, Columbia acquired the majority of his library.[10] In 1847, Smyth, along with Howe, Thornwell, Palmer, and Adger, established the seminary's theological journal, *The Southern Presbyterian Review*, and he became one of the most frequent contributors to it. He regularly delivered addresses at the seminary and filled in when professors were away. On multiple occasions, Thornwell and others urged him to accept a full-time position on the faculty. Ultimately, he 'refused to leave his Charleston church for a position on the Columbia Seminary faculty but served on its board and loyally supported the seminary in its work to train a competent and godly ministry.'[11]

After four decades of ministry in Charleston, Smyth passed away on 20th August 1873. Girardeau, who had sat under his preaching as a college student, delivered the homily at his funeral. Smyth's son Adger became mayor of Charleston; his son Augustine became a state senator; and his son Ellison became a prominent Charleston businessman like his grandfather. Columbia established

7. Ibid., p. 10.767.

8. Erskine Clarke, 'Thomas Smyth: Moderate of the Old South,' ThD diss. (Union Theological Seminary (VA), 2001), pp. 178-91.

9. White, *Leaders*, p. 264.

10. Smyth, *Autobiographical Notes*, p. 131; Augustine Smythe to E. M. Green, 10 December 1913, CBK.

11. Adger, *My Life and Times*, p. 229; Smyth, *Autobiographical Notes*, pp. 165; Calhoun, *Our Southern Zion*, p. 78.

a lectureship through Smyth's generous bequest, and the Smyth Lectures are still given annually.[12]

## Smyth's Encounters with Unitarianism

According to Sims, Thornwell was motivated to study the theology of Westminster because he fell in love with an uncompromising Presbyterian. Smyth was similarly motivated to acquaint himself with the *Unitarian* faith. When he was a student at the Institute of Belfast, he fell in love with a Unitarian named Mary.[13] In his attempt to win her heart, Smyth looked into her faith for himself. Her parents approved of the courtship, but, ultimately, Mary did not reciprocate his affection. To communicate her feelings, she wrote him a poem that read, 'Farewell, Farewell beloved one; A separate path is ours; Another course is thine to run; That doth not promise flowers.'[14]

It took years for Smyth to recover from the heartbreak, and he continued to hold Mary in high esteem. Years later, in 1844, during a trip to Belfast, Reverend Smyth visited with her once again. In addition to observing that she had become 'a very large, fine looking woman', he learned that she was still a Unitarian and asked her to examine the Trinitarian faith. She responded with an open mind, and after several correspondences with Smyth on the topic, she 'renounced her Unitarianism' and became a believer in the Trinity.[15]

Mary was not the only Irish Unitarian that Smyth saw become a believer in the Trinity. Unitarian professor James Knowles tutored Smyth when he was in college. Years later, Knowles converted to Trinitarianism and became a Baptist preacher. Smyth referred to Knowles' conversion as being 'among the many superhuman trophies to the power of divine grace'.[16]

---

12. Clarke, 'Smyth,' p. 238, 'Southern Nationalism and Columbia Theological Seminary,' *American Presbyterians* 66, no. 2 (Summer 1988), p. 127; Calhoun, *Our Southern Zion*, p. 83n.

13. Smyth, *Autobiographical Notes*, pp. 20-21.

14. Ibid., p. 21.

15. Ibid., p. 364.

16. Richard Knowles, *The Life of James Sheridan Knowles* (London: James McHenry, 1872), pp. 146-48; Smyth, *Autobiographical Notes*, pp. 395-96.

These early encounters with Unitarianism in Ireland prepared Smyth for his ministry in Charleston, where he would offer a Trinitarian response to one of America's most celebrated Unitarians: Samuel Gilman.

## Gilman and the Unitarian-Trinitarian Conflict in Charleston

### The History of the Unitarian Church of Charleston

In 1681, dissenters from the Church of England founded an Independent Church in Charleston, which became known as the Meeting House. The street in front of the church, which became the main thoroughfare in downtown Charleston, was named Meeting House Street and later shortened to Meeting Street. The original membership of the Meeting House included English Congregationalists, Scottish Presbyterians, and French Huguenots. Although a significant portion of the French Huguenots and Scottish Presbyterians eventually formed their own churches, the Meeting House continued to grow steadily, so much so that a second sanctuary was built just two blocks away on Archdale Street, and concurrent services were conducted each Sunday by the church's co-pastors. In 1813, after the death of one of its pastors, the congregation called Benjamin Morgan Palmer, Sr. to serve as co-pastor with William Hollinshead. Shortly thereafter, Hollinshead became severely ill, and, in 1815, the church called Anthony Forster to co-pastor the church with Palmer, Sr.[17]

Forster grew up near Wilmington, North Carolina, attended the University of North Carolina, and became a teacher at the Raleigh Academy, which was directed by William McPheeters, founding pastor of the Presbyterian Church of Raleigh.[18] McPheeters, whose

---

17. Samuel Gilman, 'Farewell Discourse,' in *The Old and the New* (Charleston: Samuel G. Courtenay, 1854), pp. 5-15. Benjamin Morgan Palmer, Sr. was the uncle of Benjamin Morgan Palmer, Jr.

18. Joseph Gales, ed. *Sermons, Chiefly of a Practical Nature by the Late Anthony Forster, A. M., Pastor of the Second Independent Church in Charleston* (Raleigh: J. Gales, 1821), p. vii; William S. Powell, ed. *Dictionary of North Carolina Biography: Volume 2 D–G* (Chapel Hill, NC: The University of North Carolina Press, 1986), p. 2.224.

grandson, William Marcelus McPheeters, would later become a professor at Columbia, took Forster under his wing and tutored him in theology.[19] Forster was licensed to preach by the Orange Presbytery in North Carolina. He briefly served as pastor of the Independent Church in Wappetaw, South Carolina, then as supply pastor at First Presbyterian Church of Charleston, and then as pastor of the Independent Church on John's Island, South Carolina. In 1815, he became co-pastor of the Independent Church of Charleston, along with Palmer, Sr.[20]

Forster was married to Altona Gales, the daughter of a wealthy Unitarian newspaper publisher named Joseph Gales, who became the mayor of Raleigh in 1819.[21] Gales was originally from England, where he became a close friend and disciple of Joseph Priestley. In 1795 he followed Priestley to America, settling in Philadelphia where he became a leading member of the Socinian congregation Priestley helped establish there. He moved to North Carolina in 1799, and he 'took the lead in a movement to establish Unitarianism within that state as well'.[22] Thus, like Cooper, Gales represented the Socinian wing of the Unitarian movement in the South.

Hoping to engage Mr Gales in theological conversation and convert him to the Trinitarian faith, Forster borrowed some of his father-in-law's Unitarian books, including works by Priestley. Rather than convincing his father-in-law to embrace Trinitarianism, the young Presbyterian minister converted to Unitarianism: 'His investigation was long and laborious; but the final result of it was a full and entire conviction that the doctrine of the Trinity was not a doctrine of the Scriptures.'[23] In the spring of 1816, Forster informed Harmony Presbytery of his desire to

19. 'Samuel Brown McPheeters,' in *Encyclopedia of the History of St. Louis*, pp. 3.1404-08.

20. Gales, *Forster*, pp. x-xi.

21. Ibid., pp. xi-xiii.

22. Bowers, *Joseph Priestley*, p. 87.

23. Gales, *Forster*, p. xvi.

withdraw his membership because 'he could no longer accept in good faith the doctrine of the Trinity, but instead had become Unitarian in his belief.'[24] In 1817, a growing rift between the orthodox members of the Independent Church of Charleston and those 'influenced more directly by eighteenth-century rationalism' resulted in the secession of the latter under Forster's leadership.[25]

Under Palmer's direction, the orthodox members, who held to the system of theology outlined in the *Westminster Standards*, maintained control of the Meeting Street campus, where they were known as the Independent (Congregational) Church or the Circular Church because of the shape of their sanctuary. Under the leadership of Forster, those who had embraced Unitarian views established Second Independent Church on the Archdale Street campus. There, 'discarding the use of all formulas and systems of man's invention, they declared the Scriptures, and the Scriptures alone, to be the rule of their faith and practice; leaving every individual to the free and uncontrolled exercise

---

24. Ibid., p. xviii.

25. Joanne Calhoun, *The Circular Church: Three Centuries of Charleston History* (Charleston, SC: The History Press, 2008), p. 67. At the dedication of the new sanctuary in 1854, Unitarian minister George Burnap referenced Forster with the following: 'To the elderly it is suggestive of the past, and carries their minds back, doubtless to the dawn of Unitarian Christianity in this city, and brings to their recollection the person and character of that saintly scholar and Christian, who first planted the standard of liberal opinions in the heart of this ancient commonwealth. If they appreciate their position, they must feel that no Protestant society can look back to an origin more honorable and legitimate. As the Reformation in Germany apparently sprang from the studies of a solitary monk, accidentally aroused by the discovery of a copy of the Bible in a library at Erfurt, so did this Church apparently owe its origin to the inquiries of a conscientious and fearless Protestant divine, accidentally turned to the investigation of the scriptural argument for the doctrine of the Trinity. Though a member of the Presbyterian church, he had the penetration to perceive and the honesty to avow the conviction, that the principles of the Reformation and the doctrines of the Reformers were two different things, and wholly distinct from each other' (Burnap, 'Unitarian Christianity Expounded and Defended,' pp. 115-16).

of his own judgment and conscience in the interpretation of the sacred volume.'[26]

In 1819, Forster became ill with tuberculosis, stepped down from the pastorate, and returned to Raleigh. On the 28th October 1819, with his wife acting as his amanuensis, Forster wrote the chairman of the congregation resigning the pastorate.[27] Forster passed away a few months later, on the 18th January 1820, at the age of thirty-five. His old Presbyterian mentor, William McPheeters, conducted the funeral service. Forster's successor at Second Independent Church was a recent Harvard graduate named Samuel Gilman, who led the congregation to declare its theology more openly and change its name to the Unitarian Church of Charleston.[28]

## Samuel and Caroline Gilman

Exemplary of the way in which Socinian-leaning Unitarians were increasingly collaborating with the Arian-leaning Unitarians of New England in order to reshape the South, Jefferson once wrote his friend Benjamin Waterhouse, a Harvard professor and theological disciple of Channing, to propose a strategy for winning the South for Unitarianism: Harvard must send its best and brightest divinity students southward to establish Unitarian churches and attract Southern elites to the Unitarian faith. Jefferson assured Waterhouse that 'missionaries from [Harvard] would soon be greeted with more welcome, than from the tritheistical school of Andover.'[29]

Undoubtedly, the most famous realisation of Jefferson's proposal was Harvard graduate Samuel Gilman, the son of a wealthy merchant from Gloucester, Massachusetts. At Harvard, Gilman distinguished himself as a writer and tutored the likes of Ralph

---

26. Gales, *Forster*, p. xxvi.

27. Forster to Hugh Paterson, 28 October 1819, Unitarian Church Records, SCHS.

28. Gilman, 'Farewell Discourse,' p. 16; Macaulay, *Unitarianism*, pp. 44-46.

29. TJ to Benjamin Waterhouse, 19th July 1822, accessed 21 May 2016, http://rotunda.upress.virginia.edu/founders/default.xqy?keys=FOEA-print-04-02-02-2965.

Waldo Emerson.[30] In 1836, his alma mater asked him to write an ode for Harvard's two hundredth anniversary. He obliged by writing, 'Fair Harvard,' which continues to be the official song of the university.[31]

Shortly after Forster's death, the leaders of Second Independent Church wrote the president of Harvard, John Kirkland, asking him to send them his best graduate. In response, he sent them Gilman.[32] In Charleston, Gilman quickly established himself as an ambassador of Unitarianism. After two decades in Charleston, he reflected, 'I came as an avowed Unitarian, and was expected to unfurl here the banner of Unitarian Christianity.'[33] He did so in a way that earned the respect even of those who disagreed with his doctrine. During a visit to Charleston, his mother wrote his sister, 'How often do I wish you were seated on one of the benches listening to the good advice given in the mildest possible manner by your dear brother .... His Parrish almost adore him. Many, very many, that is averse to his Doctrine say he is a good man.'[34]

This was not merely the opinion of a proud mother. Even theological opponents such as Thornwell described Gilman as having 'a genial sympathy with his kind, a spirit full of love to all that God has made beautiful ... pure, gentle, confiding, shrinking from the very thought of inflicting gratuitous pain, these qualities are everywhere so conspicuous, that one must not be told, why the circles of Dr Gilman's intimacy are so devoted to their pastor and friend.'[35]

Gilman's goal was to win over Charleston with the 'moderation, reasonableness, and respectability of Unitarianism'.[36] He was

---

30. Howe, 'Gilman,' *The New England Quarterly* 44, no. 2 (1975), p.197; Henry Foote, 'Gilman,' *The Harvard Graduates' Magazine* 24 (1915–1916), p.613; Macaulay, *Unitarianism*, p.45.

31. See Gilman, 'Fair Harvard,' in *Contributions to Literature* (Boston: Crosby, Nichols, and Company, 1856), pp. 547-48.

32. Howe, 'Samuel Gilman,' p. 197.

33. Gilman, 'Farewell Discourse,' p. 20.

34. Foote, 'Gilman,' p. 614.

35. Macaulay, *Unitarianism*, p. 8.

36. Howe, 'Gilman,' p. 198.

helped in this endeavour by his wife Caroline, who was 'among the most energetic of female editors and among the most influential novelists' of the mid-nineteenth century.[37] Charleston was 'the mecca for literature and culture in the Old South', and, as the 'most eminent woman writer' in the state, Caroline helped draw intellectuals to the Unitarian Church.[38] Her earnings as a writer and publisher of her magazine, *The Southern Rose*, helped the Gilmans afford a stately home in Charleston and a summer home on Sullivan's Island.[39]

Like Cooper and Jefferson, Gilman was optimistic about the future of Unitarianism in the South and believed that Unitarianism would 'prevail and finally triumph in the world'.[40] He asked his congregation, 'Who can doubt that, sooner or later, [Unitarianism] will be the universal creed of the Christian Church?'[41] He explained,

> It may be centuries hence, or it may only be years hence that the grand consummation will take place .... Go among the most pious of all denominations, and converse with them about their relations and obligations to God, and about their dependence on him, and you will invariably hear them speaking of him as one Being – they will be as Unitarian in their expressions as you yourself are, unless, indeed, you drive them back to their creeds, when they will perhaps make a stand, and endeavor to define and defend themselves on that ambiguous ground.[42]

The growth of his own congregation bolstered Gilman's optimism about Unitarianism's future. In the mid-nineteenth century, New Englanders were moving to Charleston in droves, and many

---

37. O'Brien, *Conjectures*, p. 267.

38. William Hoole, 'The Gilmans and the Southern Rose,' *North Carolina Historical Review* 11 (1934) pp. 126-28.

39. Their former home at 11 Orange Street is still called 'the Gilman House' (Foster, *Charleston*, p. 97).

40. Samuel Gilman, *Contributions to Religion* (Charleston: Evans & Cogswell, 1860), pp. 483-84.

41. Ibid., p. 476.

42. Ibid.

of them joined Gilman's church. In addition, native Charlestonians—pillars of the community, including a number of notable Presbyterians—became members of the Unitarian Church. For example, Samuel Dickson, founder of the Medical College of Charleston, left Smyth's church, where he had been a mainstay, and joined the Unitarian congregation. Dickson became one of the most outspoken proponents of Unitarianism in Charleston. As Charlestonians thronged to the Unitarian Church, a larger sanctuary was needed, and Gilman led the congregation to build a 'splendid Gothic building' in 1854.[43]

When Gilman passed away four years later, his funeral was 'the most solemn funeral held in South Carolina since that of Calhoun'.[44] The state's attorney general wrote, 'The funeral of Mr Gilman was like that of a great minister of state. It was the best evidence of the high estimation in which he was held, that the church, long before the hours of the service, was filled to overflowing and crowds remained outside until sundown.'[45]

---

43. Smyth, *Autobiographical Notes*, p. 180n; Holifield, *Gentlemen Theologians*, p. 65.
44. Foote, 'Gilman,' p. 616.
45. Hoole, 'The Gilmans,' p. 120.

# 6

# Gilman and Smyth Battle
# for the Soul of Charleston

IN May of 1852, the General Assembly of the Old School Presbyterian Church met in Charleston. At the opening session, retiring moderator Edward Humphrey delivered a sermon titled 'Our Theology in its Developments.' Humphrey based his sermon on Matthew 7:17: 'Even so, every good tree bringeth forth good fruit, but a corrupt tree bringeth forth evil fruit.' He sought to show that Reformed theology uniquely develops the following seven fruits: a deep and genuine piety; free church government; simple and spiritual worship; the intellectual powers of humankind; the principles of republican liberty; the boldness of confessors and martyrs; and an expanding and aggressive Christianity. In light of these fruits, Humphrey urged the assembly to propagate Reformed theology and renew its commitment to world evangelisation.[1] *The Charleston Evening News* published the sermon and many in Charleston admired it as 'a masterly, a magnificent apology for the Calvinistic theology.'[2]

---

1. Edward Humphrey, 'Our Theology in its Developments' (Philadelphia: Presbyterian Board of Publication, 1857), pp. 10-90.

2. *Charleston Evening News,* 20, 21st May 1852. At the time, Humphrey was pastor of Second Presbyterian Church of Louisville, Kentucky. He later became a professor at Danville Theological Seminary.

In response, Gilman preached a sermon titled 'Calvinistic Theology: A Discourse occasioned by the Rev. Dr Humphrey's Sermon on the Developments of Calvinistic Presbyterian Theology.' Gilman chose as his text Proverbs 18:17: 'He that is first in his own cause seemeth just, but his neighbour cometh and searcheth him.' Humphrey's discourse had led Gilman's parishioners to have 'doubts and queries', which Gilman wanted to allay.[3]

He explained, 'I felt it my duty to unburden my mind before you, and aim to secure you, as well as I may, from the danger, though probably small, of your being ever entangled in what seems to me a heavy yoke of bondage, a system of confused, unpractical, and unscriptural speculations.'[4] He sought to show his parishioners that any 'habitual student and admirer of the New Testament' must find the doctrines of Calvinism 'strange and perplexing in the extreme'.[5]

He then sought to demonstrate that Calvinism does not *uniquely* produce the fruits that Humphrey had enumerated. For example, Humphrey had posited that Calvinism *uniquely* produces humility. Gilman responded, 'Calvin and Knox were no more humble than their opponents and victims, nor Chalmers more humble than Priestley. I had the privilege of a personal acquaintance both with Stuart and Channing, and the impressions on my youthful mind of all the loveliest graces of the Christian character were conveyed by the latter with equal power as by the former. My hearers ... must decide for themselves whether, for instance, Arminian Methodists, or Calvinistic Presbyterians have most generally struck them as imbued with the "piety of humility."'[6]

Regarding Humphrey's claim that Calvinism *uniquely* produces confessors and martyrs, Gilman replied, 'But let it be remembered, that Calvinism herself was baptized in blood not

---

3. Gilman, *Contributions to Religion*, p. 159.

4. Ibid., p. 118.

5. Ibid., pp. 118-26, 119.

6. Ibid., p. 131.

her own, and sucked the gall of persecution as her maternal milk. The liberty of thought and speech which she claimed from Rome, she refused to indulge to others, and Servetus, the unoffending Unitarian, as good, as ingenious, and as learned a man as Calvin, was her initial victim.'[7] He also cited Joan Boucher, a 'good, pious, heroic woman, who did not believe in infant baptism, nor in the orthodox doctrine of the Trinity. She was condemned to the flames by a court of Calvinistic Protestant bishops.'[8] He pled, 'Let what is by-gone be by-gone. Only let us not dress up, in the present day, a picture *entirely on one side*, and hold that partial delineation forth as specifically characteristic of any contemporary denomination.'[9]

In his response to Humphrey's claim that Calvinism uniquely develops an expanding and aggressive Christianity, Gilman argued that Calvinism was actually declining rather than expanding. He asserted, 'It is curious that in almost all the regions which the preacher enumerates as having been penetrated by this expanding aggressive principle, it evidently wanted the stamina which should preserve it, or it was repudiated and evaporated after the first spasmodic effort that secured its introduction.'[10]

Gilman ascribed the waning popularity of Calvinism in the West and its failure to enjoy world-wide expansion to the fact that 'it is not in human nature to receive more than a definite modicum of Calvinism; it would seem altogether too exclusive, abstract, eccentric, unnatural, ever to become a universally popular and acceptable religion; *that* destiny is still in reserve for some system which shall only embrace, like the teachings of Jesus Christ, a very few, plain, powerful principles, comprehensible by every intellect, necessary to every condition, and welcome to every eager heart.'[11]

The system of which Gilman spoke so glowingly was, of course, Unitarianism. The purpose of his rebuttal was clear: expose the

---

7. Ibid., p. 147.

8. Ibid., p. 147.

9. Ibid., p. 149.

10. Ibid., pp. 149-50.

11. Ibid., p. 153.

'wild, strange, objectionable tenets' of Calvinism and commend Unitarianism to 'every believer in Jesus Christ, to every reflecting, sensitive, inquiring man.'[12] *The Evening News* published the sermon on its front page; the Unitarian Tract Society printed it as well.[13] A letter to Gilman from a prominent judge in another part of the state is representative of the sermon's popularity:

> My Dear Sir,
>
> The very able and beautiful sermon which you preached in reply to Dr Humphreys, and which was published in the news, has been so frequently enquired for, that I am induced to ask you to send me some for distribution. I the more earnestly make the request because I am well satisfied the Discourse is admirably and calculated to do much good and cure a great deal of error, which has been widely disseminated both here and elsewhere. In the hope that you will not regard this letter as intrusive or my petition as unreasonable,
>
> > I am Dear & Revd Sir
> > Yours most Truly & Respectfully
> > A. P. Aldrich[14]

### Smyth's Sermons in Response to Gilman

The next Saturday, the *Evening News* printed the following announcement: 'DR GILMAN'S DISCOURSE. A SERMON occasioned by the recent Discourse of the Rev. Samuel Gilman, D. D., will be delivered in the Second Presbyterian Church, *To-morrow Night*, by the Rev. THOMAS SMYTH, D. D. Service to commence at 8 o'clock.'[15] Thus, Smyth put Gilman on notice that he had prepared a response, and he invited the people of Charleston to hear it. He titled his sermon, which the *Evening News* printed on its front page, 'Unitarianism Not the Gospel: Occasioned by the

---

12. Ibid., pp. 156, 118.
13. *Charleston Evening News*, 5 June 1852; *Two Stand-Points* (Charleston: Walker & Evans, 1854), p. 23.
14. Aldrich to Gilman, 22 June 1852, Unitarian Church Records, SCHS.
15. *Charleston Evening News*, 12 June 1852.

Recent Discourse of the Rev. Samuel Gilman, D. D., in Reply to One by Rev. E. P. Humphrey, D. D.'[16]

Smyth selected 1 Corinthians 11:19 as his text: 'For there must be also heresies among you, that they which are approved may be made manifest among you.' As this selection indicates, the overarching purpose of his sermon was to argue that the Unitarianism Gilman presented in his discourse and was popularising in Charleston was nothing short of heresy. He viewed the overarching purpose of Gilman's sermon not to be a critique of Humphrey's presentation but rather 'an assertion of the religious system known by the name Unitarian', 'an aggressive attack upon the doctrines and polity of the Presbyterian Church,' and 'a proselyting effort to bring about his anticipated millennium – "those grand and promised evolutions, when all parties, no longer seeing through a glass darkly, shall behold face to face, and when the universal, world comprehending religion" of Unitarianism which will "not stagger the common reason and moral sense of mankind" shall every where prevail.'[17]

Smyth spent the majority of his sermon providing Scripture proofs for the deity of Christ and reasoning from the Scriptures that one must believe in Christ as the *divine* redeemer in order to be saved. He borrowed the language of 2 Thessalonians 2:3 and 2 Corinthians 13:5 to summarize his response to Gilman and make his appeal to the people of Charleston: 'Brethren let no man deceive you. Examine your own selves, whether ye be in the faith; prove your own selves.'[18]

The following Saturday, the *Evening News* notified the public that Smyth would preach an additional response to Gilman: 'DR GILMAN'S DISCOURSE. A concluding Sermon, occasioned by the recent Discourse of the Rev. Samuel Gilman, D. D., will be delivered by the Rev. THOMAS SMYTH, D. D., *To-Morrow Evening*, in the

---

16. Thomas Smyth, 'Unitarianism Not the Gospel,' in *Works* (Columbia, SC: R. L. Bryan Company, 1905–1912), pp. 9.295-313.

17. Ibid., pp. 304, 308.

18. Ibid., p. 309.

Second Presbyterian Church, service to commence at 8 o'clock. A Discourse on "The Responsibility of Man for his Belief," will be delivered in the same Church, *To-Morrow Morning*, by the Rev. J. B. ADGER.'[19]

Smyth titled this sermon, which the *Evening News* also printed on its front page, 'Unitarianism Another Gospel.' For this discourse, he chose Galatians 1:6–7 as his text: 'I marvel that ye are so soon removed from him that called you unto the grace of Christ unto another Gospel, which is not another: but there be some that trouble you, and would pervert the Gospel of Christ.' He argued that 'Unitarianism .... though it call itself the gospel, is not the gospel of Christ, but is another gospel and yet not another.'[20]

Smyth argued that Unitarianism is not good news for three reasons. First, it is powerless. It does not possess the supernatural power necessary to give spiritual life to those who are dead in sin. Second, it is indefinable. Unitarians cannot agree on what they believe, but rather only on what they deny – doctrines such as the Trinity, original sin, and justification by faith. Such denials are not unique: they 'are common to almost all unbelievers'. Third, it leads to uncertainty. Because it denies the authority of Scripture, Unitarianism cannot offer certainty about God, his character, or his plan of salvation.[21]

Ultimately, Smyth showed that Unitarianism and Trinitarianism cannot simultaneously be true, and that the issues about which they principally differ are not secondary but rather primary: 'They involve a total difference of sentiment in regard to the God we worship, the medium of worship, the nature of all true and acceptable worship, and the way by which alone any of our guilty and sinful race can ever become sanctified and acceptable worshippers in the church on earth, and in the church of the first born in heaven. One or the other must be false. Both cannot be true.'[22]

---

19. *Charleston Evening News*, 19 June 1852.

20. Smyth, *Works*, p. 9.322.

21. Ibid., pp. 327-337.

22. Ibid.

His message was clear: the people of Charleston had to make a choice between which system—ultimately, which God—they would follow. In that regard, he even made reference to the leader of Charleston's Unitarian movement: 'Dr Gilman I have long and well known. Our social relations have been most kind and agreeable …. And even while I feel that "woe is unto me if I stand not up for the defence of the gospel," my heart's desire and prayer to God for him is, that he may be saved.'[23]

## Gilman's Open Letters to Smyth

After Smyth's first sermon, Gilman's daughters, Lou and Caroline, wrote their father, who had commenced his summer vacation in Massachusetts, urging him not to offer a public response to Smyth. On the back of the previously referenced letter from A. P. Aldrich, which they were forwarding to their father, Lou wrote,

> Dear Father, Caroline and I think you had better not answer Dr Smyth. People will be tired and are I think already tired of him, and he is so bitter to have anything to do with. But of course you will do what is right. At Society the ladies seemed to think he could do us no harm by his horrid sermon. I long to hear what you think of it, and if you are worried by it. Lou. Frank on the contrary wishes you to tell the public what Unitarianism is, and to answer Dr Smyth. Frank says I must direct your papers to Newburyport, so I will direct no more to Boston until further orders.[24]

'Frank' was Lou's husband. Just below Lou's note, Frank wrote, 'By all means answer Dr S. I think he has called your veracity into question, & it is due to ourselves that the true and simple Unitarian faith should be explained to the public in your clear and lucid manner, & not let them be led still further into error as to our faith, by that untrue, illiberal, unchristian, & intemperate discourse. Frank.'[25]

---

23. Ibid., p. 323.
24. Lou and Frank Porcher to Gilman, n.d., Unitarian Church Records, SCHS.
25. Ibid.

Gilman agreed with Frank. On the 29th June 1852, Gilman wrote an open letter to Smyth, which the *News* subsequently printed. He accused Smyth of being uncharitable and unchristian, and called him to celebrate their unity in the truths they held in common. Specifically, in response to Smyth's assertion that Unitarianism embodies the spirit of 'anti-Christ' because it denies Christ's deity, Gilman implored his friend, 'Let us not then, sadly call each other by these old mystic names, in this enlightened Charleston of the nineteenth century.'[26]

He suggested that less quarrels would exist among Christians if they would only embrace the simplicity of the Unitarian gospel. He defended the Unitarian view of Christ as being that of the Scriptures: 'That he claims an absolute, original, independent, un-limited Almightiness, I have yet to learn, and cannot learn until I shut my Bible, and betake myself to human creeds, originating centuries after the publication of the New Testament.'[27] He promised, 'Providence permitting, I propose, on some early future occasions, to pursue the examination of the notices with which you honor me. I am here in the midst of the hospitalities of Massachu-setts, and you know as well as I, that however antagonistic South Carolina and Massachusetts may be in their public policy, yet in hospitality they run a friendly race, not very conducive to the pursuit of studious or theological tasks.'[28] He concluded,

> Whatever may be the result of these discussions, I am not sorry that a fair occasion has presented itself, in which I may try to convince my beloved and respected fellow-citizens of all denominations, that the humble individual, on whom for so many years they have bestowed so many generous confidences, has not differed from them in religious belief on light grounds— that he has sought to base his religious teachings on a studious, patient, and careful consideration of the *whole* scripture—and that neither he nor his people have ever so recklessly defied either

---

26. *Charleston Evening News*, 9 July 1852.

27. Ibid.

28. Ibid.

the Bible, or the Creator, or the Great Founder of Christianity, as they have been by many, mistakenly supposed to do. If for the very few years that can yet be remaining to me, I may but produce this limited result, it will amply reward the ambition and prayer of

Yours, very truly and respectfully,
S. GILMAN[29]

In a second open letter, Gilman sought to clarify his Christology. He emphasized his belief that a Christian can love, honor, and serve Jesus as Lord without believing that he is God. He argued that Jesus never claimed to be God; rather, he claimed inferiority to and dependence on God the Father. Thus, Jesus is to be honored because he is the 'AMBASSADOR of the Deity', not the Deity himself.[30] In a way that revealed his epistemological assumptions, he explained: 'I do not profess to know the exact nature of the connection between the Father and the Son. It may involve profound and wonderful relations, beyond what men or angels can ever penetrate or comprehend. I only object to the enforcement of propositions as standards and tests of Christianity, whose language not only seems unrequired and unwarranted [sic] by Scripture, but absolutely *contradictory to my reason*.'[31]

He ended by communicating his earnest desire for a Universal Church in which the simple teachings of Jesus would be embraced, without the encumbrances of creeds and confessions. He spoke glowingly of a Baptist Church in Charleston at which two of his parishioners had recently worshipped and who were invited to take Communion even though their Unitarian identity was known. Reflecting on the incident, Gilman declared, 'There, sir, was a practical realization of my fondly favorite scheme of a simple, universal creed. I sometimes think I see tendencies to such things, among many portions of the Church, although, as a Unitarian,

---

29. Ibid.

30. *Charleston Evening News*, 17 July 1852.

31. Ibid.

I may myself be as yet hardly admitted to the outer orbit. But I rejoice at every slightest approximation to such a result, in other denominations, and I breathe gladly the prayer, "Even so, Lord Jesus, come quickly!"[32]

### Benjamin Gildersleeve's Open Letters to Gilman

After it published Gilman's letters, the News published four open letters, which Benjamin Gildersleeve wrote to Gilman critiquing his response to Humphrey. Originally from Charleston, Gildersleeve was a Presbyterian evangelist and one of Smyth's close friends.[33]

He began by telling Gilman that his response to Humphrey was unwarranted: '[Humphrey's] object was simply to exhibit the *developed effects* of the [Calvinistic] system. But you take advantage of ground which he did not occupy to denounce and caricature the system from which these effects are alleged to arise. All this may be fair in polemics. It is what you have done. But it places you in the attitude of an assailant – not Dr H. nor ourselves who have volunteered in the defence of his positions.'[34] He also stated that Gilman was guilty of hypocrisy when he called on Smyth to exercise a more charitable form of Christianity when Gilman had referred to Calvinism as a 'repulsive system' and one which should be viewed with 'aversion and disgust'.[35]

Further, Gildersleeve pointed out that Gilman, who identified himself as a champion for the cause of Protestantism, had garnered praise from an unlikely source. *The Catholic Miscellany*, the Roman Catholic newspaper of Charleston and the first of its kind the United States, had reprinted excerpts of Gilman's sermon and expressed glowing approval of it. Gildersleeve inquired of Gilman,

> We can readily suppose that you were highly gratified at the commendation bestowed upon your performance by the Miscellany .... But has it never occurred to you that this commendation

---

32. Ibid.
33. Smyth, *Autobiographical Notes*, pp. 87, 158, 169-70, 359.
34. *Charleston Evening News*, 22 July 1852.
35. Ibid., 22, 27 July 1852.

is traceable, not to any special favour, from that source, to the peculiarities of your religious belief, but to the common aversion which you both have to the principles and order of the Presbyterian church? Like 'the expulsive power of a new affection,' mutual antipathies are for the time expelled, by the still stronger antipathy which is common to you both. They feel towards you wondrous kind when they hear you proclaiming to the world, that those whom you represent 'cannot tolerate, nor approve, nor understand the Calvinistic system, but repudiate it with something approaching to aversion and disgust,' – when they hear you describe it as 'a heavy yoke of bondage' – as 'a system of confused, and unpractical, and unscriptural speculation' – as 'entirely contrary to our spiritual powers and spiritual needs, as well as to the principles habitually adhered to by Jesus Christ and his Apostles' – when you say of it that 'if any system of religion in Christendom has ever engendered among its votaries fatal doubts of its truth it is that of Calvinism,' and when you add that 'the Hindoo Theology resembles Calvinism in its transmundane, unpractical speculations, if nothing else.' Interpersed [sic] as your *critique* is with such sweeping denunciations of the Calvinistic system, and with such caricatures of it as you might have copied from the Polemic Theology of Rome, it is not at all strange that they are lavish in their praises of your able discourse – and the more so, as it has brought them 'aid and comfort' at a time when they had been closely besieged – in consequence of their rash attack upon one of the citadels of Protestantism.[36]

In addition to pointing out the *Miscellany's* praise for Gilman's treatise, Gildersleeve dealt with Gilman's claim that Unitarianism is more practical than Calvinism. He asserted, 'You may boast, as you can, of the prevalence of Unitarianism in many churches which were once orthodox—and this is true of the very church to which you sustain the relation of pastor—but what has Unitarianism ever accomplished which entitles it to the appellation, *par eminence* of a *practical* religion.'[37] Gildersleeve compared the Unitarian

---

36. Ibid., 22 July 1852.
37. Ibid.

movement to a bird who, rather than building a nest for herself, overtakes one already built: 'Unitarians have uniformly planted themselves in churches, once Orthodox but have done little or nothing in fulfilling the [Great Commission]. Your missions to the heathen, where are they? Your labors and your efforts, and your contributions, to extend the gospel, in the new, and sparse and destitute settlements of the land, where are they? And what are the special truths of Unitarianism in the churches under your control? It is not our aim to introduce any invidious comparisons, but when you deny that orthodoxy is *practical*, you have no reason to object to questions such as these.'[38] Ultimately, Gildersleeve sought to show that Gilman's aversion to Calvinism was simply an expression of his aversion to Trinitarianism. He explained, 'Your aversion to the Calvinistic system arises in part from its maintenance of the supreme deity of Him of whom it is said, "in the beginning was the Word, and the Word was with God, and the Word was God."'[39] He posited that Gilman's basic arguments against Calvinism were essentially the arguments of unbelievers against Christianity. He concluded, 'If you abstract from the system of Christianity, and set aside as entirely indefensible the doctrines of the *Trinity*, or of the *incarnation*, of the *vicarious atonement*, of *original sin*, of *justification by faith alone*, and of the *divine purpose* with their cognates, you so narrow the grounds of difference between you [and unbelievers] that very little is left worth contending for.'[40] Gildersleeve was alerting Charlestonians to what he perceived to be the root of Gilman's agenda: not merely a critique of Calvinism, but rather an attack on the essentials of the Christian faith.

### Gilman's Open Letters to Smyth (Continued)

After the publication of Gildersleeve's letters to Gilman, the *News* published more letters from Gilman to Smyth. Gilman began

---

38. Ibid.

39. Ibid.

40. Ibid.

with an apology for the delay of his third letter: 'I have also been engrossed [at Harvard] by the festivities and exercises of Commencement week, during which I have had the pleasure of seeing much to the advantage of the distinguished President of our South Carolina College, and I believe the gratification has been mutual between himself and the prominent characters here. I will ere long send you a small poem, which I composed for a class meeting, and which is to be published by the members of my class. I hope it may prove a diversion and peace-offering in the entanglements of controversy.'[41]

Gilman insisted that he *believed all the Scripture*, which Smyth quoted in his sermons and which Trinitarians quote as support for the Trinity; he simply had a different interpretation of them. He argued that if Smyth would only set aside the Athanasian Creed, the biblical texts that he interpreted as teaching the Trinity would soon be understood as teaching the Unitarian doctrine of God.

In a fourth letter, Gilman responded to the claims of Smyth and Gildersleeve that his sermon had been unprovoked: 'I heard much of the profound impression made on the community at large by the discourse in question …. Such an influence of course was likely in some degree to extend to the members of my own flock, among whom the discourse had been considerably circulated. On further examination it more and more appeared to me singularly open to exception. Therefore, as a religious teacher, I thought it a very obvious, legitimate, appropriate, and seasonable topic of pulpit instruction. In no other way did I assail, or think of assailing Presbyterianism, than through that very discourse of its champion, which, by the power of circumstances, had previously overshadowed and engrossed the public mind.'[42]

In a fifth letter, Gilman argued that Calvinism is unnecessarily complex and speculative. Pointing out Calvinists' proclivity

---

41. Ibid., 21 August 1852. Thornwell was the president mentioned by Gilman. In the previous chapter, we noted Thornwell's thoughts on these commencement festivities.

42. Ibid., 28 August 1852.

for never-ending in-house debates, he asked, 'Can you wonder, therefore, that I should thirst for a form of Christianity that would as much as possible avoid these entangling perplexities?'[43]

In his next letter, he addressed Smyth's argument that when the Scriptures promote the worship of Jesus, they are teaching his divinity. Citing Scripture to support his argument, Gilman explained, 'In the *worship* described by Scripture as being paid to Jesus, we heartily join. *Worship*, as used in those writings, is a general term, implying profound reverence paid either to the Supreme Being, or to the bearers and mediums of any sort of precious blessing.'[44] He presented the Unitarian understanding of worship as follows: '[Jesus] explicitly directs our supreme worship to be paid to the Father. He himself worships that Father. We therefore feel it both right and safe to stand on that eternal ground. Still, we would yield the required and due homage to him, whom the Father hath sanctified and sent into the world.'[45]

In his next epistle, Gilman disclosed why and how he and many others had left Calvinism and embraced the Unitarian faith:

> Many sincere, pious, and irreproachable believers in Christianity find themselves incapable of receiving some abstruse proposition, which is enjoined in the standards of their church. An awful struggle in consequence arises in their minds. To conceal their difficulty, would savour of hypocrisy, and so increase their distress. To confess it, and still to be retained in the communion, which is not an uncommon circumstance, awakens a powerful sense of the inconsistency indulged in by themselves and their fellow believers. Voluntarily to retire from the communion, would afflict an offense and grievance on their friends and blast their own reputation. An honest and bold avowal of their doubts or convictions subjects them, ecclesiastically, to as deep a stigma and heavy a punishment, as if they were guilty of an atrocious wickedness. Now to put a mere innocent error of opinion into

---

43. Ibid., 8 September 1852.

44. Ibid., 9 October 1852.

45. Ibid.

the same category with erroneous moral delinquencies, is *not* the doctrine of Jesus Christ, not the doctrine of Paul's glorious chapter on charity, not the doctrine of the New Testament.[46]

In his eighth letter to Smyth, Gilman reiterated his belief that Calvinism is unnecessarily complex, especially when contrasted with the simplicity of Unitarianism. He pointed to disputes amongst Calvinists over doctrinal formulations as examples of why the system should be abandoned. Having re-examined the Calvinistic standards for the purpose of the debate, he wrote:

At every step of this examination, I have been more and more confirmed in the impression which pervaded my discourse: that the system of Calvinism is an unhappy, intricate, and unnecessary entanglement of verbal perplexities – stating and unstating propositions in almost the same breath – recoiling aghast from consequences which it has previously aimed to establish – and compelled to trim and balance between abstruse, metaphysical expressions, which, however, it all the time represents as essential to a sound and saving faith. It cruelly commands us to believe certain universal propositions, and then, if we dare to deduce from them particular inferences of the most obvious, legitimate, logical character, it denounces us as vile, blasphemous and infernal, for such are Calvin's and his followers' own favorite epithets against those who question and are perplexed by his dogmas. It says we must believe that God ordained everything that comes to pass and then, if we ask whether that does not make him the ordainer of sin, it pronounces us audacious blasphemers. It tells us that God appointed an exact number of sinners, from all eternity, for his own glory, to everlasting wrath and then if we wonder how unchangeably doomed sinners can be saved even through the mercy of God, it answers by thrusting us in among the devoted throng themselves. According to my conviction, it involves more than twenty of these fatal violations of logic and charity. I am thankful for the opportunity of searching and testing it anew, and looking it *longer* in the face than I could do before. Such a system, I earnestly repeat, seems repugnant to the spirit

46. Ibid., 11 October 1852.

of the New Testament—to the capacities, needs and appreciation of the ordinary mass of Christians—and to the straight forward, practical character of the present age. I reverence it indeed for its connection with much of the piety both of the presence and the past. But I see it virtually expiring, in spite of the vast efforts put forth to sustain it.[47]

He closed his scathing appraisal of Calvinism with these words to his Calvinistic friend:

> Hoping that no theological difference will be allowed to vary the usual terms of our intercourse, I remain
>
> Very truly and respectfully yours,
> S. GILMAN[48]

After returning from vacation, Gilman wrote a ninth letter to Smyth in which he dealt with the case of Michael Servetus. As we noted earlier, Humphrey had said that the Reformed faith uniquely produces professors and martyrs. Gilman had challenged that assertion. He pointed to Servetus as an example of a Christian martyr, arguing that, not only was Servetus not Reformed, he was martyred at the hands of those who were Reformed, Calvin specifically. Smyth, in his second sermonic response to Gilman, had defended Calvin against Gilman's claims.[49] Gilman sought to rebut Smyth and demonstrate Calvin's guilt in the Servetus affair:

> It is full time, my dear sir, that yourself and other Calvinists should abandon the fallacious and untenable hypothesis, or rather assertion, which, unfortunately for the clear reputation of history, has been started of late years, and with which your paragraph on this subject concludes, that Calvin had no share of guilt or responsibility in the martyrdom of Servetus. To shift the odium of the transaction from his shoulders to those of the magistrates of Geneva, is all like the conduct which you so much condemn in

---

47. Ibid., 12 October 1852.
48. Ibid.
49. Smyth, 'Unitarianism Not the Gospel,' pp. 328-29.

the Romanists, who pretend that the victims of the Inquisition are only subjects of civil punishment by the secular arm.[50]

Smyth would eventually respond by writing an entire book devoted to the defence of Calvin titled *Calvin and His Enemies*.[51] Therein he argued, 'We do not defend, in all this, the condemnation and death of Servetus. It was a great mistake; call it if you will a crime. But let the blame rest *where it belongs*; not on John Calvin, but on the men who decreed that death, and on the age which sanctioned and demanded it.'[52]

In a tenth missive, Gilman took up the issue of charitableness once again. In his sermon, Gilman had argued that Unitarianism is a more charitable version of Christianity than Calvinism. In his sermonic responses, Smyth had pointed out the uncharitableness of various Unitarians. Gilman defended some of the Unitarians that Smyth had accused, while admitting the shortcomings of others and pointing out that he never claimed that Unitarians were perfect.[53] He argued that both the Nicenians and Arians were guilty of excesses, and he pled with Smyth, 'Thus, Sir, instead of falling back among the inexplicable and unaccountable feuds of the fourth century, to bias our decisions, let us consult the scriptures for ourselves, and listen to the calm breathings of our own independent reason, for the foundation and establishment of our religious faith.'[54]

In his eleventh and final epistle in the series, Gilman reacted to Smyth's claim that 'the system of Unitarianism is so indefinite and indeterminate as to be past finding out, by any inquirer after its truth.'[55] Gilman replied that, given the variety of opinions among the orthodox, the same could be said for them. He pointed out the divisions among Trinitarians, Protestants, Calvinists, and Presbyterians, citing the Old School-New School schism as an

---

50. *Charleston Evening News*, 20 November 1852.

51. *Calvin and His Enemies* was reprinted in Smyth, *Works*, pp. 3.319-403.

52. Smyth, *Works*, p. 3.350.

53. *Charleston Evening News*, 4 December 1852.

54. Ibid.

55. Smyth, 'Unitarianism Another Gospel,' p. 333.

example. Ultimately, he renewed his invitation to the readers of the *News* to come and worship at 4 Archdale Street:

> It is not variety of opinion which is the opprobrium of any body of men – but bitterness, uncharitableness, and exclusiveness, springing out of that variety. It is, I fondly and devoutly believe, the beauty and the glory of our system, that we erect no other speculative basis of Christian communion than the Supremacy of the Father and the Messiahship of his Son. Feeling an inborn, undying confidence that the perfect excellence of this simple and truly evangelical principle will one day be universally acknowledged, we are willing while proclaiming it in all earnestness to await God's own time for its complete development and realization and to endure all the bitterness, estrangement, odium, misconception, and isolation, which the abounding advocates of more complicated and humanly devised creeds choose to shed abroad upon our names and heads. That very indefiniteness of which you complain, is in one respect our life and crown! We do not say to a fellow Christian, you shall entertain exactly the same conceptions of the person of Christ that we do. We say to the high Arian, to the low Arian, to the Sabellian, to the Humanitarian, to the Swedenborgian, and to all others who are sincerely impressed with the divinity, necessity, and saving power of the gospel, come and worship with us! We judge you not. You have struggled, as we have for the light. Christ himself never defined his own metaphysical nature. Why then should we multiply philosophical and unwarranted Shibboleths to debar you from the kingdom of heaven? Nay, even trinitarians of every hue and stamp, in their infinite multiplicity, are welcome to our communion, and they can all conscientiously worship with us, although they exclude us from their own altars, and exclude one another also, both vigorously and abundantly, which we never do, for speculative differences. As far as we go in belief, *they* can go, and there is not one of our doctrines that they cannot assent to as absolute truth. Demand not then, my respected correspondent, from Unitarians, an impracticable uniformity, which, even if practicable and realized, would banish from among us the dearest humanities of life, and deprive us of the exercise of its divinest charities.[56]

---

56. *Charleston Evening News*, 5 January 1853.

# 7

# *Smyth's Articles on the Trinity*

S MYTH could not help but respond to Gilman's letters, but he did so not through open letters in the *Charleston Evening News,* but rather through a series of articles in *The Southern Presbyterian Review.* Though he did not mention Gilman by name, Smyth was clearly responding to Gilman's arguments in the nineteen articles that he published in the *Review.* We will consider them in the order they were written, grouping them under the following headings: controversy, reason, importance, plurality, triads, testimonies, and Scriptures.

## Controversy

At the close of his sermon, 'Calvinistic Theology,' Gilman exhorted his Unitarian congregants to love, sympathise with, and respect their 'Presbyterian brethren' in spite of their differences.[1] In his letters to Smyth, Gilman called for Christians to move away from 'sectarian interpretations' and 'warring beliefs' that divide them. He spoke of unity in the Gospel existing between Socinians, Arians, Sabellians, and 'trinitarians of every hue and stamp, in their infinite multiplicity.'[2] He entreated the people of Charleston not to allow 'philosophical and unwarranted Shibboleths' to

---

1. Gilman, *Contributions to Religion,* p. 159.
2. *Charleston Evening News,* p. 5, 9 July 1852.

separate them, but rather to unite in the worship of their common Savior.[3]

In his first *Review* article, 'The Necessity and Importance of Controversy,' Smyth countered Gilman by arguing that Unitarianism and Trinitarianism are fundamentally and irreconcilably 'contrary, the one to the other.'[4] Undoubtedly with Gilman's congregation in mind, he continued, 'And yet both exist, and both claim the name, the authority, and the sanctions of Christianity. Both are found among us. Both have their ministry, their ordinances, and their worshippers, and both hold forth their claims to the allegiance of ourselves and our children. What course, then, are we to pursue? Both cannot be true. One or the other must be false, and if false, dangerous, delusive, and destructive. What are we to do?'[5]

Against Gilman's postulations that the true and simple Gospel, if faithfully communicated, would not bring controversy but rather agreement among all people on a common faith, Smyth argued, 'The Gospel is itself a standing controversy, with the cavils, the objections, the doubts, and the blasphemies of men. There is not a truth in the Gospel, nor in the Bible, nor even in natural religion, that is not controverted by the skeptical, unbelieving, proud, and self-conceited wisdom of foolish men .... Aversion to controversy, when it is based upon a professed regard for the interests of religion, is founded upon misapprehension and mistake.'[6] He encouraged his reader to beware of those who 'condemn the contending earnestly for the faith, because they contemn the faith itself.'[7]

Smyth pointed out that the preaching ministries of the prophets, Jesus, and the apostles were marked by controversy, as were the ministries of the Church Fathers and the Protestant Reformers. He warned that attempts to preach the Gospel in such

---

3. Ibid., 5 January 1852.

4. Thomas Smyth, 'The Necessity and Importance of Controversy,' *Southern Presbyterian Review* 7, no. 1 (July 1853), p. 61.

5. Ibid.

6. Ibid., pp. 68-69, 73.

7. Ibid., p. 73.

a way as to avoid all controversy ultimately leads to a loss of the Gospel itself and a failure to fulfil the Great Commission: 'It is only by controversy, and contending earnestly, that the truth, in all its purity and power, can ever be maintained and handed down to our posterity, and disseminated throughout the world.'[8]

After explaining that controversy is necessary for the spread of the Gospel, he encouraged Trinitarians to contend for the faith while resisting the temptation to have a *contentious spirit*: 'Only let our zeal for the truth be combined with charity for the persons who oppose it …. This will enable us to honour the truth, without dishonouring ourselves—to be firm and calm—and with warm heart to preserve a cool head, and a graceful tongue.'[9]

## Reason

In his next four articles, Smyth addressed the role of reason in theology. In his sermons and letters, Gilman had argued that Unitarianism is more reasonable than Trinitarianism. He explained that although he could not believe in the Trinity because it was contradictory to his reason, he could believe in a uni-personal God because it was agreeable to his reason. Thus, the doctrine of the Trinity should be abandoned for the more reasonable doctrine of a uni-personal God.[10]

Smyth addressed such claims in his second article, 'The Province of Reason, Especially in Matters of Religion.' He confronted the Unitarian position that 'reason is a sufficient, and the only necessary guide in matters of religion, and that revelation is either unnecessary and useless, and therefore untrue, or that, being to some extent, and for some purposes necessary, reason is the standard by which its doctrines and its duties are to be judged.'[11] Smyth quoted the German Socinian, Valentinus

---

8. Ibid., pp. 69-70.

9. Ibid., p. 74.

10. *Charleston Evening News*, 17 July 1852.

11. Thomas Smyth, 'The Province of Reason, Especially in Matters of Religion,' *Southern Presbyterian Review* 7, no. 2 (October 1853), p. 276.

Smalcius, who said, 'Whatever opinion agrees not with reason is inadmissible in theology, and to admit such doctrines, we neither can, nor ought to, be induced, even by the express words of the Spirit of God himself.'[12] He also referenced one of Gilman's favorite theologians, the English Unitarian John Beard, who said, 'The fundamental peculiarity of the anti-trinitarian movement is the deference paid to human intelligence as the *judge*, though not the source of religious truth.'[13]

Smyth responded to these claims as follows: 'Reason, therefore, and not any written revelation, it is affirmed, is the source, or at least the arbiter and judge of religious truth. Is it so? This question, it may be perceived, lies at the foundation of all inquiries into religious doctrine, and determines at once, whether God, in His Word, or *reason* in *each individual heart*, is to be the standard and judge of religious truth.'[14]

Smyth's criticism of the Unitarian movement was not that it encouraged the use of reason, but rather that it placed reason above Scriptural revelation. He too encouraged the use of reason, but he argued for the authority of Scripture over reason, and that students of theology should employ their reason to the fullest extent while keeping in mind that human reason is 'finite, limited, and imperfect, and in reference to all Scriptural and Divine things, weakened and darkened.'[15]

In light of this, and reminiscent of Thornwell, Smyth summoned his readership: 'Let us, then, learn the true nature and condition of man. Let us be humble. Reason is exalted when it is abased, when it is teachable, conscious of its weakness, imperfection and liability to mistakes.'[16] In a subsequent article, Smyth

---

12. Ibid.

13. Ibid; J. Beard, *Historical and Artistic Illustrations of the Trinity; Showing the Rise, Progress, & Decline of the Doctrine; With Elucidatory Engravings* (London: Simpkin, Marshall, and Co., 1846), p. 196.

14. Smyth, 'The Province of Reason,' p. 277.

15. Ibid., p. 292.

16. Ibid.

demonstrated his agreement with Thornwell that the root of heresy is hubris: 'The existence in the one godhead of the Father, the Son and the Holy Ghost, and their several relations to us in the work of salvation, is all that in Scripture we are taught or required to believe, and the reluctance of human pride to acquiesce in this simple teaching, and its vain attempt to bring the nature of God within our comprehension, is the fruitful source of Unitarianism, and of every other error on the subject of the Deity.'[17]

In 'The Bible and Not Reason, the Only Certain and Authoritative Source of Our Knowledge, Even of the Existence of God,' Smyth addressed Gilman's claim that reason leads to a belief in the existence of God, but not to a belief in the Trinity. Smyth argued that human reason could never, '*by its own unaided powers*,' attain to 'the knowledge of God's being'.[18] He attributed the almost universal recognition of a deity not to unassisted human reason, but rather to existing or traditionary revelation. He insisted, 'Every other idea of *one* God that floats in the world is derived from the tradition of the sons of Noah handed down to their posterity.'[19] According to Smyth, although the truth of God's existence 'commends itself to the intuitive powers of human reason, when brought, with its evidence before them, nevertheless, reason alone, unaided and uninstructed, is incapable of arriving at the sublime truth that there is a God.'[20]

He continued to address the theme of reason in his fourth article, 'The Bible and Not Reason, the Only Authoritative Source and Standard of Our Knowledge of the Nature of God – What it Teaches Concerning the Unity of God.' Smyth built on his previous article, arguing that if knowledge of the existence of God requires revelation, then knowledge of the nature of God,

---

17. Thomas Smyth, 'The Doctrine of the Trinity, Fundamental in its Importance' *Southern Presbyterian Review* 8, no. 2 (October 1854), p. 174.

18. Thomas Smyth, 'Existence of God' (January 1854), p. 330.

19. Ibid., p. 336.

20. Ibid., pp. 339-340.

including the unity of his being, requires revelation. Again, this was to counter the Unitarian notion that reason universally leads to a belief in the unity of God but not the Triunity of God, that while Trinitarianism was a complex and difficult creed contrary to reason, Unitarianism, in the words of Gilman, 'possesses a simple and easy creed,' agreeable to the reason of mankind.[21]

Smyth's response was simple: the idea of divine unity is no more reasonable than the idea of divine Triunity; orthodox Christians believe both of these doctrines because, and only because, *both* are *revealed* truths. Smyth explained, 'The being of God, the manner of his being, the attributes of his being, these by all its wisdom and searching, human reason never knew and never can know, until it can compass infinity, comprehend eternity, fill immensity, and attain unto omniscience, omnipresence, and omnipotence.'[22] He then offered a reply to what he believed was the best argument for the unity of God based exclusively on human reason:

> The great, and the only argument upon which the UNITY OF GOD is based by human reason, is the unity of design found throughout the works of nature. But were we not enlightened by revelation and thus enabled to obviate all difficulties, it would be easy to reply that after all it is but a small part of the universe we are acquainted with, and that that part may be under the separate dominion of one presiding Deity, but that were we able to investigate the whole, we might find its various regions under the dominion of various Deities. It might be replied secondly, that even in that part of the universe which we are able to examine, unity of design, as even Paley, the great reasoner on Natural Theology admits, goes no further than to prove a unity of *counsel* and not of being, since there might be unity of counsel among many perfect beings as well as with one. And *thirdly*, it might be replied, that there are even in this world, mixtures of good and evil, misery and happiness, goodness and severity, apparent contrarieties, interruptions and breakings up of what would seem to be wise and

21. *Charleston Evening News*, 28 August 1852.
22. Smyth, 'Nature of God' *Southern Presbyterian Review* 7, no. 4 (April 1854), p. 463.

good plans and operations, such as to have forced upon the mind of a large portion of our race, the belief in two or more distinct eternal and opposing beings to whose sway all sublunary things were subjected. And thus it will be perceived how that even in this advanced and enlightened period of humanity, it would be impossible, on principles of human reason *alone,* to establish any CERTAIN, AUTHORITATIVE and ABIDING CONVICTIONS respecting the NATURE, and especially, the UNITY OF GOD.[23]

Smyth pressed his point still further by arguing that the only people in ancient history to have a settled conviction as to the unity of God have been those who acknowledged that their belief in that unity came from divine revelation: 'The only people who, in ancient times, possessed any certain knowledge of the nature and unity of God, was the Jews and their patriarchal ancestors – a people antecedent to the very existence of any other nation whose records have reached us, and by whom, as is attested by their Scriptures, this knowledge was attributed exclusively to a divine and supernatural communication.'[24]

In his fifth article, 'On the Trinity – The Objections and Unreasonableness, Contradiction, and the Human Origin of the Word Trinity,' Smyth endeavored to show, in contradistinction to the claims of Gilman, that the doctrine of the Trinity is not contrary to reason. In reply to the accusation that the term Trinity is itself a contradiction, Smyth argued that the term is not a contradiction because it does not teach that 'three are one and that one is three,' but rather that 'in the infinite and incomprehensible Jehovah there is a unity so inconceivably different and distinct from the union of finite human natures – of which alone we know anything – as to admit of three persons, hypostases or modes of subsistence, in the one ever-blessed Godhead.'[25] He stated, 'The

---

23. Ibid., pp. 470-71.

24. Ibid., p. 472. Here and elsewhere Smyth referenced 1 Corinthians 1:21: 'The world by wisdom knew not God.'

25. Smyth, 'On the Trinity,' *Southern Presbyterian Review* 8, no. 1 (July 1854), p. 62.

very term trinity therefore, which means a TRI-UNITY, obviates the objection made against the doctrine, that it is contradictory, since it does not imply that God is one in the same sense in which he is three, or three in the same sense in which he is one, but three in a sense different from, and reconcilable with, that in which he is one, and one in a sense different from, and reconcilable with that in which he is three.'[26]

He also argued that it is not unreasonable to believe in the doctrine of the Trinity because traces of the Trinity are seen in the works of God. Like Thornwell, he evidenced a leaning towards Social Trinitarianism by articulating that the Trinity is the archetype of human society. In his assertion that traces of the Trinity are seen in various facets of the created world and the human race, he found agreement with previous theologians such as Richard Baxter and John Owen. His assertions also anticipated further elaboration on these themes by theologians such as Herman Bavinck, who said, 'There is much truth in the belief that creation everywhere displays to us vestiges of the Trinity.'[27]

In addition, Smyth offered a response to the Unitarian criticism that the term *Trinity* is not in the Bible. He pointed out that there are terms which Unitarian theologians use, which likewise are not in the Bible, but which are likewise helpfully employed as summaries of doctrines taught in the Bible:

> It would, therefore, be just and proper to deny the doctrine of the divine ubiquity or omnipresence, and many other truths, because the terms by which they are described are not found in Scripture, as to deny that of the Trinity because the *term* Trinity

---

26. Ibid.

27. Ibid., pp. 70-90; Herman Bavinck, *Reformed Dogmatics*, 4 vols. (Grand Rapids, MI: Baker Academic, 2004), p. 2.333. According to Peter Leithart, this idea is part of a tradition 'in Christian theology, present in seminal form already in Augustine and the Cappadocians and developed through the centuries under the heading *vestigia Trinitatis*,' the aim of which is 'to discover and lay bare echoes, vestiges, traces, clues to trinitarian life within the creation' (Leithart, *Traces of the Trinity*, p. vii).

is not found in Scripture …. We have no zeal for the *term* Trinity any more than for the terms person, unity of God, omnipresence, &c., if any other can as well, or better, express the ideas of which these are the conventional signs. We contend, not for *terms*, but for the doctrines expressed by the terms, and which are, in each case, no more than conclusions drawn by the irresistible power of human reason from the premises found in Scripture.[28]

He went on to cite the Fathers regarding the necessity and acceptableness of using the word *Trinity*, and he quoted Calvin, who said, 'If they call every word exotic, which cannot be found in the Scriptures in so many syllables, they impose on us a law which is very unreasonable, and which condemns all interpretation, but what is composed of detached texts of Scripture connected together.'[29]

## Importance

At the dedication of the newly enlarged sanctuary of the Unitarian Church, Gilman argued, 'We certainly *lose* nothing by this singleness and simplicity of our conceptions of Jehovah; for all that can possibly be ascribed to the three persons of the Deity, pertains, in an equal degree, and without confusion or contradiction, to that ONE mysterious Being, whom we adore as infinite in his power, perfect in his wisdom, and exhaustless in his compassionate beneficence.'[30]

Smyth answered the idea that the doctrine of the Trinity is superfluous in his sixth article, 'The Doctrine of the Trinity, Not Theoretical or Speculative, but Practical in its Nature and Fundamental in its Importance.' He argued, 'The doctrine of the Trinity must either be a "damnable heresy," or the willful rejection of it must be so. It lies at the foundation of our religion. It shapes our conceptions of the God we are to worship, and the worship

---

28. Smyth, 'On the Trinity,' pp. 73-74.

29. Ibid., pp. 71-88, 81.

30. Samuel Gilman, 'Sermon of Dedication,' in *The Old and the New* (Charleston: Samuel G. Courtenay, 1854), p. 64.

with which we are to approach him.'[31] He detailed the difference between the Unitarian and Trinitarian modes of worship, arguing that the question is 'whether it shall be through the intercession and merits of a Mediator, and by the guidance and assistance of a Holy Spirit helping our infirmities, or, directly and in our own name – whether we shall approach God, looking for acceptance through the work and righteousness of a vicarious and Divine Redeemer, and a Divine Sanctifier, or through works of repentance, prayer and praise, which our own hands and hearts have wrought.'[32]

Once again reminiscent of Thornwell, Smyth argued that the Triunity of God is not only the foundation of worship; it is the indispensable ground of human salvation:

> In the Divine Judge we behold our all-merciful Redeemer. As man we are sure of his sympathy, as God we are sure of his power; and from both united, we look for our eternal deliverance. The immense gulf, which appeared to divide the creature from his God, is closed, and we are assured of access to the throne of grace, where our Redeemer sits, to hold out the golden sceptre of mercy, that we may touch and live …. Thus strip the Redeemer of his Divinity, and the whole Gospel scheme would be doubt and darkness, inconsistency and confusion.[33]

He went on to describe how the Trinity affects every area of the Christian life: 'the nature and necessity of prayer, preaching, and the other means of grace, of the church and its ordinances, and of living, loving and experimental piety.'[34] According to Smyth, the doctrine of the Trinity is a 'central Sun, around which the whole system of Christianity, in all its glory, and in all its harmony, revolves.'[35]

---

31. Thomas Smyth, 'The Doctrine of the Trinity, Not Theoretical or Speculative, but Practical in its Nature and Fundamental in its Importance,' *Southern Presbyterian Review* 8, no. 2 (October 1854), p. 158.

32. Ibid., p. 161.

33. Ibid., p. 167.

34. Ibid.

35. Ibid., p. 168.

Surely with the history of the Unitarian Church of Charleston in mind, Smyth called on Christians, especially ministers of the gospel, not to assume that their churches would automatically remain Trinitarian, but rather to proactively maintain Trinitarian orthodoxy. He warned, 'It is only necessary for any church to allow these doctrines to be kept out of the pulpit, and to assume that they are already sufficiently and securely held, to give the enemy all the opportunity he desires to sow tares, which will ere long spring up and choke the good seed, and overspread the garden of the Lord with the weeds of putrefaction and decay.'[36]

## Plurality

In his seventh article, 'Objections to the Doctrine of the Trinity from the Unity of God, as Taught in Scripture, Answered,' Smyth examined two passages that, according to Unitarians, taught the unipersonality of God. The first was Deuteronomy 6:4: 'Hear, O Israel: the LORD our God (*Elohim*), is one.' Smyth argued that the 'one' in this passage does not refer to unity of number, but rather unity of essence, and that *Elohim* (a plural noun) points to a plurality of persons in the Godhead. With New Testament eyes, Smyth interpreted the passage as, 'Jehovah our Elohim, though three persons, is one Jehovah.'[37]

He also examined John 17:3: 'And this is life eternal, that they might know thee, the only true God, and Jesus Christ whom thou hast sent.' Smyth observed that what Christ said here was that the Father is the only true God; what he did not say is that the Father *only* is the true God. Smyth pointed out that later in the same chapter Jesus declared His unity with the Father when He said, 'I and the Father are one.' He catalogued Scripture proofs to show, 'On the one hand, we are taught in Scripture, that there is one only true God. On the other hand, we are equally taught in Scripture,

---

36. Ibid., pp. 175-76.

37. Thomas Smyth, 'Objections to the Doctrine of the Trinity from the Unity of God, as Taught in Scripture, Answered' [alt. 'Unity of God in Scripture Taught as to imply Plurality']. *Southern Presbyterian Review* 8, no. 3 (January 1855), p. 311.

that the Father and the Son, and the Holy Ghost, are alike this one only true God.'[38]

He explained the crucial difference between the way Unitarians and Trinitarians interpret John 17:3: 'Unitarians may say, that to know Jesus Christ, is to know the will of God, as delivered by Jesus Christ. But it is not knowing the will of God, but God Himself as a Saviour, that will secure us eternal life. To know Jesus Christ is, therefore, to know him as he is represented in the Gospel, as God and man; and as having become such for our redemption; and to believe in, love, and obey him as such, and thus we perceive the plain, practical, and fundamental character of the doctrine of the Trinity.'[39]

In his eighth article, 'On Elohim as a Title of God, and as Implying a Plurality in the Godhead,' he elaborated on his claim that *Elohim* implies plurality in the Godhead. Like Thornwell, Smyth posited that the appellative *Elohim* is a derivative of *Ala*, meaning 'to enter into an engagement by oath'. That, in addition to the plurality communicated in *Elohim*, intimates the divine persons covenanting with one another. He believed Genesis 1:26, 'And Elohim said, let us make man in our image, according to our likeness,' portrayed a trialogue.[40]

By holding this position, he, like Thornwell, represented Columbia's willingness to be out of step with most nineteenth-century American seminaries. In a sermon titled 'One God and Father of All,' Gilman spoke of the trend of seminaries on this topic:

> The multiplication of theological seminaries among all denominations will have a tendency, as sure as fate, [towards Unitarianism]. Instead of fearing the influence of these seminaries, I rejoice more and more at the establishment of resorts where the Bible shall be critically studied. The Andover Theological Seminary, which was founded for the express purpose of opposing the spread of Unitarianism, was one of the first to reject the idea that the text in the first chapter of Genesis, Let *us* make man in our own image, had any reference to a

---

38. Ibid., pp. 319-26.

39. Ibid., p. 327.

40. Thomas Smyth, 'On Elohim as a Title of God, and as Implying a Plurality in the Godhead,' *Southern Presbyterian Review* 8, no. 4 (April 1855), pp. 546-49, 552.

plurality of persons in the Deity .... In this way, text after text will be gradually and quietly abandoned, till not a shred will be left to weigh against St. Paul's magnificent position of one God and Father of all, who is *above* all, and *through* all, and *in* all.[41]

Thus Gilman welcomed the multiplication of seminaries, for he believed that all serious biblical scholarship would inevitably lead to the abandonment of Trinitarianism for the Unitarian system. Smyth and the other Columbia theologians were determined that Columbia Seminary would disprove Gilman's prophecy.

## Triads

In his tenth letter, Gilman had responded to a portion of Smyth's sermon, 'Unitarianism Another Gospel,' in which he compared the unipersonal monotheism of Unitarianism with that of Islam and cited a number of Unitarians' 'cordial approbation of Mohamet and of the Koran'.[42] Gilman sharply responded, 'If you go so far out of your way in search of odiums and stigmas to shed upon us, what should prevent us, in return, if such were our untoward inclination, from copying your example and adducing the instances of the Platonic and Hindoo Trinities, so as to charge upon you all the idolatries and unspeakable abominations of the Greeks and Hindoos?'[43] In his rejoinder, Gilman was raising a major Unitarian claim: Trinitarianism is the result of the importation of pagan triads into Christian theology. In articles nine through eleven of his series, Smyth responded to this claim.

From the outset, in 'The Nature and Origin of the Pagan Doctrine of Triads, or a Trinity,' Smyth conceded, 'The fact of the existence of a doctrine of a trinity of Supreme Gods, with more or less distinctness, in all the earlier forms of religious belief, is now universally admitted.'[44] Led by Beard, Unitarians used this notion to discredit Trinitarianism

---

41. Gilman, *Contributions to Religion*, p. 485.

42. Smyth, *Works*, pp. 9:331-32.

43. *Charleston Evening News*, 4 December 1852.

44. Thomas Smyth, 'Pagan Doctrine of Triads,' *Southern Presbyterian Review* 8, no. 4 (April 1855), p. 560.

and popularize the argument that the doctrine of the Trinity was an importation of pagan theology into early Christianity, and thus a corruption of its original Unitarian form. In *Historical and Artistic Illustrations of the Trinity Showing the Rise, Progress, and Decline of the Doctrine*, Beard meticulously compiled evidence, including pictorial illustrations, from ancient religions to demonstrate their historic beliefs in triadic conceptions of the divine.

Smyth used Beard's evidence to make the *Trinitarian* case. He argued that Beard's research, if rightly interpreted, actually supports the argument that Trinitarianism is not the invention of human reason, but rather the revelation of God. Smyth argued that conceptions of triplicity among ancient pagan religions were corruptions of the original revelations of the Trinity given to the Old Testament patriarchs.

Smyth referenced the *Hindu* triad (Brahma, Vishnu, and Shiva – the Creator, the Preserver, and the Destroyer) as a corruption of the original Trinitarian revelation. He also cited the ancient religion of *Egypt*, which contained the concept of a Monad, or fountain deity, Amon-Ra (Chaos) who was equivalent to Brahma in Hinduism, and three deities coming from him: Ptha (the creating power), Kneph (the preserving power), and Khem (the destroying and reproducing power). He pointed out that the Egyptian One and Three are also known as Chronos (the Monad) and Osiris (whose domain is celestial), Horus (whose domain is terrestrial), and Typhon (whose domain is infernal). He added that, similar to the Egyptian system was the *Phoenician*, wherein there was a Monad (Chaos) and three powers flowing from it: Air, Love, and Intellect.

Smyth explained that he understood the Hermetic and Orphic systems to be the intermediate links between Egyptian and classical Greek theological conceptions. He observed that in the Hermetic and Orphic conceptions, one finds the Monad Chaos, co-existent with Ether, from which sprang Ericapaeus (Power), Pothos (Love), and Metis (Intellect); in classical Greek theology, one finds a Monad (Chronos) producing a Triad: Zeus (whose domain is air), Poseidon (whose domain is water), and Hades (whose domain is darkness); and the Peruvian system, where one finds a Monad (Viracocha, the soul of the world), who is symbolised by the Sun (the chief object of Peruvian worship), who produced a Triad: Father-Sun, Son-Sun, and Brother-Sun.

He posited still further that triadic formulations were found in the Syrian, Sidonian, Tyrian, Tibetan, Indian, Chaldean, Persian, Chinese, German, Roman, Druidic, Scandinavian, and Native American cultures. His lengthy survey led him to conclude, 'All the nations of primitive antiquity worshipped a Triad of divine persons, which Triad they believed to have been in some manner inherent in, or to have proceeded from, or to have been produced by a Monad, who was recognised as the supreme source of deity …. These are, beyond all question, the most ancient mythological tenets of the most ancient heathen nations; and, therefore, they present to us the nearest approach to the primitive opinions of the post-diluvian patriarchs, or rather, let us say, the first corruption of the patriarchal religion.'[45]

In addition to these corruptions of the doctrine of the Trinity, Smyth posited that there were remnants and adulterations of other facets of revealed religion present in ancient pagan religions: the Egyptian myth of God creating all things through his firstborn, who was the word of God and who manifested himself through incarnation, infancy, and boyhood (a corruption of patriarchal revelations regarding the second person of the Trinity); the Hindu Avatar likewise an adulterated version of a divine messianic incarnation (as foretold to the patriarchs and fulfilled in Christ); the various sacrificial rites of pagan religions as corruptions of the sacrifices revealed to the patriarchs, which are likewise fulfilled in Christ; the various ancient myths regarding a hero who escapes from a flood or other calamity by finding refuge in a boat, a cavern, the moon, or the hollow of a Lotus leaf, and who is the One Father (monadic) of Three Sons (triadic) who re-peoples the earth (corruptions of the Noahic flood narrative).[46]

---

45. Smyth, 'Presumptive Arguments for the Trinity,' *Southern Presbyterian Review* 9, no. 1 (July 1855), pp. 1-5; 'Pagan Doctrine of Triads,' pp. 562-64.

46. Ibid., pp. 564-65. Regarding pagan notions of incarnate deities, see Smyth, 'The Primitive Revelation of a Divine and Incarnate Saviour Traced in the History and Rites of Bacchus,' *Southern Presbyterian Review* 3, no. 4 (April 1850) pp. 658-71.

Smyth was not the only Columbian to hold such views. With regard to the incarnation, Palmer, for example, explained to his New Orleans flock, 'All systems of religion, the Jewish, the Hindoo, and the heathen, have their incarnations. The first of these three having incarnations that were true, yet transitory; the other two having incarnations that were only the shadows of the true, and altogether unreal. But all of them alike are founded upon that original revelation which was made in the beginning of the ages, of the coming time when God should appear upon earth as man.'[47] At a commencement service at Louisiana State University, Palmer similarly said that incarnation was a central principle of many religions, including the pantheism of Greece and Rome, as well as the religions of the East, and that these were corruptions of primitive revelations of Christ.[48]

In a series of public lectures, titled 'The Origin and Inwardness of Idolatry,' Palmer detailed the history of pagan triads, concluding, 'This belief in triads must have originated from the doctrine of the Trinity, Father, Son and Holy Ghost, which was revealed to the patriarchs of the antediluvian age, and which survived, only to be perverted and corrupted in the forms already named. Or, the traditions of the Garden of Eden having been handed down through the ages, survived in this belief of a triune god, in the story of Adam and Eve and their firstborn.'[49]

Smyth summarized his primitive revelation argument as follows:

> We have shown abundant proof of the universal belief in the doctrine of a Trinity, or at least of a Triad, with some obscure notions of an Avatar or Incarnation, among the Gentile nations, from the earliest times, long previous to the era of the Mosaic dispensation, and therefore not derived from that source; this can be accounted for only by the supposition, that this doctrine,

47. Benjamin Palmer, Jr., *A Weekly Publication Containing Sermons*, 2 vols. (New Orleans: Clark & Hofeline, 1875–1876).

48. *Daily Picayune*, 30 June 1873.

49. *Daily Picayune*, 16 November 1896. Ibid., 23 November 1896.

together with that of the Incarnation, formed the chief tenets of the ancient patriarchal religion, held and taught while mankind constituted but one family, or one community, and carried with the various branches as they separated from the parent stem. Let it be noted, that as successive migrations took place, the tribes wandered to a distance from the chief seat of the nation, they necessarily sunk into greater degrees of barbarism, and their religion became more and more corrupt.[50]

And in his eleventh article titled 'The Doctrine of the Trinity either the Offspring of Reason or of Primitive Revelation,' he once again summarized his case: 'Why should not those images and notions be much rather considered as drops from the rich stream of Divine revelation, which at the beginning of the ages came down from Heaven to men? From the primitive source, might they not have descended to all nations? The remarkable unanimity of these traditions speaks strongly in favor of a common historical origin.'[51]

A weakness in the Columbians' thesis is that they were arguing that the doctrine of the Trinity was preserved more discernibly in other religions than in the Hebrew religion as recorded in the Old Testament. Why would the doctrine of the tri-personal nature of God be more distinctly preserved and manifested in other religions than in the religion of the Triune God Himself and His covenant people?

Smyth anticipated this objection, and he posited that, after the patriarchal revelations regarding the Trinity had been corrupted, God, in his wisdom and grace, published a new revelation to humankind through the written Word, and, although it contained many of the truths originally revealed to the patriarchs, it did not *expressly* contain a restatement of the doctrine of the Trinity. Rather, it was assumed by and contained in the Mosaic and subsequent Old Testament revelations, but in such a way that only

---

50. Smyth, 'Pagan Doctrine of Triads,' pp. 575-76.

51. Thomas Smyth, 'The Doctrine of the Trinity either the Offspring of Reason or of Primitive Revelation,' *Southern Presbyterian Review* 9, no. 2 (October 1855), p. 250.

the 'spiritually enlightened discerned it, and thus it was effectually preserved from being again corrupted by the materializing process natural to the darkened mind of fallen man.'[52]

Smyth understood this concealment to be part of God's preparation for fuller revelation of God's Triunity: 'The sublime doctrine of the Unity of the only living and true God was thus maintained, the Jews kept from lapsing into idolatry, and the false worship of heathen nations kept in check, while reforming influences were from time to time infused into the heart and mind of the world, preparatory for the full and clear manifestation of Divine truth in the pure system of Christianity, so far as to the weak and finite mind of man the infinitely mysterious, yet infinitely true doctrine of TRINITY IN UNITY AND UNITY IN TRINITY, can be manifested.'[53]

According to Smyth,

> [The Old Testament] does not formally state the doctrine of the Trinity. It does not present it in a categorical proposition. It seems to assume and take it for granted, and to use language which pre-supposes it and is adapted to it. And if it is objected that a doctrine so fundamental would, if true, be very clearly and unequivocally defined, in a revelation given by God, we reply that this objection would apply as forcibly to the doctrine of the Divine existence, and, supposing it to be the true doctrine, to the absolute, personal unity of God. The objection, therefore, refutes itself, since it requires that if God is in his nature a personal unit incapable of any distinction of persons, he would in his revelation of himself so fully state and define this unity as to leave no possible ground for ambiguity or doubt. But this, we have seen, he has not done. The very contrary, we have seen, has been done. Even in proclaiming the unity of his Godhead in opposition to all polytheistic notions; and even while commanding that no other Gods shall be worshipped; and even while denouncing his indignation against such, as a jealous God; he nevertheless uses language which implies, if it does not affirm, a plurality—a Trinity—in that ineffable unity. This form

---

52. Smyth, 'Pagan Doctrine of Triads,' p. 576.
53. Ibid.

of language is, we have seen, inwrought into the very texture, the weft and woof of revelation.[54]

## Testimonies

In articles twelve through fourteen, Smyth catalogued testimonies from previous generations regarding the doctrine of the Trinity. In 'Testimony of the Early Fathers to the Doctrine of the Trinity,' he posited,

> If we can ascertain those views which were held by the *primitive* church, on the subject of the Trinity, we have the highest assurance that these must have been delivered by Christ and his apostles, and must contain the real doctrine of the Holy Scriptures. And if we find that those views are not those of the Unitarians, but are, in all that is essential, those of Trinitarians, then we may safely conclude that the Trinitarian, and not the Unitarian doctrine, is that taught in the word of God. In a very important sense, Tertullian's declaration is correct, as it regards Christian doctrine: 'Whatever is first, is true – whatever is later, is adulterated.'[55]

Smyth chronicled the development of and challenges to the doctrine of the Trinity and catalogued the Scriptural interpretations of early church fathers, as well as their creeds, liturgies, and hymns to show that the early church almost universally held to the essentials of modern day Trinitarianism.[56]

In 'Testimony of the Reformers to the Doctrine of the Trinity,' Smyth argued, 'We must regard the unanimous agreement of

---

54. Smyth, 'The Trinity of the Godhead the Doctrine of the Scriptures, (Continued),' *Southern Presbyterian Review* 11, no. 2 (July 1858), pp. 187-88. For more recent discussions of triads in ancient religions, see 'Trimurti' and 'Trinity' in *Encyclopedia of Religion and Ethics*, pp. 457, 458; 'Triads,' in *Encyclopedia of Religion*, pp. 15.39-44; 'God' in *Encyclopedia of Global Religion*, pp. 1.472-73; 'Yupa in Hinduism' and 'Divine Totality and Its Components,' in *Asian Mythologies*, pp. 37-39, 163-65; Ter Haar, *Ritual & Mythology of the Chinese Triads*, pp. 44, 66, 204, 291; Eliot, *Timeless Myths*, pp. 37-42.

55. Smyth, 'Testimony of the Early Fathers to the Doctrine of the Trinity,' *Southern Presbyterian Review* 9, no. 3 (January 1856), pp. 313-14.

56. Ibid., pp. 313-44.

all the reformed churches on the doctrine of the Trinity, both as to form and importance, as an irresistible assurance that their interpretation of the Bible is correct, and that this is verily the doctrine that is according to Godliness.'[57] He quoted at length from various Reformed confessions to show that the Reformed churches of the sixteenth and seventeenth centuries universally held to and stressed the importance of the doctrine of the Trinity. He concluded his article with beautiful words taken from the *Savoy Declaration* and the *1689 Baptist Confession*: the 'doctrine of the Trinity is the foundation of all our communion with God, and comfortable dependence on him.'[58]

In 'Testimony of the Ancient Jews on the Trinity,' Smyth suggested, 'the ancient Jews did not believe in the present Jewish dogma of an absolute personal metaphysical unity of God.'[59] Smyth agreed with Owen that the Targumists were Trinitarian. He quoted Philo and the Talmudical writings to demonstrate that many of the Jews believed in something approaching a Trinitarian concept of God and a conception of the Messiah as an incarnate Yahweh. He concluded, 'It is thus evident, from evidence drawn from a variety of sources independent of one another, and as accessible to Christian as to Jews, that the ancient Jews, both before the time of Christ, immediately after, and during the early ages, did not believe in an absolute unity in the Godhead, but in a plurality of divine subsistence, and which they limited to THREE, in the One undivided Godhead.'[60]

## Scriptures

In his third open letter, Gilman had promised Smyth that, if he would just set aside the Athanasian Creed and examine the Scriptures for

---

57. Smyth, 'Testimony of the Reformers to the Doctrine of the Trinity,' *Southern Presbyterian Review* 9, no. 4 (April 1856), p. 474.

58. Ibid., p. 492. *Savoy Declaration*, 2.3; *1689 Baptist Confession*, 2.3.

59. Smyth, 'Testimony of the Ancient Jews to the Trinity,' *Southern Presbyterian Review* 10, no. 1 (April 1857), p. 94.

60. Ibid., pp. 102-05; John Owen, *An Exposition of the Epistle to the Hebrews with Preliminary Exercitations*, 7 vols. (Edinburgh: Banner of Truth, 1991), pp. 1.114, 2.273.

himself, he would emerge from his studies a convinced Unitarian. In articles fifteen through nineteen, Smyth rebuffed Gilman's claim. He compiled Scripture proofs to show that the Bible teaches 'God is one; the unity of the Godhead, as Scripturally defined, teaches plurality of persons; the distinctions in the Godhead are personal, not nominal; the three persons of the Godhead are equal in all that constitutes God; and the three Divine persons of the Trinity are not three Gods, and therefore that they are one God.'[61]

He reiterated that his purpose was only to state the revealed facts of Scripture, not to explain the inexplicable mystery of the Trinity. He showed that the Bible attributes the works of creation and resurrection to each of the three persons of the Godhead and yet to *one* God, and he posited, 'Reject the doctrine of the Trinity, and the statements of Scripture on this subject can not be reconciled. Admit it, and all is clear.'[62] Like Thornwell, Smyth emphasized his belief that Scripture most clearly reveals the Trinity through the covenant of grace.[63]

## Summary

On 17 July 1966, Milton Rahn, president of the Unitarian Universalist Fellowship of Savannah, Georgia, delivered an address at the Unitarian Church of Charleston to honor the memory of Samuel Gilman. Rahn began his address with these words: '"I trust," wrote Thomas Jefferson in 1822, "that there is not a young man now living in the United States who will not die an Unitarian." A few months earlier John C. Calhoun observed that Unitarianism would be the

---

61. Smyth, 'The Trinity of the Godhead the Doctrine of the Holy Scriptures (1858),' p. 92.

62. Ibid., p. 231.

63. Smyth, 'The Distinctions in the Godhead Personal and Not Nominal,' *Southern Presbyterian Review* 12, no. 2 (July 1859), pp. 302-10. For additional sermons dealing with Trinitarian themes we have already covered, see Smyth, 'The Divinity of Christ,' in *Works*, pp. 9.255-92; 'Dr Watts Not a Unitarian,' in *Works*, pp. 9.347-62; 'On the Fellowship and Communion of Believers with the Father, Son and Holy Ghost,' in *Works*, pp. 9.407-24; 'Baptism a Testimony to the Doctrine of the Trinity in Unity,' in *Works*, pp. 10.333-37.

religion of the whole country within fifty years. These statements of prophecy seem almost absurd, looking at history in view of later events, but these men were sincere in their observations.'[64]

As we have seen, Gilman also made such predictions, believing that Unitarianism would become the dominant religion in Charleston, throughout the United States, and around the world. However, as Rahn intimated, Unitarianism in Charleston declined sharply after the death of Gilman. On the other hand, Trinitarianism prospered in Charleston throughout the rest of the nineteenth century. Second Presbyterian Church grew steadily and planted other churches in Charleston, including a flourishing outreach to the black population called Zion Church, which was the largest church in South Carolina at the time. In a way that paralleled Thornwell's success in Columbia, Smyth accomplished what he set out to do in Charleston: impede the Unitarian movement and advance the cause of the Trinitarian faith.[65]

64. Rahn, 'Savannah Unitarians' Debt to Dr Samuel Gilman,' 1. Unitarian Church Records, SCHS.

65. Macaulay, *Unitarianism*, pp. 178-83; Calhoun, *Our Southern Zion*, p. 225; George Howe, *History of the Presbyterian Church in South Carolina*, 2 vols. (Columbia, SC: W. J. Duffie, 1883), pp. 2.590-610.

# New Orleans

✠

## Benjamin Morgan Palmer and Theodore Clapp

# 8

# *The Palmer Family and Unitarianism*

WE now travel southwest from the Palmetto state to New Orleans, Louisiana, where Thornwell's and Smyth's colleague, Benjamin Morgan Palmer (1818–1902), sought to counteract the Unitarianism that Theodore Clapp (1792–1866) had popularized there.

Palmer was born in Charleston on 25th January 1818 to Edward and Sarah Palmer, both of whom descended from New England Puritan families. He was named for his uncle, Benjamin Morgan Palmer, Sr., minister of the Circular Church of Charleston.[1] His father was a Congregational minister and pastored various churches in South Carolina's low country. He 'got his intellect and intensity of character from his mother' and excelled as a student and debater at Walterboro Academy.[2]

Beginning in 1832, he attended Amherst College in Massachusetts for two years before returning home where he taught school. When he was eighteen, his cousin Isaac Axson, a graduate of Columbia and later a pastor at Independent Presbyterian Church in Savannah, inquired about Palmer's relationship with

---

1. We will typically refer to B. M. Palmer Sr. as 'Palmer, Sr.' and B. M. Palmer Jr. as 'Palmer'.

2. Charles Hutson to Johnson, 8 June 1904, BMP Papers, WSML.

Jesus. During their conversation, Axson said, 'My cousin, you are growing up fast to manhood; is it not a good time to give yourself to the Savior, when you are soon to choose the course in life which you shall pursue?'[3] A few months later, Palmer placed his faith in God's Son and received His Spirit's assurance of the Father's love. Many years later, Palmer stated that this assurance 'came to stay, and through five and fifty years it has deepened in the soul to which it came as the balm of heaven.'[4]

Shortly after his conversion, Palmer recommenced his studies, this time at the University of Georgia, from which he graduated at the top of his class in 1838. Believing God was calling him to preach, he attended Columbia Seminary and graduated from there in 1841. In the same year, he married Mary McConnell, the stepdaughter of Columbia professor George Howe. As a seminarian, Palmer sat under Thornwell's preaching at First Presbyterian Church.

After graduating from Columbia, he briefly served as supply pastor of the Presbyterian Church in Anderson, South Carolina. He then served as pastor of First Presbyterian Church of Savannah. In 1843, when Thornwell became president of South Carolina College, First Presbyterian of Columbia called him to be Thornwell's successor. He pastored there until 1855 and taught at Columbia from 1853 until 1856. In 1855, he toured the Southwest to raise support for the seminary. During his travels, he became acquainted with the congregation of First Presbyterian Church of New Orleans, and they called him to be their pastor. He accepted the call in December of 1856, and he served there until his death in 1902.

During the Civil War, Palmer returned to Columbia, where he once again preached at First Presbyterian and taught at the seminary. He taught church history and, after the death of Thornwell, systematic theology. Over the years, Palmer turned down calls to pastor churches in Charleston, Baltimore,

---

3. John Wells, *Southern Presbyterian Worthies* (Richmond, VA: Presbyterian Committee of Publication, 1936), p. 143.

4. Ibid.

Cincinnati, and Philadelphia, as well as offers to teach at Danville and Princeton.[5]

The people of New Orleans highly esteemed him. On 25th January 1898, the city paused to celebrate his eightieth birthday. *The Daily Picayune* described the event: 'One of the grandest outpourings of the population of New Orleans, one of the largest and most spontaneous of responses of the representatives of the highest and best among all ranks of society to do honor and to convey personal tribute of esteem, were evidenced yesterday, when Dr Palmer's hospitable mansion, on Henry Clay avenue, was thrown open, so as to allow a mighty host free entrance to pay individual as well as common call upon the hale and hearty octogenarian pastor.'[6]

On Sunday, 4th May 1902, Palmer preached from John 10:2, 'My sheep hear my voice and I know them, and they follow me.' In closing, he appealed to those in attendance to embrace Christ as Savior, and he declared that he would 'be willing that it should be his last sermon, if he could by it bring even one sinner to Christ.' The next day, a streetcar accidentally struck and severely injured him. He passed away a few weeks later.[7]

---

5. Thomas Johnson, *The Life and Letters of Benjamin Morgan Palmer* (Richmond, VA: Presbyterian Committee of Publication, 1906), pp. 45-169; 'Dr Palmer's Career,' *Daily Picayune*, 29 May 1902.

6. 'Dr Palmer's Birthday,' *Daily Picayune*, 26 January 1898. As an example of Palmer's celebrity, consider the following newspaper advertisement for Grover & Baker sewing machines: '*From the Wife of the Rev. Dr Palmer, Pastor of the First Presbyterian Church, New Orleans:* I take pleasure in recommending Grover & Baker's Sewing Machines to all who have not purchased one. I have been using one for five years, and would not part with it for any amount of money. MRS M. A. PALMER. Prytania street, New Orleans' (*Daily Picayune*, 25 January 1860).

7. 'The Last Time Dr Palmer Preached,' *Daily Picayune*, 28 May 1902. By this time, Palmer was co-pastoring the church with his nephew, Wallace T. Palmer. 'The venerable divine was run down early on the afternoon of Monday, May 5, by a Carrollton avenue street car and dragged for fully a block. His right big toe was cut off, two gashes inflicted in the forehead, one on either side, and his right leg broken in two places just above the ankle' (*Dallas Morning News*, 29 May 1902).

*The Daily Picayune* declared: 'There is left not one who can take the place once so fully and completely occupied by Dr Palmer, and it is much to be doubted if it can ever be filled, but will remain forever vacant as a memorial of the grand and unique man who stood among the foremost of his age in service and in duty.'[8] New Orleans 'had not seen such a large gathering for a funeral since the death of the Confederate president, Jefferson Davis. Streetcars stopped running, businesses closed, and the flag on City Hall floated at half-mast, as thousands of people of all classes and denominations filled the First Presbyterian Church and overflowed into Lafayette Square.'[9]

## The Palmer Family: A Microcosm of the Unitarian-Trinitarian Conflict

In 1621, the *Fortune* sailed from England to Plymouth, Massachusetts. One of the passengers was William Palmer, whose son Samuel became one of the first graduates of Harvard and a Congregational minister. One of Samuel's sons was Job Palmer (1747–1845). Shortly before the Revolutionary War, Job moved from Massachusetts to Charleston, where he became a successful businessman and the lead deacon at the Circular Church.[10]

Growing up, he watched Puritan New England increasingly become Unitarian. In Charleston, he was embroiled in the controversy that led to the division of the Independent Church and the formation of Charleston's Unitarian Church. In light of the increased popularity of the Unitarian movement, he was especially burdened to promote the Trinitarian faith within his own family. Thus, when he was eighty-eight years old, he wrote a lengthy letter to his posterity seeking to show them from Scripture the reality and the love of the Triune God. He wrote,

> To my descendants who may see this paper after my decease, I leave it and what it contains, as a memorial of my tender

---

8. *Daily Picayune*, 28 May 1902.

9. Calhoun, *Our Southern Zion*, p. 325.

10. 'Job Palmer to his Descendants, 1835,' Circular Congregational Church Records, SCHS.

regard for them, and my earnest desire and prayer for their eternal welfare; and strongly recommend to them, and more especially to those of them, if any such there should be, who have doubts in their minds of the Supreme Divinity of the Lord Jesus Christ and of his suffering to make an atonement for sin, that they read the following passages of Scripture carefully, and prayerfully, that their minds may be led to a knowledge of the truth as it is in Jesus Christ, and that their hearts may be disposed to embrace it.[11]

After expounding a multitude of Scriptural passages to communicate the manifold love of the Trinity, he concluded, 'Oh may God in his mercy grant it may be many, all of you, at the right hand of our glorious Redeemer when he is seated on his throne to judge the world and to make up his jewels, this is the fervent desire and prayer of your aged ancestor.'[12]

## Mary Palmer Shindler

Job Palmer's oldest son was Benjamin Morgan Palmer, Sr. (1781–1847), who, as we have discussed, led the Trinitarians during the division of the Independent Church in Charleston. He pastored the Circular Church from 1813 until 1835, when, due to failing health, he resigned from the pastorate and retired to Orangeburg, South Carolina.[13]

One of his daughters was Mary Palmer Shindler (1810–1883). Palmer, Sr. and his brother Edward, the father of Benjamin Morgan Palmer, Jr., married sisters. Thus, Mary and Benjamin Morgan Palmer, Jr. were *double* first cousins. As a child, Mary exhibited rare intellectual ability and wrote stories that were printed in *Rosebud*, Caroline Gilman's magazine for children. Mary went on to study at the finest female academies in Charleston and New England.[14]

---

11. Ibid.

12. Ibid.

13. 'The Circular Church,' *Charleston Daily Courier*, 16 July 1853.

14. Shindler-Palmer Papers, RWSL. Because Mary's last name was changed several times we will simply refer to her as 'Mary'.

In 1835, she married Charles Dana, and the couple settled in Iowa. In 1839, Charles and their infant son, Charlie, died of cholera. After that, Mary moved back to Charleston and lived with her close friends, Senator John C. Calhoun and his wife Floride.[15] She attended the Circular Church, which was by then pastored by her father's successor, Reuben Post, who, like Palmer, Sr., was a graduate of Princeton.[16] Over the next few years, Mary wrote prolifically, publishing poems, hymns, and works of prose that earned her national renown.[17]

While living with John and Floride Calhoun, she became more acquainted with several prominent Unitarian families in Charleston. Most significantly, Mary grew in her relationship with her long-time friend and literary mentor, Caroline Gilman, and she became increasingly interested in the Gilmans' Unitarian faith.[18]

Members of the Circular Church began to notice that Mary, who was a member of the choir, was strangely silent during the singing of the Doxology for several Sundays in a row. As she spent more time with the Gilmans and other Unitarians in Charleston, rumors that she had converted to Unitarianism began to spread.[19]

Finally, in January of 1845, Mary wrote her parents telling them that she had become a Unitarian. After that, she began to share the news of her conversion with others. Because of the way her father and grandfather had so publicly stood for Trinitarianism,

---

15. Linda Sundquist, *The Poetess of Song: The Life of Mary Shindler* (Livermore, CA: Wingspan Press, 2006), pp. 73-74. Kay Bailey Hutchison, former United States Senator from Texas, is Mary's great-great granddaughter; she wrote the foreword to *Poetess of Song*.

16. Calhoun, *Circular Church*, p. 73.

17. Dana, *The Southern Harp*; *The Northern Harp*; *The Parted Family*; and *Charles Morton*.

18. Sundquist, *Poetess of Song*, pp. 73-74, 95. Calhoun 'espoused Unitarian views', though he 'did not necessarily flaunt them' (Macaulay, *Unitarianism*, p. 7).

19. Mary Dana, *Letters Addressed to Relatives and Friends, Chiefly in Reply to Arguments in Support of the Doctrine of the Trinity*, 2nd ed. (Boston: James Munroe and Company, 1846), pp. 39-42.

and because of her international reputation as a Christian writer, her conversion to Unitarianism shook the city of Charleston and became known on both sides of the Atlantic.

Over the next several months, Mary wrote many letters to her family, friends, and other concerned citizens who had written her, in which she tried to explain her conversion to Unitarianism. Because of the public nature of her conversion, she felt compelled to explain herself in print. In 1845, shortly after the death of Job Palmer, and while her increasingly popular cousin, whom she referred to as 'Cousin Ben', was serving as pastor of the First Presbyterian Church of Columbia, Mary published thirty of her letters in a book titled *Letters Addressed to Relatives and Friends, Chiefly in Reply to Arguments in Support of the Doctrine of the Trinity.*[20]

An advertisement in a Charleston newspaper read:

> *Mrs Dana's New Work on the Doctrine of the Trinity.* We have before us this interesting publication just from the press of Munroe & Co., Boston.
>
> This is the latest treatise on the important subject of the Trinity – and by an entire new hand; and what renders the book remarkable and peculiarly interesting, is, that it was written by a lady, and one of our own native citizens. Such a work from such a quarter, is quite a unique in this country.
>
> The arguments are set forth in a somewhat new and beautiful light, evince not only a settled conviction in the mind of the author of the truth of the doctrines which they support and defend, but so much independence, honesty and genuine piety, that they can hardly fail to win their way to the heart, and to secure for the author, the respect and admiration of the reader.
>
> The work may be obtained at Greer's, No. 135 King street.[21]

The first letter in the book was her initial communication to her parents informing them of her change. She wrote, 'My kind

---

20. See Sarah Palmer to Mary, 21 November 1865, Shindler-Palmer Papers, RSWL.

21. *The Southern Patriot*, 18 October 1845.

and venerated parents: It has become my solemn duty to make to you an announcement, which, I fear, will fill your hearts with sorrow …. I do not now believe that my blessed Lord and Saviour Jesus Christ is the Supreme God …. In other words, after long and earnest deliberation, much diligent study of the Holy Scriptures, and fervent prayer to God for the assistance of his spirit, I conscientiously and firmly reject the doctrine of the Trinity.'[22] In a subsequent letter she wrote, 'I have decided to go on next Sabbath morning to the Unitarian Church, and have thought it honest and right to tell you so.'[23]

Throughout *Letters*, Mary demonstrated that she was well acquainted with both Trinitarian and Unitarian apologists. She was especially captivated by the eloquent arguments of her friend and new pastor, Samuel Gilman, and the writings of Harvard president, Jared Sparks. As a disciple of Gilman, she adhered to Channing's Unitarianism, but she revered Priestley as well.

What is most pronounced in her letters is her renunciation of the 'dreadful' Calvinism in which she had been raised. She wrote:

> I knew the Assembly's Catechism by heart at a very early age; but I was too young, light-hearted, and thoughtless, to receive from it any very definite ideas; and the words which were engraved upon my memory were mere sounds, conveying, to my mind, very little sense. It is now my business and my aim to forget them, though they often haunt me like phantoms of the past.[24]

And again she wrote:

> I regard [Calvinism] almost as I would some venomous serpent, from whose fangs I have but narrowly escaped. Too long has it been coiling itself around my struggling spirit. That its poisonous fangs have not reached my vitals, I owe to that wonderful Providence of God which has protected me from harm, and, at length, provided a way of escape. He has given me strength to

---

22. Dana, *Letters*, pp. 1-2.

23. Ibid., p. 72.

24. Ibid., p. 111.

struggle on, till, at length, I have thrown the monster from me. I bless God for my escape.[25]

Her goal became helping others experience her newfound freedom from the 'tyranny' of Calvinism, and she earnestly desired to be 'instrumental in doing something to promote the interests of liberal and enlightened Christianity'.[26] Reflecting on her conversion, she explained, 'When I sit down seriously to compare the system of doctrines with which I have so long been fettered, with those under the influence of which my freed spirit now joyfully springs to meet its benevolent Creator, I cannot but exclaim, "thanks be to God who hath given me the victory, through my Lord Jesus Christ!"'[27] She was optimistic that more and more people would experience that victory as well: 'I sincerely hope and trust that the unfortunate peculiarities of [Calvinism] will, after a time, become entirely obsolete. May the period soon arrive! It will be a joyful day for Christendom, and I devoutly believe it will occasion joy in Heaven.'[28]

Mary maintained that her adoption of Unitarianism was the result of careful study of the New Testament, which she referred to as 'the most powerful and convincing Unitarian book in the world'.[29] On the other hand, she revealed Unitarianism's priority of reason over revelation. Echoing the sentiments of her new pastor, she wrote, 'The modern doctrine of the Trinity is, to me, so plainly a contradiction, that I deem it *impossible* it could be found in a revelation from God.'[30] She similarly demonstrated the influence of Enlightenment thinkers such as Hume: 'It appears to me that Hume was not far from the truth when he jeeringly asserted, that the popular theology had "a kind of appetite for absurdity, and

---

25. Ibid., p. 131.

26. Ibid., p. 112.

27. Ibid., p. 13.

28. Ibid., pp. 111, 132.

29. Ibid., p. 38.

30. Ibid., p. 78fn.

contradiction.'"[31] She surmised, 'Our reason is the highest gift of God; let us see to it that we neglect not "the gift that is in us." If we make no use of our reason, would not our Heavenly Father justly charge us with the guilt of hiding our talent in the earth?'[32]

Led by Gilman and Dickson, the Charleston Unitarian Book and Tract Society widely distributed *Letters*. Albert Mackey, a leading Charleston physician and an officer in the society, wrote that there was a great demand for the 'invaluable letters of Mrs Dana', and testified, '[*Letters*] exercises a favorable impression in the advancement of our doctrines, and has, we believe, been the means in more than one instance, not only of awakening a spirit of enquiry into the truth of Unitarianism, but of giving a more liberal tone to the opinions of several of our opponents who have read it.'[33]

We have not been able to locate the original letters between Mary and her friends and family, which form the substance of *Letters*. In the published compilation of the letters, except for those addressed to her parents, she does not reveal who her correspondents were. We imagine that Palmer, Jr. was among those relatives seeking to persuade her back to the Trinitarian faith. We know for certain that the two cousins spent time together shortly after the second publication of *Letters*.[34]

In December of 1846, Mary wrote Francis Lieber, a renowned professor of history and politics at South Carolina College, introducing herself and asking to meet with him during a visit in Columbia. In Lieber, Mary found another intellectual who would sympathize with her anti-Calvinistic views. It was widely known that Lieber was no fan of the Thornwell-led Presbyterian takeover of the college. He complained of Thornwell's 'bitter, biting, acrid,

---

31. Ibid., p. 238. See David Hume, *The Natural History of Religion*, ed. H. E. Root (Stanford, CA: Stanford University Press, 1956), p. 54.

32. Ibid., p. 221.

33. *Annual Report* (Charleston, SC: Walker & Evans, 1855), p. 10; *What is the Worth of Doctrine?* (Charleston, SC: Walker & Burke, 1848), pp. 8, 21.

34. According to Sundquist, the original letters are not extant. Sundquist, telephone interview, 17 June 2015.

scratching, tearing, grating, grinding, harrowing, inflaming, Hyper-Calvinism.'[35] He wrote a friend saying, Thornwell is 'a man, of whom Mr Breckinridge once printed, that since Calvin there had been no man like him. I hope so.'[36] Mary introduced herself to Lieber by writing, 'I am the daughter of the Revd. Dr Palmer of Charleston, and first cousin of the Revd. Mr Palmer, of your city, whose house will be my home during my stay there.'[37] We imagine that Cousin Ben and Mary had many conversations about her faith during her stay in his home.

Towards the end of 1847, the year in which both her parents died, there was a remarkable turn of events in Mary's life: rather quietly, she returned to 'a belief in the Trinity in which she had been raised'.[38] In the early part of 1848, she was publicly confirmed in the communion of the Episcopal Church, and, shortly thereafter, on 18th May 1848, she married Robert Shindler, an Episcopal minister in Orangeburg, who later became rector of Christ Church in Nacogdoches, Texas.[39]

Trinitarians entreated Mary to publish a refutation of her previous arguments for Unitarianism and use her popularity to promote the cause of the Trinitarian faith, but she never did. Instead, 'she quietly left behind her period of "religious rebellion" and moved toward a faith more closely linked to the world of her youth.'[40] In spite of Mary's return to the Trinitarian faith, 'Biblical Unitarians' continue to use *Letters* to promote and defend their faith.[41]

---

35. O'Brien, *Conjectures*, p. 1129.

36. Ibid.

37. Ibid., p. 360.

38. Sundquist, *Poetess of Song*, p. 100.

39. Ibid.

40. Ibid., p. 101.

41. Anthony Buzzard, telephone interview, 12 June 2015. Buzzard's publications include *The Doctrine of the Trinity: Christianity's Self-Inflicted Wound* and *Jesus Was Not a Trinitarian*. See 'Mary Dana Book,' accessed 21 May 2016, http://www.biblicalunitarian.com/marydanabook.pdf; 'A Review,' accessed 8 September 2016, http://www.21stcr.org/multimedia/artitcles/mary_dana _book_review.html.

After her return to the Trinitarian fold, Mary became interested in Spiritualism. She began seeking the guidance of mediums and participating in séances. She chronicled her experiences and promoted this new element of her spirituality through a book titled *A Southerner Among the Spirits*, the dedication of which read, 'To my dear spirit father and mother, the Rev. B. M. Palmer, D.D., and Mrs Mary S. Palmer; and to my spirit husband, the Reverend R. D. Shindler, at whose request this work has been prepared; and to my numerous relatives and friends in the angel-world, I affectionately dedicate this record of my experience in investigating the wonderful and heart-cheering phenomena of Spirit communion.'[42]

Mary believed that she had a 'Spirit Band', a group of departed souls who were guiding her through this life and into the next. The Spirit Band included family members, as well as famous Christians such as Robert E. Lee and John Wesley.[43] Mary did not believe Spiritualism was in conflict with the Trinitarian faith. That she was not alone in this belief is evidenced by the fact that the Southern Baptist Publication Society published *A Southerner Among the Spirits*.[44]

On 16th July 1853, almost six years after the death of Palmer Sr., *The Charleston Daily Courier* printed a lengthy history of the Circular Church, occasioned by a renovation of the church's sanctuary. The detailed article recounted the division of the church under the ministries of Palmer, Sr. and Forster due to 'the adoption or manifestation of Unitarian tenets' by the latter, with

42. Mary Shindler, *A Southerner Among the Spirits: A Record of Investigations into the Spiritual Phenomena* (Memphis, TN: Southern Baptist Publication Society, 1877), p. iii.

43. Shindler-Palmer Papers, RWSL; Mary S. Shindler Papers, SCHS.

44. *Spirits*, pp. i, xi. Girardeau, on the other hand, called the Spiritualist movement 'demoniacal' (*Sermons*, George A. Blackburn (Columbia, SC: The State Company, 1907), p. 111).

'Dr Palmer, and the Trinitarians of his congregation, retaining the [Circular Church], and Mr Forster, and his adherents, taking the [Archdale Street Church] as their place of worship.'[45]

The article also reprinted the words inscribed on Palmer, Sr.'s gravestone, including the following: 'He was orthodox in his creed, luminous in exposition, graceful and elegant in diction, in exhortation, impressive and affecting, in prayer fervent, evangelical and sublime.'[46] On 25th July 1853, the *Courier* printed a subsequent article titled 'Appendix To the Circular Church'. The article included a 'Tribute to the Memory of the Rev. Benjamin M. Palmer, D. D.,' provided by the Circular Church. It spoke of him as an 'intrepid, zealous, and uncompromising champion' of orthodoxy.[47]

A few weeks later, Gilman wrote an article for the *Courier* in response to the articles on the Circular Church. He wanted to correct certain portions concerning Palmer Sr. and reveal 'a change of doctrinal opinions entertained by that excellent and pious man, for some time previous to his decease.'[48] Gilman stated, 'For a year or two previous to Dr Palmer's death, I had long conversations with him, sought not by myself, but by him, in regard to the doctrine of the Trinity, and the opinion of Unitarian Christians.'[49] Gilman went on to allege that Palmer Sr. eventually embraced the Unitarian faith.[50]

Two days after the publication of Gilman's article, the *Courier* published a response co-authored by Bazile Lanneau and Bazile Edward Lannaeu. Bazile Lanneau was one of the writers of the history of the Circular Church published by the *Courier*. He was

---

45. 'Circular Church,' *Charleston Courier*, 16 July 1853.

46. Ibid.

47. 'Appendix To The Circular Church,' *Charleston Courier*, 25 July 1853.

48. 'The Late Rev. Dr Palmer,' *Charleston Courier*, 13 August 1853.

49. Ibid.

50. Ibid. For Gilman's entire article, see Appendix 3.

a prominent Charleston attorney, a leader in the Circular Church, and the son-in-law of Palmer Sr.[51]

Bazile Edward Lanneau was the son of Bazile Lanneau, and, thus, the grandson of Palmer, Sr. He was an alumnus of Columbia Seminary, where he studied under and lived with his cousin and mentor, Palmer, Jr., and he later became Instructor of Hebrew at the seminary.[52] In their response, the Lanneaus defended the orthodoxy of Palmer Sr. and rebuked Gilman for his accusations. They forcefully rejected the allegation that there was any evidence that Palmer Sr. had 'passed from Orthodox to Unitarian sentiments'.[53] They spoke of Mary's return to the Trinitarian faith and, ultimately, sought to reclaim the reputation of Palmer Sr. as a faithful defender of Trinitarian orthodoxy.[54]

### Edward and Sarah Palmer

Job Palmer's son Edward attended Andover Seminary because it was founded by northern Congregationalists to counteract the Unitarianism being taught at Harvard. After his graduation from Andover, Edward served Congregational churches with fidelity to Trinitarian orthodoxy.[55]

Following in his father's footsteps, Edward strove to ensure that his children embraced and maintained the Trinitarian faith. As one of Palmer's relatives explained, 'Young [Benjamin] Palmer's comrades and friends, then, went to the South Carolina College at Columbia. But these were the days of Dr Cooper's influence in that institution; and, so great was the Rev. Edward Palmer's fear of the contagion of infidelity on his son's mind, that he decided

---

51. *Charleston Courier*, 29 April 1829.

52. Johnson, *Palmer*, pp. 134, 167.

53. *Charleston Courier*, 15 August 1853.

54. For the Lanneaus' complete article, see Appendix 4.

55. See Christopher Duncan, 'Benjamin Morgan Palmer: Southern Presbyterian Divine,' PhD diss. (Auburn University, 2008), p. 9.

not to send him to a college which bore the reputation of being a vestibule to perdition.'[56]

Thus, in 1832, Edward and Sarah Palmer sent Benjamin, then fifteen years of age, to Amherst College in Massachusetts, which was founded by orthodox Congregationalists who 'viewed the growth of Unitarianism in the eastern part of the state as the greatest theological and societal threat of their time' and had founded Amherst with the specific mission of equipping young men, including future ministers, to combat Unitarianism and uphold historic Christianity. After his conversion, Benjamin finished his college studies at the University of Georgia, which, as we noted previously, was strongly influenced by the Presbyterian Church.[57]

The anti-Unitarianism of Palmer's parents is summarized in one of the last phrases uttered by his mother, Sarah. On her deathbed, 'More than once, speaking of Christ as a complete Savior, she exclaimed: "What a wretched religion the Unitarian has – he has no God for his Savior!"'[58]

It was in this familial context, so marked by the Unitarian-Trinitarian conflict, that Palmer grew up, entered the ministry, and developed his ministerial emphases. Ironically, his family history was not unlike the history of the church that he would pastor for almost fifty years.

---

56. Hutson to Johnson, 8 June 1904, BMP Papers, WSML.

57. Duncan, 'Palmer,' pp. 19, 30-31.

58. Johnson, *Palmer*, p. 104.

# 9

# Theodore Clapp and the History of First Presbyterian Church of New Orleans

I N addition to understanding Palmer's family background, understanding the history of First Presbyterian Church of New Orleans, where he pastored from 1856 until 1902, is vital for understanding the context and character of his ministry. In 1818, the year of Palmer's birth, the Mississippi Presbytery tasked Sylvester Larned, a recent graduate of Princeton, with planting a church in New Orleans. At the time, with the exception of Christ Church Episcopal, which was established in 1805, all of the churches in New Orleans were Roman Catholic.

Larned was a gifted preacher, and the number of those who regularly attended his preaching steadily grew. In January of 1819, the congregation began construction of a large sanctuary on a choice site on Saint Charles Street. The new edifice was dedicated seven months later. However, in the summer of 1820, yellow fever swept through the city. Larned contracted the illness, and, on 27 August 1820, he preached his last sermon. His text was Philippians 1:21: 'For me to live is Christ, and to die is gain.' He died four days later, one day shy of his twenty-fifth birthday.[1]

---

1. Elma Kolman, 'The History of the Presbyterian Church in New Orleans (1817–1860),' MA thesis (Tulane University, 1939), pp. 3-13.

After the death of Larned, the congregation called Theodore Clapp to be their minister. Clapp, who was born on 29 March 1792, grew up in Easthampton, Massachusetts, where his Calvinistic parents taught him the *Shorter Catechism*. When he was eighteen, the Calvinistic clergyman who tutored him in Latin told him that, given his intellect, he should train for the ministry in order to defend Christianity against the Unitarianism emanating from Harvard. From that time, he began contemplating the ministry, and, after graduating from Yale College, he entered Andover Seminary. As a seminarian, he lived with and was tutored by Andover professor, Leonard Woods.[2]

In 1817, after graduating from Andover and being licensed to preach by a Congregationalist association, Clapp became a tutor in Lexington, Kentucky, where he also engaged in itinerant preaching. One Sunday morning in 1821, he preached an impromptu sermon in the ballroom of a hotel, where two trustees from the fledgling New Orleans congregation happened to hear him. Clapp impressed them, and they encouraged the leadership of the church to consider him as their next pastor. They invited Clapp to visit New Orleans and preach to the congregation. He initially declined their overtures, but, in February of 1822, he visited and preached for several Sundays, after which the congregation unanimously called him as their pastor.[3]

In November of 1823, the congregation, which consisted of twenty-four members, officially adopted the *Westminster Standards*. The Mississippi Presbytery particularized the congregation as the First Presbyterian Church in the City and Parish of New Orleans.

Meanwhile, Clapp began reading the Unitarian views of Channing, whom he believed to be 'an author pre-eminently great, who has done more for the cause of pure Christianity with his pen than any other American,' and he increasingly entertained doubts about whether the Scriptures actually taught

2. Clapp, *Autobiographical Sketches*, pp. 8, 18, 32, 398.
3. Ibid., pp. 26-27, 32.

the Calvinistic faith in which he had been reared. He began to confide in a number of acquaintances and church members about his doubts regarding original sin, eternal punishment, and the doctrine of the Trinity. As early as 1824, he began hinting at his doubts from the pulpit.[4]

As Clapp provided glimpses of his views, whispers of heresy arose from within the church and the presbytery. This went on for almost eight years before the Mississippi Presbytery tried him for heresy. At the trial, his accusers did not have to work very hard to prove his unorthodoxy. In his response to the charge that he denied the doctrine of the Trinity as taught in the *Westminster Standards*, Clapp argued,

> I have simply denied Tritheism; that there are three persons, (meaning by person, a distinct separate agent) in the God-head .... You pronounce my views erroneous; that is, you avow and teach that there are three separate, distinct agents in the Godhead. It is an incontrovertible position, that the doctrine of a plurality of separate and equal agents in the Divine Nature is polytheism. I am no polytheist, moderator; the God whom I profess to honour and adore is a Unit, undivided and indivisible.[5]

Clapp defended himself further:

> If I were to say that a reception of the doctrine of the Trinity is essential to salvation, would it not be virtually declaring, that in my opinion the salvation of a Unitarian is an impossibility? Do we read in the Bible that none but Trinitarians will be admitted to the kingdom of the Messiah?[6]

---

4. Theodore Clapp, *A Report of the Trial of the Rev. Theodore Clapp, Before the Mississippi Presbytery at their Sessions in May and December 1832* (New Orleans, LA: Hotchkiss & Co., 1833), p. vii; *Autobiographical Sketches* (Boston: Phillips, Sampson & Company, 1858), pp. 160-71; Macaulay, *Unitarianism*, p. 50.

5. Clapp, *Trial*, pp. 50-51.

6. Ibid., p. 52.

In a letter to the chairman of the committee assigned to investigate his teaching, Clapp candidly wrote:

> I would not unchurch a person, or keep him from the communion table, merely because he did not believe in the doctrine of the Trinity, if he embraced the other essential doctrines of the Gospel and led a Christian life. I would as soon be settled over a Unitarian church as any other; I would as soon exchange pulpits with a Unitarian clergyman as any other, if I believed him to be a good man.[7]

One witness at the trial, a prominent judge and member of First Presbyterian, testified to what he heard Clapp say in one of his sermons:

> He stated he did not believe in a Trinity of persons or agents composing the Godhead, but that he believed in a Trinity of *Facts*, which I understood him to explain this way: that it is a fact that there is one God, the creator of all things; a fact that there is a Redeemer; and a fact that there is a Sanctifier: that these are modifications of *one God*, but in what manner those operations are performed he said he could not explain. That these *facts* correspond with the Father, Son, and Holy Ghost of the Trinitarians, called by them three persons in the Godhead, which he said amounted in his judgment to Tritheism.[8]

Another witness, who had resided with the Clapp family during the year 1830, testified that Clapp declared in a private conversation, 'I am not a Trinitarian.' Another witness said, 'I have heard him reject the term Trinity as an unscriptural word, calculated to give a false impression.' And another testified that Clapp had said he 'thought the word Trinity an unhappy expression'.[9]

The presbytery found Clapp guilty of denying the doctrine of the Trinity as taught in the *Standards*. The presbyters concluded:

---

7. Ibid., p. 136.

8. Ibid., p. 189. See also *Minutes of the General Assembly*, vol. 7 (Philadelphia: Geddes and Bailey, 1833), p. 7.192.

9. Clapp, *Trial*, pp. 196, 220, 223.

It appeared in evidence that his exhibitions of this doctrine had led many to believe that he denied it. It appeared in evidence that he denounced a trinity of persons in the Godhead as Tritheism; that he maintained only a trinity of facts; that it is a fact that there is a Creator, a fact that there is a Redeemer, a fact that there is a Sanctifier – that these are *modifications* of one God – that there are no *personal* properties in the Godhead. This is the long exploded doctrine of Sabellius. His denial of being a Sabellian does by no means change the nature of his doctrine.[10]

Ultimately, the presbytery unanimously sustained all charges brought against Clapp: 'the guilt of avowing and teaching doctrines inconsistent with the system of doctrines which he had voluntarily adopted, and the guilt of slander and falsehood.'[11] They found him guilty of denying the Trinity, original sin, the decrees of God, substitutionary atonement, eternal punishment, the Sabbath, and the efficacy of intercessory prayer. The presbytery suspended him from the exercise of ministerial functions, with the hope that he would demonstrate repentance. However, the very evening of the presbytery's decision, Clapp disregarded his suspension and preached at the Methodist Episcopal church in Natchez, Mississippi, where the presbytery was meeting. In response, the presbytery deposed him 'from the office of the Gospel ministry for contemptuous disregard of the decision of the Presbytery'.[12]

Though deposed by the presbytery, Clapp had gained a loyal following in New Orleans, and the overwhelming majority of his congregation had come to love him and his Unitarian views. In February of 1833, the congregation of the First Presbyterian Church of New Orleans thumbed its nose at the Mississippi Presbytery and voted 86 to 26 to retain Clapp as their pastor. The

---

10. Ibid., p. 352.

11. Ibid., p. 370.

12. Clapp, *Trial*, pp. 352, 372. One of Clapp's obituaries described the events as follows: 'The mind of Dr Clapp having undergone some change on the subject of doctrines, he rendered himself obnoxious to the Presbytery, and was at length arraigned before the Synod and tried for heresy' (*New Orleans Times*, 19 May 1866).

majority also kept the church property, including the communion silver, and re-established themselves as the First Congregational Church of New Orleans. After several more name changes, the church finally adopted the name First Unitarian Church.[13]

After being deposed by the presbytery and affirmed by the majority of his congregation, Clapp settled into a new chapter of ministry in which he more publicly expressed his views and vision. On 4 July 1834, he declared from his pulpit that he did not believe in the doctrines of endless punishment and the Trinity. He confessed that he could 'no longer believe in, avow, teach, or defend the peculiar doctrines of the Presbyterian church,' and that he deemed it his 'duty to wage against them, both in and out of the pulpit, a war of utter extermination.'[14]

Like many of the other Unitarians in our study, Clapp saw himself as one who had been divinely emancipated from Calvinism: 'Heaven was pleased to guide me through the mazes of error and superstition, in which I had wandered from childhood, into the broad, beautiful fields of evangelical truth.' He believed his role as a preacher was to remove the Calvinistic 'veil of darkness and deformity' from the face of God. And, like his fellow Unitarians, he was optimistic about the future of their movement, believing that if his version of the faith could be widely disseminated, Christianity would be universally accepted, and the longed-for millennial age would be ushered in.[15]

Like Gilman's, Clapp's optimism was fuelled by his own success. Not only did his congregation stick with him after his deposition, several of the city's most prominent citizens later became members of 'Parson Clapp's Church'. As Clapp's fame as an orator grew, so did the congregation, with over a thousand in attendance each Sunday. When prominent citizens from outside the state would visit New Orleans,

---

13. Today, it is the First Unitarian Universalist Church of New Orleans.

14. Clapp, *Autobiographical Sketches*, pp. 171-72.

15. Ibid., pp. 13, 161, 321, 413; Clapp, *Trial*, p. 14.

they would make a point to visit three places: the American Theatre, the French Opera House, and, on Sunday, Parson Clapp's Church.[16]

Clapp became a leader in many areas of New Orleans' civic life. He was elected as the president of the College of New Orleans and helped establish what became Tulane Medical School, which held its first classes and graduations at the Unitarian Church. He also served the Medical School as a trustee and a part-time professor of anatomy. In 1856, he retired from his pastorate and moved back to Kentucky, his wife's native state. He died in Louisville on 17 May 1866 and was buried there, but, in March of 1867, his body was exhumed and brought back to New Orleans, where he was buried at Cypress Grove Cemetery. Many thousands of people attended his funeral at the Unitarian Church.[17]

Although the overwhelming majority of Clapp's congregants stayed with him after his deposition, a handful of the church's members decided to make another attempt at establishing a Presbyterian Church in New Orleans. In the early months of 1834, twenty-three beleaguered souls re-established the First Presbyterian Church of New Orleans and secured a plot of land on Lafayette Square, just down Saint Charles Street from their former church. Soon thereafter, the congregation called Joel Parker to be their pastor. The Mississippi Presbytery installed Parker on 27 April 1834, and he served the church until the spring of 1839, by which time the church had grown to 142 members.[18]

In Parker, the presbytery found a man who would stand in sharp contrast to their former minister and his church down the street. In 1829, while pastoring in Rochester, New York, Parker stood against a surge of theological liberalism and wrote a book against Universalism.[19] While some in New Orleans supported

---

16. 'Service for Theodore Clapp, Founder of Unitarianism in New Orleans' (*Daily Picayune*, 1 April 1907).

17. 'Remains of Dr Theodore Clapp,' *New Orleans Times*, 24 March 1867.

18. 'Dr Palmer's Career.'

19. Parker, *Lectures on Universalism*. Palmer frequently addressed Universalism,

Parker's stand for orthodoxy, many accused him of sectarianism and bigotry, and twice he was burned in effigy on Lafayette Square. In spite of Parker's overall unpopularity in the city, First Presbyterian survived and, after his departure, grew slowly under two subsequent ministers.[20]

Thus, in 1856, when Palmer became the pastor of the church, he stepped onto uncommon yet eerily familiar territory. He would be pastoring a church, which, like the church pastored by the uncle for whom he was named, was deeply marked by Trinitarian–Unitarian divisions. As previously noted, only two Unitarian Churches in the South were stable enough to remain intact through the Civil War: the Unitarian Church of Charleston and the Unitarian Church of New Orleans. The former came out of a split from the church pastored by Benjamin Morgan Palmer, Sr., and the latter came from a split in the church eventually pastored by Benjamin Morgan Palmer, Jr.

Palmer entered his new pastorate with the knowledge that he was doing so in the shadow of the *original* Presbyterian Church of New Orleans in whose pulpit had laboured the city's most prized orator, a former Presbyterian whose testimony became, 'I cannot believe in the Athanasian doctrine of the Trinity.'[21] He was acutely aware of the church's history, Clapp's popularity, and Parker's difficulties.[22] The year 1856, Clapp's final year and Palmer's first year in New Orleans, would mark a significant transition in the Crescent City as attention began to shift down Saint Charles Street from 'Parson Clapp's Church' to the *second* First Presbyterian Church and the man who soon replaced Clapp as the city's favorite preacher.

---

which Clapp had taught in New Orleans. See 'The Universalist's Death' (*Selected Writings of Palmer*, pp. 12-16); notes on 'Universal Salvation Disproved,' 'Certainty of Future Punishment' (BMP Papers, CBK); 'Certainty and Suddenness of God's Wrath' (*Sermons*, pp. 1.3-12). See Clapp, 'A Discourse on Retribution (*Daily Picayune*, 28 May 1848).

20. Kolman, 'Presbyterian Church in New Orleans,' pp. 75-92.

21. Clapp, *Autobiographical Sketches*, p. 247.

22. See Johnson, *Palmer*, pp. 174-181.

Whereas Clapp had drawn dignitaries to the Unitarian Church, Palmer's oratory began drawing them to the Presbyterian Church. Mark Twain, for example, admired Palmer's eloquence and always went to hear him preach when he was in New Orleans.[23] More importantly, Palmer used his pulpit to do what Thornwell and Smyth were doing in Columbia and Charleston: proclaim the adorable Trinity in order to repel the Unitarian movement and revive the Trinitarian faith.

Not long after Palmer's arrival, members of the Unitarian Church, including former Presbyterians, began visiting his church. After the morning service on Sunday, 10 May 1857, he jotted down the following in his diary: 'Hall filled completely, with large attendance of Unitarians.'[24] As we will see, Palmer reached out to these and other Unitarians by consistently and lovingly preaching on Trinitarian themes from his New Orleans pulpit.

---

23. Mark Twain, *Mark Twain's Notebooks & Journals, volume 2 (1877–1883)*, edited by Frederick Anderson, Lin Salamo and Bernard L. Stein (Berkley, CA: University of California Press, 1975), p. 2.485.

24. BMP Journal (1857), BMP Papers, CBK.

# 10

# *Palmer's Stand for the Trinity in New Orleans*

ON Monday, 8 December 1856, the following announcement was printed in the *New Orleans Daily Creole*:

> DR PALMER – This gentleman delivered his first sermon yesterday, in Odd Fellows' Hall, in the new relation about to be consummated with the first Presbyterian Church of this city.
>
> His discourse presented the reasons for glorying in the Cross of Christ. We have never heard the great doctrine which lies at the centre of all Christian theology—the Atonement—more beautifully or more grandly presented than in this effort of Dr Palmer.
>
> The audience was unusually large, thronging the vast Hall until there was no more room.[1]

In his journal, which he kept for the first six months of his ministry in New Orleans, Palmer noted that there were over 1,500 in attendance and that he preached from Galatians 6:14 on 'Glorying in the Cross'. He added, 'Spoke freely, but with less spiritual

---

1. 'Dr Palmer,' *New Orleans Daily Creole*, 8 December 1856. The congregation was meeting in the Hall of the Odd Fellows, a fraternal organisation, because a fire destroyed their sanctuary in October of 1854. Palmer led the congregation to build a new, much larger sanctuary, which was dedicated on 1 November 1857.

feeling than I could wish; perhaps owing to the distractions of a new house and a new audience.'[2]

The next week *The Daily Crescent* reported,

> It has been many years since we have seen as great a commotion in our religious community, as now exists in reference to the Rev. Dr Palmer, the new Pastor of the First Presbyterian Church. The beauty and force of his oratory, and his unusual ability in arguing the truths of religion, have not only captivated his congregation, but have made such an impression upon the community at large, as to cause Odd Fellows' Hall to be crowded every time he preaches. Yesterday the Hall was crowded to its utmost capacity, and in the audience were to be seen distinguished members of other religious persuasions, as well as people who profess no religion, all absorbed in the profoundest attention.[3]

Palmer felt better about this sermon: 'Had unexpected and unusual freedom and power in delivery, and came home with a grateful heart for the manifest assistance and favor of God.'[4] Sadly, we have not been able to locate these inaugural sermons. Perhaps, like many of Palmer's sermon manuscripts, they were destroyed during the Civil War. Or, perhaps he used little or no notes to preach them, as preaching with minimal notes increasingly became his habit.[5]

In our analysis of Palmer's preaching, we will utilize the sermon notes and manuscripts that are available, as well as newspaper articles containing portions or abridgements of sermons. We will primarily interact with his published sermons, which contain the vast majority of Palmer's New Orleans sermons that are available in their entirety. Ninety-two of his sermons from the mid-1870s were transcribed and published as *A Weekly Publication Containing Sermons* in two volumes. Unless otherwise noted, the sermons that we will interact with come from these volumes. In addition, some of his sermons from 1883 were transcribed and published as *Sermons, 1883.*

---

2. BMP Journal, 7 December 1856.

3. *Daily Crescent*, 15 December 1856.

4. BMP Journal, 14 December 1856.

5. Duncan, 'Palmer,' pp. 5, 50, 161.

In his *Review* articles on the Trinity, Smyth admonished his fellow ministers not to assume that their churches would remain Trinitarian by default; he exhorted them to regularly and explicitly emphasize the Trinity in their pulpit ministries. With the history of both his family and his church in mind, Palmer was sure to heed Smyth's exhortation.

From his extant sermons, we are able to discern that Palmer's method of emphasizing the Trinity was not merely to periodically preach a sermon specifically devoted to the doctrine of the Trinity (annually on Trinity Sunday, for example). Rather, his method was to regularly preach the major doctrines of Scripture from an explicitly Trinitarian perspective. This was his approach in his writing ministry as well. Thus, what follows is a consideration of how Palmer preached and wrote on various themes in an overtly Trinitarian way to win the lost and build up the saints.

## The Trinity and Epistemology

Like Thornwell and Smyth, Palmer emphasized the themes of incomprehensibility, mystery, and paradox as necessary components of orthodox theology. Thus, like his Columbia colleagues, he located the root of Unitarianism in a rationalistic epistemology that placed reason over revelation: 'Proceeding upon the fundamental maxim that they will accept nothing which they do not understand, they absolutely postpone the Gospel as a practical scheme, so that it is never reached.'[6] He told his congregation that, when it comes to the doctrine of God as revealed in Scripture, it is reason's wisdom to 'rejoice in a truth which it apprehends, though it does not comprehend.'[7] Echoing Thornwell, he grounded his theological epistemology in pneumatology, declaring that, although the doctrine of the Trinity is incomprehensible, the believer, through the 'illumination of the Holy Spirit', is 'borne forward to this persuasion of the truth as we find it in the Word of God'.[8]

---

6. Benjamin Palmer, Jr., *A Weekly Publication Containing Sermons*, 2 vols. (New Orleans: Clark & Hofeline, 1875–1876). 'Worldly Wisdom Opposed to the Gospel' (p. 1.525).

7. 'Eternal Life, the Gift of God' (p. 2.35).

8. 'The Sealing of the Spirit' (p. 1.267).

Palmer consistently expounded Scripture to show that the Bible teaches the Trinity rather than the 'naked theism' of Unitarianism.[9] One of the ways he reinforced this was by regularly referring to Scripture's God by names such as 'the Trinity',[10] 'the adorable Trinity',[11] the 'adorable and incomprehensible Trinity',[12] 'the august Trinity',[13] 'the Three',[14] 'the adorable Three',[15] 'the eternal Three',[16] 'the Tri-une God',[17] and 'the Tri-une Jehovah'.[18] He also communicated the Triune nature of God with phrases such as 'the tri-personal subsistence of the Godhead',[19] 'the tri-personal constitution of the Godhead',[20] 'a three-fold distinction of persons',[21] 'the tri-une existence of the Godhead',[22] and 'His triune subsistence'.[23] Given the 'polemic history' of his church,

---

9. 'Evidences of Conversion' (p. 2.255).

10. 'Grieving the Spirit' (p. 1.42); 'The Sealing of the Spirit' (pp. 1.261, 267); 'The Grandeur of Faith' (p. 1.487); 'Worldly Wisdom Opposed to the Gospel' (p. 1.525); 'Christ, the Resurrection and the Life' (p. 1.530); 'The Organic Unity of the Church' (p. 1.569); and 'Trinity of Graces' (p. 1.597).

11. 'The Faithful Saying' (p. 1.152); 'Christ's Prayer for His People' (p. 1.382); 'Adoption Conferred by Christ' (p. 1.423); 'Harmony of God's Attributes in the Plan of Grace' (p. 1.500); 'The Sin of Unbelief' (pp. 2.77-78); 'Christ's Love to his People' (p. 2.94); 'Truth, the Law of the Intellect' (p. 2.318); 'Love, the Law of the Heart' (p. 2.335); and 'Communion with the Blood of Christ' (p. 2.373).

12. 'Warrant and Nature of Public Worship' (p. 1.362).

13. 'The Secret of the Lord' (p. 1.140).

14. 'Grieving the Spirit' (p. 1.39); 'Christ's Love to his People' (p. 2.94).

15. 'Christ's Prayer for His People' (pp. 1.382, 383); 'Confession and Forgiveness' (p. 2.56); 'Necessity of Christ's Departure from Earth' (p. 2.215); and 'Freedom through Christ' (p. 2.290).

16. 'Adoption Conferred By Christ' (p. 1.422); 'Christ the Builder of the Church' (p. 1.544).

17. 'The Church, the Kingdom of Truth' (p. 2.4); 'God Just, yet a Saviour' (p. 2.242).

18. 'The Church, the Kingdom of Truth' (p. 2.16).

19. 'Law and Love' (p. 1.286); 'Attraction of the Cross' (p. 1.507).

20. 'Christ the Builder of the Church' (p. 1.544).

21. 'Trust in God's Name' (p. 1.631).

22. 'The Everliving Priest' (p. 2.447).

23. 'Death of Believers' (p. 2.190); sermon notes for 'Christian Progress' (BMP Papers, CBK).

he made clear from the pulpit that the God that was to be worshipped at First Presbyterian Church was none other than the *Triune* God.[24]

Like Thornwell and Smyth, Palmer posited that the doctrine of the Trinity is intimated in the Old Testament. Representative of Columbia, Palmer held that *Elohim* points to the Triune nature of God, that the *Shema*, through its employment of both 'single and plural names' for the Godhead, not only teaches divine unity, but also 'conveys the hint of a plural subsistence', and that '"Let us make man in our image and after our likeness," was the language of the councilors when the THREE sat down to ordain the existence of such a being.'[25] He also believed that the work of the Trinity in creation anticipated the work of the Trinity in redemption.[26]

## The Trinity and Soteriology

According to Palmer, Old Testament narratives, appellatives, types, and shadows intimated the Trinity. 'It was reserved, however, for the "fulness of time" to make the disclosure complete, in the redemption of our lost race' for it is only through the revelation of the 'scheme of grace' that we realize 'the Jehovah-Elohim of the Old Testament is the Father, Son and Holy Ghost of the New.'[27] Not only did Palmer believe that the economy of grace reveals the Trinity; he believed that the Triunity of God makes the economy of grace possible. He explained to his congregation that the plan of redemption '*is a scheme which can be executed only by a Triune God. The parts are so various, and the offices to be discharged are in such antithesis, that they cannot be consolidated upon a single*

---

24. 'The Trinity of Graces' (p. 1.597).

25. See *Theology of Prayer* (Richmond, VA: Presbyterian Committee of Publication, 1894), p. 188; *The Threefold Fellowship and the Threefold Assurance* (Richmond, VA: Presbyterian Committee of Publication, 1902), p. 7; and 'The Rule of Christ's Kingdom' (p. 2.136).

26. 'Christ's Universal Dominion' (pp. 2.384-85); 'Eternal Life, the Gift of God' (p. 2.35).

27. *Theology of Prayer*, pp. 188-89.

agent.'[28] He fleshed this out by thinking through the doctrine of substitutionary atonement:

> [The plan of salvation] is such a scheme as could be devised and executed only by a Triune Being; and the proof is that, whenever rejected, the doctrine of Atonement and the doctrine of the Trinity have always been rejected together. A compulsory logic binds them indissolubly as twin-truths, for the parties to the scheme must be found within the Deity; and yet the offices to be discharged are so distinct, that they cannot be consolidated upon a single agent .... The God of the Socinian cannot therefore be the author of this system of grace; and he who trustingly rests his hope of eternal life upon its provisions, must adoringly worship forevermore the Triune Jehovah – Father, Son and Holy Ghost. The soul is filled with awe in contemplating the majesty of such a salvation, glorious as the God who is its author. And if its foundation is laid within the mystery of his own being, what power on earth, or in hell, can shake the everlasting pillars on which it is securely placed? Let the voice be muffled in deepest reverence which undertakes to utter the dreadful alternative: not until a schism shall occur in the Godhead, and the Persons of the adorable Trinity shall be wrenched apart, and their glorious unity be dissolved forever; not until this shall occur, which it would be blasphemy to conceive if it were not uttered only to be rejected with a holy horror, can that grace fail to save which was devised in the counsels of the eternity past, and whose results are to be gathered into the glories of the eternity which is to come.[29]

In her *Letters*, Palmer's cousin Mary, responding to what she perceived to be harshness in the orthodox view of God, said

---

28. 'God Just, yet a Saviour' (p. 2.242). In his notes for 'Christ a Prophet', he reminded himself to 'show how this Trinity of Persons is essential to the scheme [of redemption], and that it is wholly a doctrine of divine revelation.' See similar notes for 'Access through Christ to the Father', 'The Sight of God's Glory,' 'Messianic Prophecies,' 'The History of Christ.' In notes for 'God's Greatness in the Resurrection of Christ,' he reminded himself to explain that 'all the Persons of the Godhead' were glorified in Christ's resurrection because all were 'engaged in it' (BMP Papers, CBK).

29. *Theology of Prayer*, pp. 197-98.

that the God of Unitarianism is more loving than the God of Trinitarianism.[30] Palmer begged to differ. He argued that by denying the eternal sonship of Christ, Unitarians completely miss the amazing love revealed in the Gospel:

> Ah! I wonder, when men derogate from the honor of the Lord Jesus Christ, and seek to make Him less than divine, that they are not appalled at the mischief which they are attempting; for they are robbing themselves of the only measure by which to ascertain the greatness of God's love. Take away the Son-ship of Jesus Christ, which makes Him the Father's equal in nature and in glory, and you have no adequate measure of the proportions of God's mighty love to our race. Put all the creatures in heaven and upon the earth together; and in the aggregate of their powers you still create but one gigantic finite being, who cannot be the measure of God. Therefore our faith clings to the supreme divinity of our Lord; not only because it is indispensable to the salvation in which we rejoice, but because without it man is forever deprived of any measure by which he can conceive of the vastness of God's love to the sinner.[31]

Regarding the atonement, Mary had written:

> The atonement in which I believe, does not require an infinite sacrifice – an Almighty victim – the death of *a God!* I am aware that I am using contradictory terms, but I cannot avoid it under the circumstances. To meet Trinitarians on their own ground, contradictory propositions are unavoidable. If God saw fit to provide the means of atonement, or reconciliation, I do not see why he could not choose just what instrument he pleased. Its efficacy would be abundantly guaranteed from the fact that it was provided by our Almighty Father. And even on the supposition that Christ died as an 'expiation' or substitute, which, of course, I do not admit, I cannot see any reason why the substitute might not be just what the Supreme Ruler chose to provide.[32]

---

30. Dana, *Letters*, pp. 110, 113, 148, 183, 190-91, 269.

31. 'Law and Love,' pp. 1.283.

32. Dana, *Letters*, pp. 195-96.

To counteract such sentiments, Palmer preached that the atonement accomplished by the Trinity is the ultimate demonstration of the love of God for sinners, a love that Unitarianism does not possess:

> When you have been impressed with the dignity and glory of this only begotten Son, add to it that boundless love which has always been interchanged between the Father and this Son, lying through all eternity in the Father's bosom, and declared to be his delight. I dare not press the thought, and yet I would not exclude it, imperfectly comprehended as it is; how much the blessedness of the infinite God depends upon that mysterious subsistence by which He is the Father, the Son and the Holy Ghost. Within the economy of the Godhead itself, there shall be verge and scope for the play of the affections, even of an infinite heart. The Father, as the Father, shall always have an infinite person in His Son, upon whom His infinite affections can forever terminate; and that Son shall reciprocate this infinite affection upon the person of the Father; and so, in the social existence and communion of the Godhead, there is the play of these affections as they exist only in the bosom of God. Think, then, of the Son, in His awful majesty as the Father's equal, and then of the ineffable fellowship between the two, as they are supremely blessed and happy in each other .... Now put these different elements together – God's uncreated, eternal Son, the object of the Father's delight, going across the entire breadth of the law, and taking upon Himself the curse in our stead – and then you have the measure by which to ascertain the proportions of God's love.[33]

## The Trinity and Christology

Palmer was unabashedly Christ-centered in his preaching. In 'Certainty of the Promises of Christ', he gave a spirited *apologia* for his Christ-centeredness:

> The philosophers of the earth, and the men who are busy with the impertinences of this pitiful world, are sometimes overtaken with surprise that Christians think and talk and sing so much about

---

33. Palmer, 'Law and Love,' p. 1.284.

Jesus Christ. Why, my hearers, he is the *all* to us, and the *in all*. He is our glorious Head; He is our adorable Trustee. He went down into the bowels of the curse, and bore the inflictions of justice in our stead. He holds in the heaven of His Father our eternal life, which is to expand forever in holiness and blessedness. Why should we not talk about Him? Why should we not think about Him? Why should He not be our song, our praise and our joy? Jesus Christ, the Son of God, our Elder Brother, our Redeemer, our Friend, is to us 'the chiefest among ten thousand, and the one altogether lovely.' Better than all the schools of philosophy, better than all the teachings of the Academy and of the Porch, are those lessons of life and love which His own hand has engraved upon these pages of Scripture. We are not ashamed of Him.[34]

Palmer's sermons were Christocentric, but they were not Christomonistic. Palmer preached Christ in terms of his relationship with the Father and the Spirit. His *Trinitarian* Christocentricity led him to elucidate the roles of the Father and Spirit in salvation. Against Unitarian notions of the Spirit, Palmer argued that the Spirit is 'not as a mere influence going out from God' but rather a 'Person of the adorable Godhead … co-equal with the Father and the Son.'[35] The Spirit especially reveals *Christ* through the written Word of God and by His illuminating power as God. As God, the Spirit 'could teach us all science, and yet He does not. He could communicate all philosophy, but He does not. He simply takes the things which belong to Jesus Christ and shows them unto us.'[36] Most significantly in Palmer's preaching, the Spirit unites believers to Christ and 'conducts all the correspondence in that fellowship we have with the Father and with his Son.'[37]

Palmer's *Trinitarian* Christocentricity also led him to underscore the infinite Fatherliness of God and, especially, the filial nature of the Christian faith revealed in the doctrine of adoption. He relished in

---

34. 'Certainty of the Promises of Christ' (p. 1.358).
35. 'Christ's Restoring Work' (pp. 2.162-63).
36. 'The Sealing of the Spirit' (p. 1.273).
37. 'The Other Comforter' (p. 1.214).

the way that the incarnate Son confers sonship to believers: 'As the Sonship is real with Himself, so is it true and real with those upon whom it is bestowed.'[38] And he consistently expounded and applied the doctrine of adoption in Trinitarian terms: *What glory, and what security, too, is there in our adoption!* Decreed by the Father, acquired and bestowed by the Son, and wrought within us by the Holy Ghost!'[39] He stressed his belief that adoption, which he held to be the apex of Triune grace, is not a legal fiction, but a life-giving fact: 'Adoption into the family of God is no legal fiction, such as obtained in human jurisprudence, the shadow without the substance. On the contrary "power is given to as many as believe in His name, to BECOME the sons of God; which ARE BORN, not of blood, nor of the will of the flesh, nor of the will of men, but of God" (John 1:12,13).'[40]

Though he emphasized the distinctive roles of the divine persons in the economy of grace, Palmer was careful to communicate the perichoretic reality of the Trinity, utilizing terms such as 'interpenetration' to communicate the coinherence and cooperation of the divine persons.[41] He cautioned, 'Whatever emphasis you put upon the distinction of persons, you must remember that it is a diversity in unity.'[42]

As we mentioned before, one of the features of Social Trinitarianism is its emphasis on 'the primacy of the Father as the "fount of divinity".'[43] In this regard, Palmer and the other Columbians once again evidenced leanings toward the Social Trinity view, and, in their understanding of the Father as the fount of divinity, they differed from Calvin and his Christological doctrine of *autotheos*.

In his sermon 'The Gospel, God's Power and Wisdom,' Thornwell ruminated as to why the second person of the Trinity would

---

38. 'Adoption Conferred by Christ' (p. 1.425).

39. Ibid.

40. 'Looking at the Unseen' (p. 2.401).

41. *Theology of Prayer*, pp. 291; 'Adoption' (pp. 1.421-22); 'The Attraction of the Cross' (pp. 1.515-16).

42. 'Christ's Prayer for his People' (p. 1.384).

43. Davis, 'Perichoretic Monotheism,' p. 63.

be the member of the Godhead to become the incarnate mediator between God and men. He explained:

> God and Man he must be to meet the exigencies of our case. One person of the adorable Trinity must become incarnate, and wisdom pitched upon the Second as the most suitable and proper. It was not fit that the Father, who is of none, neither begotten, should be placed in an attitude of subjection to His own Eternal Son, who by an ineffable and eternal generation received the essence of Divinity from the Father. It was not fit that the Holy Ghost, who eternally proceeded from the Father and the Son, should be placed in an attitude of authority over the Son, as would have been the case had He become incarnate and had the Son fulfilled His functions in the plan of salvation; so that none could so appropriately assume our nature as the Second person in the blessed Godhead.[44]

Similarly, Palmer self-consciously followed the 'old theologians' in describing the Father as the '*fons et origo* of Deity'.[45] In so doing, Palmer was in fact echoing Calvin himself, who had written, 'inasmuch as the Father is first in order, and from himself begot his wisdom ... he is rightly deemed the beginning and fountain-head of the whole divinity.'[46] However, Palmer also posited, 'The designations Father and Son amongst men ... imply the derivation of substance from one to the other. The same relations in the Deity import a like derivation of the divine essence from the Father to the Son, but without succession in time or separateness of existence. There can be no succession of moments in a being who is infinite and eternal. But the whole divine essence must be conceived by us as existing eternally in both, yet as being in the Son from the Father.'[47]

---

44. James Thornwell, *Collected Writings*, edited by John B. Adger and John L. Girardeau, 4 vols. (Richmond, VA: Presbyterian Committee of Publication, 1871). 'The Gospel, God's Power and Wisdom,' *CW*, p. 2.323.

45. *Theology of Prayer*, p. 210.

46. *Institutes*, p. 1.13.25.

47. *Theology of Prayer*, p. 201.

Calvin had articulated the matter differently: 'We say that deity in an absolute sense exists of itself; whence likewise we confess that the Son since he is God, exists of himself, but not in respect of his person; indeed, since he is the Son, we say that he exists from the Father. Thus his essence is without beginning; while the beginning of his person is God himself.'[48]

Thus, we can say that Thornwell and Palmer did not articulate Calvin's *autothean* Christology.[49] Why this was the case is uncertain. As Brannon Ellis has pointed out, some of Calvin's own contemporary Trinitarians 'rejected the language of aseity for the eternal Son, not because they wanted to distinguish or even differentiate him essentially from the Father, but because they understood Calvin at least by implication to be denying the Son's generation from the Father, *upon which procession his true distinction from the Father and his consubstantiality with the Father depend*.'[50] According to Ellis, similar concerns were held by subsequent theologians such as Warfield, who believed that 'the internal logic of Calvin's autothean language seems to lead inexorably to a denial of the divine processions and immanent personal taxis in the interests of the absolute equality of Father, Son, and Spirit.'[51]

Dabney of Union was likewise hesitant to employ Calvin's language, and his discussion of the Son's aseity points to the difficulty of the matter. Dabney understood the ante-Nicene fathers to have regarded the Son and the Spirit 'as deriving their personal subsistence from the eternal act of the Father in communicating the divine essence to them in those modes of subsistence.'[52] He

---

48. *Institutes*, p. 1.13.25.

49. The same may be said of William Swan Plumer, who taught at Columbia from 1867 until 1875. See William Plumer, *The Rock of Our Salvation* (New York: American Tract Society, 1867), pp. 50-51, 229.

50. Brannon Ellis, *Calvin, Classical Trinitarianism, and the Aseity of the Son* (Oxford: Oxford University Press, 2012), p. 62.

51. Ibid., p. 8. See Benjamin Warfield, *Calvin and Augustine* (Philadelphia: P&R Publishing, 1956), pp. 283-84.

52. Dabney, *Systematic Theology*, p. 203.

posited that 'this view was embodied in both forms of the Nicene Creed, of A.D. 325 and 381, where the Son is called "God of God, Light of Light, and very God of very God"; language never applied to the Father as to the Son.'[53] Dabney touched on the complexity of the issue, one that 'cannot be comprehended by us', when he stated his belief that the Fathers regarded the Son to be 'self-existent God', 'the one self-existent essence' *because* 'the Father put His whole essence in the two other modes of subsistence.'[54] Dabney interpreted the Fathers as believing that the Son received his essence from the Father, but, because this communicated essence is self-existent, the Son is, mysteriously, self-existent.On the other hand, unlike Dabney and the Columbia divines, Hodge of Princeton explicitly affirmed Calvin's *autothean* Christology, maintaining, 'Christ is properly called *autotheos*' due to the 'verity, supremacy, and independence of his Godhead.'[55] To our knowledge, extant material does not provide a reason why the Columbia divines did not champion Calvin's *autothean* language in the way Hodge did. Perhaps, like Warfield, they saw in it a loss of the reality, or at least the significance, of divine processions. Or, perhaps, like Dabney, they believed in the possibility of communicated aseity. What we most certainly find in Palmer and the other Columbians is a settled conviction that 'the Father, Son and Spirit, are the one God, the same in substance, equal in power and glory.'[56]

## The Trinity and Hamartiology

A striking feature of Palmer's preaching is the way he communicated an expressly Trinitarian hamartiology. Palmer portrayed sin in deeply personal—or, more specifically, *tri-personal*—terms. Building on the idea that the covenant of grace reveals the divine persons and their roles in redemption, Palmer preached that sin

---

53. Ibid., p. 204.
54. Ibid., pp. 202, 204.
55. Charles Hodge, 'On the Sonship of Christ,' *The Biblical Repertory 5, no. 1* (1829), p. 441. See also, Hodge, *Systematic Theology*, p. 1.6.6.
56. 'Christ's Prayer for his People' (p. 1.384).

is directed against the person and work of each member of the Godhead. In a sermon titled 'The Sin of Unbelief,' he explained how '*unbelief is an offence against each Person of the God-head in their official distinction and work.*'[57] Regarding the sin of unbelief, he declared,

> It is committed against the Father who sent His Son and sealed Him as the Mediator – who accepted this work at His hands, and gave the proof in His resurrection and ascension to glory – who discharges the function of Supreme Lawgiver, in holding the sinner under the penalty until he accepts this righteousness of his surety, and in fully justifying the believer the moment by faith he appropriates it as his own. In the refusal to embrace Christ as his personal Saviour, the unbeliever, plants himself in opposition to the office and work of the Father, which in the Covenant of Grace, He assumed as His personal function.
>
> It is even more obviously an offence against the Son. All His offices are rejected; His sacrifice is disallowed; His grace is despised; His offers are declined; His person is spurned. The enormity of this crime against the Person and work of our blessed Lord, provokes the searching exclamation of the Apostle '– Of how much severe punishment, suppose ye, shall he be thought worthy, who hath trodden under foot the Son of God, and hath counted the blood of the covenant, wherewith he was sanctified an unholy thing, and hath done despite unto the Spirit of grace!' (Heb. 10:29.) How little does the sinner understand the malignity of that indifference to Christ – which, according to the judgment here rendered, not only pretermits the Saviour's claims, but is an open assault upon His person and a profanation of His blood!
>
> Even this does not exhaust the criminality; for it is equally a sin against the Holy Spirit. This person of the God-head not only concurs with the other two in devising the scheme of salvation, but He discharges offices peculiar to Himself. His agency is concerned in the conception of the man Jesus, (Luke 1:35) – in anointing him to His work, as Mediator, (Isa xlii:1, and lxi:1, and Luke iv:14, and John iii:34,) – in effecting His resurrection from the grave,

57. 'The Sin of Unbelief' (p. 2.77).

(Rom. viii:2,) – in sanctifying the offering He rendered for sin, (Heb. ix.14,) – and in applying this redemption, in the whole work of renewing, sanctifying and glorifying the sinner. What estimate can we form of the malignity of unbelief, when it is seen to be directed against the separate agency of each Person of the adorable Trinity, as these unite in their Personal distinction to execute the scheme of mercy! Well may it be said, 'This is THE condemnation!' With good reason is he condemned ALREADY, who hath not believed in the name of the only begotten Son of God.[58]

According to Palmer, sin is not only transgressing a written law; it is turning a cold shoulder to the Triune God and his love.[59] Sin is committed against the Father and 'grace in its inception', against the Son and 'grace in its execution', and against the Spirit and 'grace in its application'.[60]

## The Trinity and Evangelism

In almost all of Palmer's extant weekly sermons, there is, in some fashion and at some point – typically at the conclusion of the sermon – a call to the unconverted to repent of sin and believe in Jesus for salvation.[61] Through his evangelistic pulpit ministry, he embodied the teaching of Goulding, who regularly admonished his students, 'Let every sermon preached contain so much of the plan of salvation that should a heathen come in who never had heard the gospel before, and who should depart, never to hear it again, he should learn enough to know what he must do to be saved.'[62]

---

58. Ibid.

59. 'Christ, the Final Judge' (pp. 1.109-10).

60. 'Grieving the Spirit' (pp. 1.41-42).

61. See *Sermons*, passim. In his notes on 'God's Greatness in the Resurrection of Christ', his last note is, 'Appeal to saints to have deeper views of Christ and their union with Him. Appeal to sinners to receive this Christ and share with him in His glory.' On the back of his notes for an evangelistic sermon titled 'Final Spoliation of the Sinner,' he wrote, 'This sermon owned of God in the conversion of the wife of my friend and brother, J. D. Wilson' (BMP Papers, CBK).

62. Goulding, 'Thomas Goulding,' (Columbia, SC: Presbyterian Publishing House, 1884), pp. 185-86.

Palmer believed that the ultimate result of the fall was loss of fellowship with the Trinity, and, thus, the ultimate result of the gospel is restoration of that fellowship. Therefore, he regularly evangelized in explicitly Trinitarian terms. The following is representative of the way he often drew his sermons to a close:

> My unconverted friend, it is a great pleasure, even though the thing be badly done, to preach God's precious Gospel to you. I take you to record that my habit is rather to woo you, if I may, with its attractive voices, rather than to hold up the glittering sword and hurl against you the anathemas of judgment. Would to heaven, I had persuasion enough in my voice, to-day, to bring you to an acceptance with us of these immense privileges! Oh, that you with us could be made willing in this, the day of His power, to hold communion with the Father and with the Son and with the eternal Spirit! And to know, as no other can teach it to you, except the Divine Spirit Himself, what is that love of Christ to the believer, which He compares to the Father's love to Himself![63]

As he evangelized, Palmer presented the attractiveness of Trinitarian love in contrast to the 'bleak dreary waste of deism', the 'dank air' of the rationalist's 'charnel-house', and the 'mechanical morality' of the Unitarian.[64] Ultimately, he presented the Triune God of grace in contrast to the gods of other religions. In the nineteenth century, 'a tradition of philosophy taught that there was a common content to the word "God," shared (it was assumed) by all religions. Specifically Christian ideas, such as the doctrine of the Trinity, were regarded as secondary to this common core of belief.'[65] To graduates of the University of North Carolina, Palmer offered an alternative to this prevailing belief by distinguishing the Trinity from all other deities. In a manner similar to the way he would have heard Thornwell address the

---

63. 'Christ's Love to His People' (p. 2.102).

64. 'The Other Comforter' (p. 1.216); 'Christ's Love to His People' (p. 2.102); 'Self-Righteousness Grounded in Ignorance' (p. 2.158).

65. Stephen Holmes, *The Quest for the Trinity: The Doctrine of God in Scripture, History and Modernity* (Downers Grove, IL: InterVarsity Press, 2012), p. 3.

graduates of South Carolina, Palmer addressed the graduates of North Carolina:

> [Christianity] presents to man the living Jehovah as the object of worship: not the personification of this or that single trait; not the deification of this or that power of nature; not a Pantheus wearing the universe as His outside garment; not the symbol merely of such abstract conceptions as absolute intelligence, or illimitable being, but a living, personal God, a spirit infinite and eternal, separate from matter, creating all things by the word of His power, and by whom all things consist. It is not simple being, and then it is Brahm; it is not pure intelligence, and then it is Buddha; it is not a destroyer, and then it is Siva; it is not a restorer, and then it is Vishna; it is not a malignant hater, and then it is Kali; it is not an arbitrary and mighty ruler, and then it is Allah; but it is the one living and true God, glorious in holiness, fearful in praises and doing wonders: one God, Father, Son and Holy Ghost, infinitely blessed in the communion of the Trinity, the living Jehovah, maker of Heaven and Earth, the creator, preserver, Redeemer; the lawgiver, ruler and judge, the everlasting father and unfailing portion of all who trust, and love, and worship him.[66]

## The Trinity and the Christian Life

Palmer believed that the Christian life should be understood in Trinitarian terms, and he explored that theme in his book, *The Threefold Fellowship and The Threefold Assurance.*

He beautifully portrayed how the believer's spiritual satisfaction and security are rooted in the Triune life and activity of the Godhead:

> Upon [Christ's] ascension to heaven there follows the dispensation of the Holy Spirit, turning the hearts of the children of men from sin to holiness, and preparing the redeemed for the saints' inheritance in glory. As this grace descends to the sinner from the Father, through the Son, by the Holy Spirit, so again it ascends through the indwelling Spirit, by faith in Christ the Son,

---

66. Palmer, 'Christianity, The Only Religion for Man' (Raleigh, NC: The Carolina Cultivator, 1855), pp. 20-21.

to be presented blameless and without spot before the Father. Thus by two currents, descending and ascending, the redeemed soul moves forever within the bosom of the Godhead. Thus, both in counsel and in act, we find the scheme of grace springing out from the very nature and form of the Divine Being himself. It is such a salvation as could only be devised by the God who is revealed to us, and as executed by him in his threefold distinction as Father, Son and Holy Ghost. What amazing security does this view give the whole system of grace, seeing that it cannot fail in a single point except through a schism in the Godhead itself. The hand trembles that writes the daring suggestion; which is only saved from blasphemy by the assurance that he who searches the heart knows it is written only to give the most intense emphasis to the truth which it declares.[67]

The believer's fellowship with God should not be understood as fellowship with a unipersonal deity, but rather as fellowship with each person of the Trinity: 'If now the Triune God be thus engaged in working out this great salvation, there should be in Christian experience a recognized fellowship with each of the Divine Persons to whom the requisite offices have been assigned and by whom they have been discharged.'[68]

The Christian is first and foremost an adopted child of the Father: 'Probably no word in our science of theology more completely covers all parts of the system of grace than does this word adoption.'[69] The Father has made this adoption possible through the incarnation of His Son: '[Christ] is the one mediator through whom God descends to the creature and the creature ascends to God ... He is not a God afar off, but nigh at hand. He is the God manifest in the flesh; who wore our nature that he might be of kin to us, our elder brother, bone of our bone and flesh of our flesh.'[70] Our spiritual vitality comes from our union

---

67. *Threefold Fellowship*, p. 18.

68. Ibid.

69. Ibid., pp. 39-41.

70. Ibid., p. 64.

with the incarnate Son: 'The spiritual life of the Christian is thus a continuous flow from Christ, in whom is the treasury of this life through all eternity, ever flowing from this divine source and communicated by the indwelling Spirit.'[71]

The Holy Spirit creates a bond between the believer and the incarnate Son through the gift of faith. Through the work of regeneration the Spirit of adoption makes the believer 'really a child of God', creates 'an easy and delightful intercourse with our Father in heaven', and bears a direct witness to our spirit assuring us of the Father's adopting, unfailing love.[72]

## The Trinity and Worship

At the dedication service of their new sanctuary, Palmer made clear to his New Orleans congregation that the edifice would be used for the worship of the *Triune* God. In his dedicatory sermon he explained that the warrant for *corporate* worship springs from the fact that humanity is made in the image of the Trinity. Representative of Columbia's Social Trinity leanings, he posited that the corporate worship of God's people springs from and reflects the object of their worship, the Godhead who 'is Himself infinitely perfect and ineffably blessed, in the social existence of the Trinity.'[73]

The saint is not left to 'solitary communion with his Maker', but rather is graciously called into the society of God's people in the corporate 'worship of the sanctuary' wherein the society of the Trinity is magnified in the diverse yet unified society of His worshipping church.[74] Palmer closed the dedicatory service

---

71. Ibid., pp. 59-60. See also 'Feeling After God,' in *The Treasury: A Magazine of Religious and Current Thought for Pastor and People*, 1885, p. 2.531. Palmer often pointed out that the believer's union with the Triune God is made possible through Christ's incarnation. Thus, he spoke explicitly against doceticism, which denies the genuine humanity of Christ. See 'Christ's Prayer for his People – Continued' (pp. 1.395-96); 'The Throne of Grace' (pp. 1.462-63); notes on 'Partakers of Christ' and 'Fatherly Discipline,' BMP Papers, CBK.

72. *Threefold Fellowship*, pp. 78, 85, 89.

73. 'Warrant and Nature of Public Worship' (pp. 1.367-68).

74. Ibid.

with these words: 'To God, the Father Almighty, the maker of heaven and earth – to God, the Son, the brightness of the Father's glory, and express image of His person – to God, the Holy Ghost, proceeding from the Father and the Son – to the service of the adorable and incomprehensible Trinity, we solemnly dedicate this building, with all that appertains to it.'[75]

Almost two decades later, Palmer preached a sermon in honor of Joseph Maybin, the senior elder of the church, who had passed away. Maybin was one of the two elders who had seceded from Clapp's church to start the *second* First Presbyterian Church in 1832.[76] Palmer concluded the eulogy,

> But the feature of Mr Maybin's piety which I would signalize above all others, was his personal love for Christ. He believed firmly the doctrine of the Trinity; and it would not be difficult to find in the polemic history of this Church, in her early period, a conspicuous reason for this fact. But you, who were accustomed to his prayers in our informal services, will recall the adoration with which he would recognize the awful mystery of the Godhead – the mellow tones in which he would pour forth his adoring praise to God the Father, God the Son, and God the Holy Ghost, rejoicing in the personality of each and in the blessed unity of all. Then, out of the bosom of that great truth, grasping as he did the grace and the preciousness of God's redeeming love, he poured out the whole wealth of his heart upon the person of Jesus Christ. In all private intercourse, in all public discussion, whether he spoke upon the street or spoke in the assembly, there always came out his burning, passionate attachment to the Lord Jesus Christ. Ah! Faith always contemplates a person, and no doctrinal creed can make a Christian. Until you can see within the bosom of that creed God in Christ, our Elder Brother, taking hold upon our misery and ruin, there can be no Christian experience. But this man, through the whole twenty years in which I have been associated

---

75. Ibid., p. 1.380.

76. 'Dr Palmer's Career.' For Maybin's role in Clapp's deposition, see Clapp, *Trial*, pp. 146, 152, 158, 255.

with him, manifested, as conspicuous above all other traits, a personal love for the Saviour.[77]

Thus, it seems that not only Palmer, but also the members of his church, given their polemic history and the subsequent Trinitarian emphasis of their pastor, delighted in the Triune God of love and the Trinitarian nature of worship.

This was certainly Palmer's goal. His cousin had explained to her bewildered father why she had *stopped* singing the Doxology: 'The singing of the Trinitarian doxology is the distinguishing mark of a Trinitarian Church—a concise and regularly repeated confession of faith—the *Shibboleth* of Trinitarianism.'[78] Palmer agreed with his cousin regarding the importance of the Doxology for Trinitarianism. Yet, he *gloried* in the singing of it, for, while other elements of worship may be implicitly Trinitarian, he believed that the Doxology, like a Trinitarian benediction, is an act of worship in which 'the thought is directed to Jehovah in His plural subsistence, and the reference to the three Persons of the God-head is an *explicit* reference.'[79]

Through his Trinitarian preaching and through the inclusion of explicitly Trinitarian elements of worship such as the Doxology and Trinitarian benedictions, Palmer provided his flock with weekly reminders that Christian worship is worship of the 'Adorable Three'.[80] *Every* element of corporate worship, even the giving of tithes and offerings, is to be offered to the *Triune* God: 'We worship the Father, the Son and the Holy Ghost, not only in these psalms of praise and in these accents of prayer, but as well in the consecration of our substance.'[81]

For Palmer, the way the Trinity is revealed in the gospel informs the way He is to be worshipped by those who are being

---

77. 'The Trinity of Graces: Discourse in honour of Mr Joseph Maybin' (p. 1.597).

78. Dana, *Letters*, p. 50.

79. 'Communion with the Blood of Christ' (p. 2.373).

80. See 'Christ's Prayer for His People' (pp. 1.382, 383); 'Confession and Forgiveness' (p. 2.56).

81. 'Organic Unity of the Church' (p. 1.580).

transformed by the gospel. He believed that salvation comes to the Church from the Father through the Son by the Spirit, and, therefore, the Church responds with thanksgiving and praise to the Father through the Son by the Spirit. In his dedicatory sermon, Palmer quoted Owen regarding the way in which the gospel orders Christian worship:

> This is the general order of Gospel worship, the great rubric of our service. Here, in general, lieth its decency, that it respects the mediation of the Son, through whom we have access, and the supplies and assistance of the Spirit, and regard unto God as a Father. He that fails in any one of these, breaks all order in Gospel worship. This is the great canon, which, if it be neglected, there is no decency in whatever else is done in this way.[82]

Therefore, Palmer emphasized the role of the incarnate eternal Son when he spoke of worship just as he did when he spoke of the Gospel. He emphasized the heavenly reality of earthly worship, the way in which the Mediator lifts up the worship of the Church on earth, mingles it with that of the Church in heaven, and presents it without blemish before the throne of God: 'The praises of this earthly house, and of these human hearts, are pronounced in the kingdom of God's glory, in the temple not made with hands, by the eternal Son, in that holy language in which the Father and the Son and the Spirit speak to each other in the communion of the Trinity.'[83] And again he explained, 'We recognize this in our worship, which we reverently offer in the name of the Mediator who undertakes to present it for us before the throne of His Father.'[84]

He explained:

> Eternal provision is made for the worship which shall be worthy of man to utter, and which shall be worthy of God to receive. When the High Priest of our profession takes the worship of these

---

82. 'Warrant and Nature of Public Worship' (pp. 1.375-76).

83. 'The Grandeur of Faith' (p. 1.487).

84. 'Faith in God and the Mediator' (p. 2.366).

contrite hearts upon the earth, and the worship of the glorified as they gather round His throne – when He pours it all into His own golden censer, and lights the incense from the altar of burnt offering upon which He 'offered Himself once for all in the end of the world to take away sin,' – when, with that unspeakable dialect which is known only to the Father, to the Son, and to the Holy Ghost in the eternal and most intimate communion of the God-Head, He the advocate, goes through the veil into 'the holiest of all,' and there speaks to God the praise of the creature on earth, or of the creature in heaven; – then is laid a foundation for their worship and their praise.

Sneer then at the Cross if you will; but remember upon that Cross hangs the sacrifice which makes worship possible to the creatures, and acceptable to the God to whom it is presented. Sneer if you will at the sufferer's form, quivering there in its anguish upon its ragged spikes; who will come down from that Cross, and with his resumed life shall appear eternally in the presence of the Father, as the channel through which our worship shall ascend in a manner which God can afford to accept. My brethren, the Cross – how precious it is! – under all aspects in which you choose to view it, how precious the Cross, and how precious the faith which clings to the Cross![85]

Palmer taught his flock that Christ's on-going incarnation at the Father's right hand enabled them to draw near to God and worship Him with reverence, confidence, and joy:

It is the priestly function of Christ, our Head, to conduct this worship on our behalf. We can render back in praise no more of the Divine glory, than is shed down upon our own hearts by the Holy Ghost; and Christ must stand as the intervenor, through whom, as 'the brightness of the Father's glory,' it must first stream upon us. When He has enriched us with all these communications of love and grace, He is our interpreter before the Father. Clothed with our nature, He represents us in the furniture of all our sanctified affections and desires. What our poor speech is so

---

85. 'Offence of the Cross, Unreasonable' (p. 2.91).

inadequate to utter, He translates into the language of the God-head. The stammering praises we seek to embalm in song He gathers in His golden censer, and waves before the eternal throne. It is this that heartens the believer's worship on earth, and fills with such unspeakable bravery the spirit which would utterly sink beneath the sense of its own unworthiness.[86]

Palmer fleshed out his view of Trinitarian worship in his book *Theology of Prayer*.[87] We should remember that Palmer's presbytery had convicted Clapp of denying the efficacy of intercessory prayer. In *Theology of Prayer*, Palmer showed that Christian prayer is efficacious and not merely therapeutic. He labored to do this in order to 'refute the various objections urged by different classes of sceptics' and counteract the teaching that there is 'no other virtue in prayer than the reflex moral influence which it exerts on the worshipper himself.'[88]

Palmer believed that Christian prayer is efficacious *because it is Trinitarian*: *to* the Father, *through* the Son and *by* the Spirit. The Spirit creates a 'living sympathy' between the interceding Christ in heaven and the praying saints on earth: 'He takes the desires which are in the heart of Jesus Christ, and works them into our hearts so that they become our desires. He takes the plea which is upon the lips of the great Advocate above, and seals it upon our lips as our prayer in Christ's blessed name.' As the Spirit of God's Son, the Holy Spirit communicates to God's children the very confidence of the beloved Son himself to encourage us to approach the throne of grace and say, 'Abba, Father.'[89]

As we already noted, because he wanted any definition of God to be explicitly Trinitarian, Thornwell found a defect in question four of the *Shorter Catechism*. Similarly, because he wanted any definition of *prayer* to be explicitly Trinitarian, Palmer cited

---

86. 'Christ a Priest after the Power of an Endless Life' (pp. 2.452-53).

87. For an abridged and modernized version, see Needham and Harman, *What Happens When I Pray?* (London: Grace Publications Trust, 1997).

88. *Theology of Prayer*, pp. 5, 81, 143.

89. Ibid., pp. 200, 318-19, 331-46.

a deficiency in question 98, which asks, 'What is prayer?' and answers, 'Prayer is an offering up of our desires unto God, for things agreeable to his will, in the name of Christ, with confession of our sins, and thankful acknowledgment of his mercies.' Palmer's dissatisfaction arose from the fact that the role of the *Spirit* is not included. Thankfully for Palmer, the *Larger Catechism*'s definition of prayer includes a reference to the Spirit's role, though it leaves out the phrase 'for things agreeable to his will'. Thus, Palmer combined the *Shorter* and the *Larger* to achieve an acceptably Trinitarian definition of prayer: 'Prayer is an offering up of our desires to God, *for things agreeable to his will*, in the name of Christ, *by the help of his Spirit*, with confession of our sins and thankful acknowledgment of his mercies.'[90]

For Palmer, the efficacy of prayer does not reside in the merit of the worshipper, but in the object and mode of that worship – to the loving Father, through the incarnate Son, by the Spirit of adoption. Because he believed in the efficacy of Trinitarian prayer, he believed that corporate prayer is a 'thermometer of spiritual life in a congregation'.[91]

## Summary

Palmer's ministry in New Orleans paralleled what Thornwell and Smyth were doing in Columbia and Charleston. Given the history of his family and his church, he was determined to heed Smyth's exhortation to proactively preach and apply the Trinity. He especially sought to reach out to Unitarians with the message of Trinitarian love, and, as he noted in his diary, Unitarians began visiting his church during the early months of his ministry in New Orleans. Palmer's goal was to woo them into the Trinitarian faith and, in some cases, *back* into the Trinitarian fold, but how successful was he?

---

90. Ibid., pp. 13.

91. Johnson, *Palmer*, p. 434. The weekly schedule at Palmer's church was Sunday School at 9:30 a.m.; Sunday worship at 11 a.m. and 8 p.m.; and Wednesday prayer meeting at 8 p.m. ('First Presbyterian Church,' *Daily Picayune*, 29 September 1872).

For several days after his death in May of 1902, *The Daily Picayune* ran full-page articles devoted to Palmer – reports of his funeral, eulogies from other ministers, biographical sketches, and histories of his ministry. One article in particular lets us in on the rest of the story about the Unitarians Palmer had written about in his diary: 'The greater number of the members of the Unitarian church, which was formed by Dr Clapp, returned to the fold of Presbyterianism through Dr Palmer's exposition of the real principles of Presbyterianism.'[92]

The article goes on to explain that this was 'due to the wonderful influence and power exercised by Dr Palmer, for his great powers of mind and gentle heart in those terrible days of doubt and upheaval in the church when he first began to work in New Orleans, quietly yet surely drew the wanderers back to the fold of their childhood. His faith strengthened the faith of the faithful and calmed the fears of the doubting. His discourses, burning with fire, thronged the church Sunday after Sunday.'[93]

The Unitarian movement in New Orleans, so vigorous in the days of Clapp, dwindled as Unitarians were converted to Trinitarianism under Palmer's ministry.[94] Trinitarianism rapidly expanded throughout the city. Not only did First Presbyterian Church grow in new membership, it planted *thirteen* churches in and around New Orleans, with a 'total enrolment of communicants approximating 29,000'.[95] Thus, like Thornwell in Columbia and Smyth in Charleston, Palmer succeeded in New Orleans in subduing the Unitarian movement and spreading the fame of the adorable Trinity.

---

92. 'Dr Palmer's Career.'

93. Ibid.

94. For details of the decline of Unitarianism in New Orleans, see Macaulay, *Unitarianism*, pp. 177-83.

95. 'Dr Palmer's Career.'

## 11

# *Historical Significance and Contemporary Relevance of the Columbians' Stand for the Trinity*

IN this concluding chapter we will briefly summarize the importance of the Columbians' efforts relative to the history of the Unitarian-Trinitarian conflict in the nineteenth century South. We will also summarize a few of the ways that Christians today might apply facets of the Columbians' stand for the Trinity.

## Historical Significance

Writing in 1902, Unitarian scholar George Cooke lamented the breakdown of the Southern Unitarian movement: 'Unitarianism has made little progress outside of New England, and those regions to which New England traditions have been carried by those who migrated westward. The early promise for growth of Unitarianism in the south, from 1825 until 1840, failed ....'[1]

Cooke and other historians have tried to understand the reasons for this failure. According to Cooke, dreams of a Unitarian South were not realized because 'there was no background of tradition for its encouragement and support. Individuals could think their way into the Unitarian faith, but

---

1. Cooke, *Unitarianism in America*, 145.

their influence proved ineffective when all around them the old tradition prevailed as a stubborn conviction.'[2] Peter Williams, on the other hand, has argued that the temporary success of Unitarianism in Charleston and New Orleans was due to the 'charisma' of Gilman and Clapp, and, when they passed from the scene, the movement simply petered out.[3]

Macaulay also wrestled with why the number of Southern Unitarians dramatically declined: 'Did the verbal sticks and stones thrown by orthodoxy kill them off in large numbers? Did they pack up and move North? Did they die off by plague or storm?'[4] According to Macaulay, sectionalism played a major role in Unitarianism's decline during the years around the Civil War. Southerners tended to associate Unitarianism with 'all things Northern' and rejected it on those grounds.[5]

There are surely many factors that lead to the decline of one movement and the growth of another, but our study has revealed that investigations regarding the decline of Unitarianism and the progress of Trinitarianism in the nineteenth-century South should factor in the efforts of the Columbians to stand for orthodoxy against Unitarian encroachments. In Columbia, Charleston, and New Orleans, the three Southern cities where Unitarians were making the most gains in the 1825–1840 timeframe mentioned by Cooke, the Columbians stepped in and attempted to reverse Unitarian advancements. In the decades that followed in each of these cities, the Unitarian movement, which had been marked by an optimistic resolve to exterminate Trinitarianism from the South, began to decline while Trinitarianism regained its momentum and enjoyed increased expansion and influence. However one chooses to characterize the Columbians' efforts – whether as mere stubbornness, populist charisma, sticks and stones, sectionalism,

---

2. Ibid.

3. 'Unitarianism,' in *Encyclopedia of Religion in the South* (Macon, GA: Mercer University Press, 1984), p. 790.

4. Macaulay, *Unitarianism*, p. 3.

5. Ibid., p. 65.

Spirit-wrought revival, or perhaps some combination thereof – the Columbians should have a prominent place in discussions about Unitarian losses and Trinitarian gains in the nineteenth-century American South.[6]

## Contemporary Relevance

Throughout our study we have touched on the practical and pastoral implications of the Columbians' stand for the Trinity. The Columbians modelled the fact that the Trinity is not a peripheral matter or simply a doctrinal box to check, but rather the *sine qua non* of Christian faith and practice. We have seen a robustly Trinitarian approach to Christianity in which all aspects of orthodoxy and orthopraxy are considered and developed Trinitarianly. Now we will briefly suggest a few ways in which Christians, especially ministers who want to *pastor*, *worship*, and *preach* Trinitarianly, might find some assistance from Columbia's pastor-scholars.

### Pastoring Trinitarianly

Many people struggle with knowing whether God really loves them. The sermons we have referenced on the love of the Triune God, as well as resources such as *The Threefold Fellowship and The Threefold Assurance*, can help ministers think through ways of sharing the good news of the adopting love of the Father, the unmerited grace of the Son, and the assuring fellowship of the Spirit with those who are lost, lonely, or doubting, so that they can grow in the confidence and victory that the Triune God delights

---

6. The Columbians were certainly not the only Trinitarians in America or the South who sought to counteract the nineteenth-century Unitarian movement. We have noted the efforts of John Holt Rice of Union, who laboured to prevent the Unitarian designs of Thomas Jefferson at the University of Virginia. Similarly, Samuel Miller of Princeton sought to help Presbyterians in Baltimore, Maryland, respond to the Unitarianism being popularized there by Jared Sparks. See Samuel Miller, *Letters on Unitarianism Addressed to the Members of the First Presbyterian Church in the City of Baltimore* (Trenton, NJ: George Sherman, 1821).

to give His people.[7] Just as it was the corrective for the burgeoning Unitarian movement of the nineteenth century, sharing the soul-satisfying love of the Trinity is the corrective for today's empty yet prevalent Moralistic Therapeutic Deism.[8]

Pastors could also help Christians flesh out the Columbians' doctrine of the Trinity as the archetype of human society in their own society. Recently, Trinitarian denominations have publicly confessed sins of the past and communicated a renewed desire to promote racial reconciliation through the Gospel. With redemptive irony, Christians today could apply the Columbians' Trinitarian doctrine in a way that the Columbians themselves failed to do in order to help the church and society more fully reflect the love, honor, and harmony of the Trinity.[9]

## Worshipping Trinitarianly

In *Worship, Community & The Triune God of Grace*, James Torrance observed that the 'most common and widespread' form of worship in Christian churches today is 'in practice unitarian',

---

7. For further assistance on how the Triune God fellowships with the lonely, satisfies the soul, and gives meaning to life, see Thornwell, 'Necessity of the Atonement' (*CW*, p. 2.243); Palmer, 'Feeling After God' (*The Treasury*, p. 2.531); 'Communion with God, Alone Perfect' (p. 1.257ff); 'Warrant and Nature of Public Worship' (pp. 1.367-68); 'Blessedness of being with Christ' (*Sermons, 1883*, pp. 5-12); Smyth, *The Complete Works of Thomas Smyth*, edited by J. W. Flinn, 10 vols. (Columbia, SC: R. L. Bryan Company, 1905–1912), 'On the Fellowship and Communion of Believers with the Father, Son and Holy Ghost' (*Works*, pp. 9.407-24).

8. See Smith and Denton, *Soul Searching* (Oxford: Oxford University Press, 2005), pp. 162-65.

9. See 'Overture p. 43: Pursuing Racial Reconciliation and the Advance of the Gospel,' in *Actions of the 44th General Assembly (2016) of the Presbyterian Church of America*, accessed 10 October 2016, http://www.pcahistory.org/ga/actions/44thGA_2016_Actions.pdf; 'Report on Race Relations,' from *the 213th Meeting of the General Synod of the Associate Reformed Presbyterian Church*. This report suggested many reasons why Christians should cultivate good race relations, including the church's calling to reflect the unity and diversity of the Trinity in its life and witness. Accessed 10 October 2016, http://theaquilareport.com/arp-synod-approves-report-on-race-relations/.

with 'no doctrine of the mediator or sole priesthood of Christ, is human-centered, has no proper doctrine of the Holy Spirit, is too often non-sacramental, and can engender weariness.'[10] As we have seen throughout our study, the Columbians left a trove of examples and resources for Christians who want to move away from such trends and cultivate God-honoring, soul-refreshing Trinitarian worship. The chapel sermons of Thornwell, the articles of Smyth, and the sermons and writings of Palmer, especially his *Theology of Prayer*, provide a theology of worship that emphasizes restorative communion with the Father through the mediation of the incarnate Son by the gracious help of the Holy Spirit.

The Columbians modelled the use of overtly Trinitarian elements of worship, such as the Doxology and other expressly Trinitarian hymns, as well as Trinitarian benedictions and prayers, to cultivate *Trinitarian* worship in their churches. They also presented robustly Trinitarian views of the sacraments, which ministers today could use to develop their own sacramentology and craft their sacramental homilies and prayers.

## Preaching Trinitarianly

Michael Quicke has observed, 'Sadly, much current preaching and worship seem to speak of God in *fewer* than three persons .... Too often the focus has been on Jesus alone, neglecting his relationship with the Father and the Spirit.'[11] In addition, 'While orthodox preachers reject Unitarianism, which views God as one person only and denies the divinity of Christ and of the Holy Spirit, they can practice forms of worship and preaching that appear closed to the continuing work of Christ and the Holy Spirit. Preachers need to ensure that the structure of worship and preaching gives due weight to Father, Son, and Holy Spirit.'[12]

---

10. *Worship, Community & The Triune God of Grace* (Downers Grove, IL: InterVarsity Press, 1996), p. 20.

11. Quicke, *Preaching as Worship* (Grand Rapids, MI: Baker, 2011), p. 74.

12. 'Trinity,' in *New Interpreter's Handbook of Preaching* (Nashville, TN: Abingdon, 2008), p. 500.

Similarly, according to Robin Parry,

> There is a need to train teachers and preachers to give talks and sermons with an overt Trinitarian syntax …. Sermons and talks, whether on topics or specific biblical texts, need to seek to bring out the roles of the different persons of the Trinity. They need to make explicit the dynamic connections between the persons of the Trinity and move back and forth between the Three and the One. This can be done in an evangelistic sermon as well as in a talk on ecology, the cross, caring for our neighbor, walking worthy of the Lord, Christian hope, or whatever. My contention is that regular exposure to such an overt Trinitarian syntax will shape Christians who learn to think in a Trinitarian way, relate to God in a Trinitarian way, and read Scripture in a Trinitarian way. Trinitarian sermons working hand in hand with Trinitarian praying and singing will, over time, reinforce each other and shape Trinitarian Christians.[13]

As we have seen, Smyth similarly encouraged preachers in his day to preach in an overtly Trinitarian way in order to shape overtly Trinitarian Christians. Our study has provided a multitude of examples of how Smyth and his Columbia colleagues put this into practice. Anyone who wants to help remedy what Sanders has called the 'current plight of Trinity forgetfulness', and who is looking for examples of Christians who have winsomely and effectively emphasized the Trinity in doctrine and practice, would do well to consider the Columbians and their stand for the adorable Trinity.[14]

---

13. Robin Parry, *Worshiping Trinity: Coming Back to the Heart of Worship* (Eugene, OR: Cascade Books, 2012), p. 153-54.

14. Sanders, *The Deep Things of God*, p. 19.

# Appendix 1

# *Cooper's Dying Letter to his Physician*

December 15<sup>th</sup> 1838

Dr M. H. Deleon

Dear Dr,

You and I are by this time both sensible that my leaky old vessel has received a shot between wind and water, that leaves no alternative, but whether the final submersion shall be effected by asthma or dropsy. As I have neither art nor part in this matter, I leave my two enemies to squabble in their own way. But I think I may venture to appeal to you, that however debilitated are my legs in the basement story, my brains in the attic have not received much injury.

The intimation you gave me the other day, that some of my religious friends had been making enquiry of you whether I did not feel some compunctions of conscience, on account of my heterodox opinions and publications, makes me apprehensive that some fanatic or other may trump up a story about my repentance and convertion [sic] from infidelity. My recantation would be a precious prize for the orthodox, who have a strong propensity to believe a great deal more than is true. But let this letter remain privately in your secretary, unless some public calumny should require to be contradicted. I state therefore to you, that much of my leisure has been occupied for many years, in a laborious, anxious, long-continued search into the historical proofs on which Christianity, and religion generally, are supposed to be based. I have pursued this search with untired perseverance, and from an honest, truth-seeking motive; I have read all the books of character on both sides, from the time of Queen Anne, to the present time, and I have been unsparing of labour, in my continued references to the numerous ancient authorities of the first four centuries. Of the frauds, the falsehoods, the forgeries, of the Christian writers, I have met with abundant evidence; but of satisfactory proof in favour of their supernatural and miraculous pretentions, <u>none</u>.

Having employed in this study many years, much labour, and a competent share of learning, honestly and deliberately, I hold that I have earned a right to my own opinions. Mine have been formed on the evidence such as I have found it; others have as much right to differ from me, as I have from them; and I do not wonder that so many good and wise, and honest men, hold firmly the Christian doctrines as the evidence on that side of the question, and on that alone, has been pressed upon their minds from their earliest infancy; and they have had neither leisure, opportunity, nor inclination, to examine any further than they have been taught by their parents, their parsons, and the world at large.

Throwing no blame, therefore, upon others, I hope none will be thrown upon me, for embracing opinions which have been forced upon my conviction. And in that conviction, I shall die.

Further than this, dear Dr, I have nothing to say.

Yours, most truly,

Thomas Cooper[1]

---

1. Thomas Cooper Papers, SCL.

# Appendix 2

# Matthew Williams' Impressions of Thornwell's Preaching

Matthew Williams was a professor of mathematics, natural philosophy, and astronomy at South Carolina College under Thornwell's presidency. In his unpublished diary, Williams often commented on the chapel sermons of Thornwell as well as the preaching of other ministers in the city of Columbia. Williams' diary, which he kept from 1852 through 1853, indicates that Thornwell regularly preached for the weekday chapel services and preached at the Sunday service held for the students in the chapel. Thornwell also held a prayer meeting each Monday evening for faculty and students. Entries in Williams' diary include the following:

> Heard Dr Thornwell preach this morning. I was surprised to see (as I thought) a change in his manner, a change which I certainly did not consider for the best. There was a great increase of action which gave to his manner the appearance of labour. I hope he will think better of it and determine stare super antiquas vias ....
>
> Dr Thornwell dined with us today. He is a delightful companion. Went to the Methodist Church at night. Heard a Mr Johnson preach. It was sheer nonsense ....
>
> The exercises of the college were resumed this morning. The bell rang at the usual hour for prayers. About a hundred students and all the Faculty except Drs Henry and Reynolds were in attendance. Dr Thornwell made us a neat and appropriate speech ....

Dr Thornwell delivered a most excellent sermon in chapel. I am sorry so few were present to hear it ....

Dr Thornwell preached his commencement sermon today in the College Chapel. The house was packed with people from gallery to pavement ....

His sermon was an admirable effort. I hope it did good. I hope so in spite of the obvious fact that many persons of both sexes were there not to hear the great truths of the revelation expounded and defended but to see and be seen ....

We had a grand procession today from the state house to the site of the new College Chapel when the ceremony of laying the cornerstone was performed. We afterwards marched back to the state house where Dr Thornwell delivered a beautiful and highly finished address ....

Heard Dr Thornwell preach in the College Chapel this morning. His text was from Proverbs. 'The sluggard shall desire and have nothing.' The sermon was a capital one and very appropriate ....

Went in the morning to College Chapel and heard an excellent sermon from Dr Thornwell on repentance. Heard my new pastor Rev. Murchison this afternoon. He seems to be a good man but is, without doubt, a very weak one. His text was part of the dialogue between our Saviour & the Samaritan woman at the well. It was a poor specimen of preaching considered in any point of view ....

I listened to Dr Thornwell this forenoon preach one of the greatest sermons I ever heard. It was preached in the College Chapel. The audience was composed almost exclusively of students. It was a great effort ....

Cold, unpleasant day. Attended prayer meeting at Dr Thornwell's this evening ....

I attended the Chapel in the forenoon. Dr Thornwell preached an excellent sermon. It was appropriate and I trust reached the hearts and consciences of his audience ....

Heard Dr Thornwell preach in the College Chapel in the forenoon and Rev Mr Parsons in Washington St Church (Methodist) in the afternoon. It would be invidious to institute comparison between these preachers. The learned president of the College <u>deserves</u> his high reputation for profound learning, for extensive research, varied attainments, and powerful eloquence. Mr

Parsons is a young man without the advantage of early training. Yet his sermon was a good one and perhaps was as fruitful of good results as the more learned, more artistic, more finished, and more eloquent sermon of Dr Thornwell – I say <u>perhaps</u>, because of the nature of the congregations addressed by these very different clergymen. I do not mean to say that Mr Parsons was more deeply imbued with the Spirit of Truth. By no means. Nothing could be more earnest than Dr T's manner. It was impossible to resist the conviction that he felt deeply, the solemn truths he so earnestly insisted upon. But a collection of College boys is not so easily touched ....

Went to the Chapel in the forenoon. Heard Dr Thornwell in an excellent sermon. Went to Washington St Church (Methodist) in the afternoon; Rev C Murchison preached. It was a very moderate sermon. A thing of shreds and patches ....

Went this morning to Washington St Church. Rev C. Murchison preached. I hope he edified others. I am sure his sermon did me but little good. I must – I <u>must</u> endeavour to impel this prejudice against my pastor. Whence comes it? I cannot understand it .... Rev C Murchison ....disgusted many of the audience by relating <u>funny</u> anecdotes. I went in the afternoon to hear Dr Palmer at the Presbyterian Church. His discourse was a good one ....

Heard Dr Thornwell in the morning & Rev. C. Murchison in the afternoon. The first sermon was excellent; the second was not.[1]

---

1. Matthew J. Williams Papers, David M. Rubenstein Rare Book & Manuscript Library, Duke University.

# Appendix 3

# *Gilman's Newspaper Article on Palmer Sr.*

The Late Rev. Dr Palmer

*Messrs. Editors*:

Having, whilst on a long tour for my health, observed in recent numbers of the *Courier* some historical notices of the Circular Church, and of the relations sustained towards it by the late Rev. B. M. Palmer, D. D., I felt it my duty to communicate a few facts, which happen to come to my knowledge, in regard to a change of doctrinal opinions entertained by that excellent and pious man, for some time previous to his decease. Although cognizant of the same facts at the time when numerous testimonials to his character appeared soon after his death, in the *Courier* and elsewhere, I yet did not care to disturb the sensibility of many of his surviving friends, by uttering what they might have deemed a rudely discordant note, and I therefore maintained a respectful and sympathising silence. But as kindred topics are made to bear rather a prominent position in the various documents to which I have just alluded, it appeared to me at the distance of time, and under the altered circumstances and aspects of the case, that the interests of plain truth and fair justice to all parties constrained me, as a conscientious man, to keep silence no longer, especially as I never again shall have so fit an opportunity to break it. To such motives alone, instead of any mere sectarian interest I may feel in the subject, I trust that both you and the public will do me the justice to ascribe the present communication. I respectfully submit, also, whether this communication, as a statement of facts, be not an appropriate, and even necessary sequel to the historical reminiscences which have called it forth?

For a year or two previous to Dr Palmer's death, I had long conversations with him, sought not by myself, but by him, in regard to the doctrine of the Trinity, and the opinions of Unitarian Christians. Though we had never before been on terms of any sort of intimacy, he now favored me with a visit of the large part of a day at my house on Sullivan's Island, and I had the pleasure of visiting with him at his residence in Orangeburg. During these interviews, he gave me distinctly to understand that he considered the doctrine of the supreme divinity of Jesus to be untenable, adopting, as it appeared to me, something like the views of the higher Arians, as inculcated by the celebrated Dr Samuel Clarke. He had also unquestionably abandoned the doctrine of the separate personality of the Holy Spirit, denying, of course, none of its offices and influences, but ascribing them to the immediate agency of the Supreme Father of all, in accordance with the well known views entertained by Dr Watts during the later periods of his life, and with the representations of the belief of the primitive church by the Chevalier Bunsen, in his recent essays on Hippolytus. I understood him, also, to have abandoned the views of the ultra Calvanists [sic] as to the vicarious nature of the atonement. So frank and decided was he in his statements and remarks, that while my surprise was somewhat excited, I could not mistake the purport of his communications, and mentioned it soon after to my family and one or two other friends. There was nothing constrained in his conversation, and he enjoined on me no kind of concealment. My own impressions as to his change of opinions coincided also with those of a member of his own family, who assured me, after the Doctor's death, that, in consequence of that change, he, (Dr Palmer,) had for some time contemplated relinquishing the annual benefaction received by him from the Congregational Minister's Fund, and that he undoubtedly would have done so, had his life been spared a little longer. I was also informed by the same individual, to whose testimony I confidently appeal for the correction of any inaccuracy in my recollections on all these points, that certain manuscripts, left behind by the Doctor, would be found to record some of the changes of opinion above specified. How far my statements may have been corroborated by the examination and personal knowledge of those who have enjoyed better opportunities for deciding than myself, I am unable to say. I have, however, the satisfaction to hope and trust, that whatever is the exact truth on this subject, it will be as willingly recognised by them, as by

Your respectful and obedient servant,
SAMUEL GILMAN

*Jonesborough, (Tenn.) August 6, 1853.*[1]

---

1. *Charleston Courier*, 13 August 1853.

# Appendix 4

# *The Lanneaus' Rebuttal of Gilman's Article on Palmer Sr.*

*Messrs. Editors*:

In the *Courier* of Saturday last, appears a communication over the signature of 'Samuel Gilman,' impeaching the religious views and memory of the late Rev. B. M. Palmer, of this city – occasioned, it is alleged, by the recent prominence given to the 'History of the Circular Church,' of which he was for so many years its able and esteemed Pastor.

It was natural to expect the extreme sensitiveness of Dr Gilman, from the tendency of the recent publications – all of which have a direct bearing upon the issue made years ago, between the Churches involved, and the 'faith once delivered to the Saints.' But it must be left to a discerning public, to whom the lamented dead was so well and familiarly known, to determine the *propriety* of the *attack* now, for the second time, made upon the memory of one still embalmed in many living hearts; especially, when from the article referred to, nothing more appears than the author's *recollections* and *impressions* of conversations that passed between himself and the now silent dead. Dr P.'s friends must be excused if they require something more stable and satisfactory, since nothing is easier than to attack an individual's opinions and character, and challenge his friends to prove his *innocence*.

The subscribers are far from designing to impeach Dr Gilman's *veracity*, and to relieve any such appearance, the following circumstances may be mentioned. It is undoubtedly true, that the change in his daughter's sentiments brought Dr P. into nearer contact with Unitarians and their writings; the effect of which was to *mitigate* a bitterness of feeling which he formerly entertained towards them, springing in a great degree, from the difficulties in the Circular Church during his Pastorship. That he *spoke* with greater *moderation* of them and their sentiments, and displayed towards them, especially his *daughter's guests*, Christian courtesy and good feeling, is undoubtedly true. But this would not surprise Dr G., could he give the *orthodox* clergy *in general*, more credit for sincerity and liberality of feeling, (while sternly maintaining principle) than they generally receive at the hands of some religionists. Added to this, it must be said, that Dr P. was a man of free-spoken candor, always making due concessions when truth demanded it, and cheerfully abandoning a bad proof even of truth, when satisfied of its inconclusiveness. That this should have led Dr G., with his sanguine attachment to his own views, to construe too favorably, expressions dropped in the course of conversation, and thus made 'the wish father to the thought,' is quite conceivable. Without denying his *impressions*, the undersigned cannot but feel that the basis of them is *insufficient*. But of a change in his *actual* views of the controverted topics, there is not only no proof, but abundant evidence to the contrary.

It may not be out of place to add, that, to the certain knowledge of the subscribers, the main cause of Dr P.'s change of residence from the city to the country, was to rid himself, if possible, of the painful mortification and grief of heart occasioned by the change of religious views of the member of his family referred to, and the hope cherished, that retirement, and serious, prayerful reflection, would enable both reason and an enlightened conscience to resume their sway. This feeling of deep concern for his daughter's welfare continued to his dying day. It is also well known, that since Dr P.'s death, his daughter has *abandoned* her former views, and is now a member of the Episcopal Church.

The allusion made to Dr Palmer's intended relinquishment of the annuity of the 'Clergy Society,' is *entirely new*, and may have had its origin in this fact, that, from his *extreme conscientiousness* he contemplated asking a *reduction* of the sum allowed him, as he considered himself able, and was actually engaged in supplying a church in a neighboring parish with the 'bread of life,' for which he received a small salary. It was to the *extent* of the stipend received that the proposed reduction had reference, and was only alluded to by him a *few weeks* prior to his decease, in a letter to a friend. With regard to the existence of certain manuscripts, containing a record of 'some of the changes of opinion' alleged, no manuscripts have been discovered by any member of the family, other than duplicates of private letters, which it was his habit to keep, even to the month of his death. These letters, as far as they show anything upon the subject, while they evince such a change of feeling as is above described, and show him to be somewhat engaged in a re-examination of the subject, reveal no *change* of opinion whatever; much less that he was a 'year or two before his death a high Arian,' or had modified his views upon the subject of the Atonement; while his last sermons and the whole tenor of his preaching, prayer and conversation (as the inmates of his family and community in which he lived well know) tend directly to the opposite conclusion.

Unless, therefore, the ingenuousness of his whole life forsook him in his last months, it is morally impossible that he can have passed from Orthodox to Unitarian sentiments. This, the 'exact truth' upon the subject, it is hoped will be willingly recognized by Dr G., as it is well known by 'those who have enjoyed better opportunities for deciding, than himself.'

B. LANNEAU
B. E. LANNEAU
*Charleston, August 15, 1853.*[1]

---

1. *Charleston Courier*, 15 August 1853.

# BIBLIOGRAPHY

## Manuscript Collections

Circular Congregational Church Records. South Carolina Historical Society, Charleston, South Carolina.

Columbia Seminary Notebooks. Reformed Theological Seminary Library Archives, Jackson, Mississippi.

Thomas Cooper Papers. South Caroliniana Library, University of South Carolina, Columbia, South Carolina.

Samuel Gilman Papers. South Caroliniana Library, University of South Carolina, Columbia, South Carolina.

Thomas Jefferson Papers. Library of Congress, Washington, DC.

Thomas Cary Johnson Papers. The William Smith Morton Library, Union Theological Seminary and Presbyterian School of Christian Education, Richmond, Virginia.

Historic New Orleans Collection. New Orleans, Louisiana

Benjamin Morgan Palmer Papers. C. Benton Kline, Jr. Special Collections and Archives, John Bulow Campbell Library, Columbia Theological Seminary, Decatur, Georgia.

Benjamin Morgan Palmer Papers. The William Smith Morton Library, Union Theological Seminary and Presbyterian School of Christian Education, Richmond, Virginia.

James Henley Thornwell Papers. C. Benton Kline, Jr. Special Collections and Archives, John Bulow Campbell Library, Columbia Theological Seminary, Decatur, Georgia.

James Henley Thornwell Papers. South Caroliniana Library, University of South Carolina, Columbia, South Carolina.

Mary S. Shindler Papers. South Carolina Historical Society, Charleston, South Carolina.

Shindler-Palmer Papers. Ralph W. Steen Library, Stephen F. Austin State University, Nacogdoches, Texas.

Smyth Family Papers. South Carolina Historical Society, Charleston, South Carolina.

Thomas Smyth Papers. C. Benton Kline, Jr. Special Collections and Archives, John Bulow Campbell Library, Columbia Theological Seminary, Decatur, Georgia.

Stoney Family Papers. South Carolina Historical Society, Charleston, South Carolina.

Unitarian Church Records. South Carolina Historical Society, Charleston, South Carolina.

Matthew Jouett Williams Papers. David M. Rubenstein Rare Book and Manuscript Library, Duke University, Durham, North Carolina.

## Newspapers

*The Charleston Daily Courier*, Charleston, South Carolina.

*The Charleston Evening News*, Charleston, South Carolina.

*The Daily Crescent*, New Orleans, Louisiana.

*The Daily Picayune*, New Orleans, Louisiana.

*The Dallas Morning News*, Dallas, Texas.

*The New Orleans Daily Creole*, New Orleans, Louisiana.

*The New Orleans Times*, New Orleans, Louisiana.

*The Southern Patriot*, Charleston, South Carolina.

## Primary Sources

*A Memorial of the late Rev. William H. Adams, For Twelve Years Pastor of the Circular Church*. Charleston, SC: Walker, Evans & Cogswell, 1880.

Adger, John B. 'Calvin Defended Against Drs Cunningham and Hodge.' *The Southern Presbyterian Review* 27, no. 1 (January 1876): pp. 133-69.

———. 'Calvin's Doctrine of the Lord's Supper.' *The Southern Presbyterian Review* 36, no. 4 (October 1885): pp. 785-800.

———. 'The Christian Doctrine of Human Rights and Slavery.' *Southern Presbyterian Review* 2, no. 4 (March 1849): pp. 569-87.

———. 'Memorial of James Henley Thornwell, D.D., LL.D.' In *Memorial Volume of the Semi-Centennial of the Theological Seminary at Columbia, South Carolina*, pp. 188-94. Columbia, SC: Presbyterian Publishing House, 1884.

———. *My Life and Times, 1810–1899*. Richmond, VA: The Presbyterian Committee of Publication, 1899.

*The Aeneid of Virgil*. Translated by Allen Mandelbaum. New York: Random House, 2004.

Alexander, William McFaddin. 'Palmer's "The Threefold Fellowship and Assurance."' *The Presbyterian Quarterly* 16 (1902–1903): pp. 132-35.

Allibone, S. Austin. *A Critical Dictionary of English Literature and British and American Authors*. Philadelphia, J. B. Lippincott & Co., 1874.

Bavinck, Herman. *Reformed Dogmatics*. 4 vols. Grand Rapids, MI: Baker Academic, 2004.

Baxter, Richard. *The Practical Works of Richard Baxter*. 23 vols. London: James Duncan, 1830.

Beard, J. R. *Historical and Artistic Illustrations of the Trinity; Showing the Rise, Progress, & Decline of the Doctrine; With Elucidatory Engravings.* London: Simpkin, Marshall, and Co., 1846.

Blackburn, George A., ed. *The Life Work of John L. Girardeau, D.D., LL.D.* Columbia, SC: The State Company, 1916.

Buckingham, J. S. *The Slave States of America.* 2 vols. London: Fisher, Son, & Co., 1842.

Burnap, George Washington. 'Unitarian Christianity Expounded and Defended.' In *The Old and the New: Or, Discourses and Proceedings at the Dedication of the Re-Modeled Unitarian Church in Charleston, S.C. on Sunday, April 2, 1854. Preceded by The Farewell Discourse Delivered in the Old Church, on Sunday, April 4, 1852*, pp. 113-139. Charleston, SC: Samuel G. Courtenay, 1854.

———. *Expository Lectures on the Principal Passages of the Scripture Which Relate to the Doctrine of the Trinity.* Boston: James Munroe and Company, 1845.

Butler, Joseph. *Analogy of Religion, Natural and Revealed.* New York: Harper & Brothers Publishers, 1860.

Calvin, John. *Genesis.* Vol. 1, *Commentaries.* Grand Rapids, MI: Baker Books, 2003.

———. *Institutes of the Christian Religion.* Edited by John T. McNeill. Translated by Ford L. Battles. 2 vols. Louisville: Westminster John Knox, 2006.

Clapp, Theodore. *A Report of the Trial of the Rev. Theodore Clapp, Before the Mississippi Presbytery at their Sessions in May and December 1832.* New Orleans, LA: Hotchkiss & Co., 1833.

———. *Autobiographical Sketches and Recollections, During A Thirty-Five Years' Residence in New Orleans.* Boston: Phillips, Sampson & Company, 1858.

———. 'Slavery: A Sermon Delivered in the First Congregational Church in New Orleans, 15 April 1838.' New Orleans: John Gibson, 1838.

*Columbia South Carolina City Directory.* Columbia, SC: R. W. Gibbes, 1859.

*Constitution of the Theological Seminary of the Synod of South Carolina and Georgia.* Columbia, SC: 1844.

Conway, Moncure Daniel. *Autobiography, Memories and Experiences of Moncure Daniel Conway.* New York: Cassell and Company, 1904.

Cooper, Thomas. 'A Review of Dr Priestley's Theological Works.' In Joseph Priestley, *Memoirs of Dr Joseph Priestley*, 2 vols., pp. 2.482-825. London: J. Johnson, 1806.

———. *An Account of the Trial of Thomas Cooper, of Northumberland: on a charge of libel against the President of the United States, 1800.* Philadelphia: John Bioren, 1800.

———. 'Address to the Graduates of South Carolina College, 1821.' Columbia: 1821.

———. 'Address to the Graduates of South Carolina College, 1830.' Columbia: 1830.

———. 'Exposition of the Doctrines of Calvinism.' New York: 1834.

———. *Reply to Burke's Invective in the House of Commons, on the 30th of April 1792.* London: J. Johnson, 1792.

———. 'The Scripture Doctrine of Materialism.' Philadelphia: 1823.

———. 'A Summary of Unitarian Arguments.' In *Tracts: Ethical, Theological, and Political*, pp. 465-526. Warrington, PA: W. Eyres, 1789.

Cunningham, William. *The Reformers and the Theology of the Reformation.* Edinburgh: T&T Clark, 1862.

Dabney, Robert L. *Systematic Theology.* Edinburgh: Banner of Truth, 1996.

———. 'The Doctrinal Contents of the Confession.' In *Memorial Volume of the Westminster Assembly, 1647–1897,* pp. 87-114. Richmond, VA: The Presbyterian Committee of Publication, 1897.

Dana, Mary S. B. *Charles Morton, or The Young Patriot.* New York: Dayton & Newman, 1843.

———. *Letters Addressed to Relatives and Friends, Chiefly in Reply to Arguments in Support of the Doctrine of the Trinity,* 2nd ed. Boston: James Munroe and Company, 1846.

———. 'Mary Dana Book.' http://www.biblicalunitarian.com/marydanabook.pdf.

———. *The Northern Harp: Contributions of Original Sacred and Moral Songs.* New York: Dayton & Newman, 1843.

———. *The Parted Family and Other Poems. An Offering to the Afflicted and a Tribute of Love to Departed Friends.* New York: Dayton & Saxton, 1842.

———. *The Southern Harp: Consisting of Original Sacred and Moral Songs.* Boston: Parker and Ditson, 1841.

Davidson, James Wood. *Living Writers of the South.* New York: Carleton Publisher, 1869.

Edes, Grace Williamson. *Annals of Harvard Class of 1852.* Cambridge, MA: Privately Printed, 1922.

Flinn, Andrew W. 'A Sermon Delivered the third of April, 1811, at the Dedication of the Second Presbyterian Church, Charleston, S.C.' Charleston, SC: J. Hoff, 1811.

Foote, Henry Wilder. 'Samuel Gilman, Author of "Fair Harvard."' *The Harvard Graduates' Magazine* 24 (1915–1916): p. 613.

Foote, William Henry. *Sketches of North Carolina, Historical and Biographical, Illustrative of the Principles of a Portion of Her Early Settlers.* New York: Robert Carter, 1846.

Forrest, Mary. *Women of the South Distinguished in Literature.* New York: Charles B. Richardson, 1866.

Fraser, A. M. 'Dr Thornwell as an Ecclesiologist.' In *Thornwell Centennial Addresses,* pp. 31-52. Spartanburg, SC: Band and White Printers, 1913.

'Fundamental Articles of Faith of the Independent or Congregational Church of Charleston, and Articles and By-Laws for its Government.' Charleston, SC: J. Noff, 1818.

Gales, Joseph, ed. *Sermons, Chiefly of a Practical Nature by the Late Anthony Forster, A. M., Pastor of the Second Independent Church in Charleston.* Raleigh: J. Gales, 1821.

Gilman, Samuel. *Contributions to Literature: Descriptive, Critical, Humorous, Biographical, Philosophical, and Poetical.* Boston: Crosby, Nichols, and Company, 1856.

———. *Contributions to Religion: Consisting of Sermons, Practical and Doctrinal.* Charleston: Evans & Cogswell, 1860.

———. 'Hymn and Ode: For the Occasion of the Solemnities in Respect to the Memory of Hon. John C. Calhoun, 1850.' Printed by the citizens of Richland District, 1850.

———. *The Old and the New: Or, Discourses and Proceedings at the Dedication of the Re-Modeled Unitarian Church in Charleston, S.C. on Sunday, April 2, 1854. Preceded by The Farewell Discourse Delivered in the Old Church, on Sunday, April 4, 1852.* Charleston: Samuel G. Courtenay, 1854.

———. 'Sermon Preached November 26, 1843, at the Ordination of Mr Dexter Clapp, over the Unitarian Church at Savannah, GA. by Henry W. Bellows, Minister of the First Congregational Church in New York: with The Charge, by Samuel Gilman, D. D. of Charleston, S. C.' New York: Charles S. Francis and Company, 1843.

Girardeau, John L. 'The Christo-centric Principle of Theology.' *The Presbyterian Quarterly* 6, no. 19 (January 1892): pp. 1-20.

———. *Discussions of Theological Questions*. Edited by George A. Blackburn. Richmond, VA: Presbyterian Committee of Publication, 1905.

———. 'Sermon on the Occasion of the Ordination of the Rev. F. P. Mullally, and the Installation of Rev. J. H. Thornwell, D.D., and Rev. F. P. Mullally, as Co-Pastors of the First Presbyterian Church, Columbia, S.C.' Columbia, SC: Steam-Press of Robert M. Stokes, 1860.

———. *Sermons*. Edited by George A. Blackburn. Columbia, SC: The State Company, 1907.

Goulding, F. R. 'Memorial of Thomas Goulding, D. D.' In *Memorial Volume of the Semi-centennial of the Theological Seminary at Columbia, South Carolina*. Columbia, SC: Presbyterian Publishing House, 1884.

Hale, Sarah Josepha. 'Mary B. Shindler.' In *Sketches of all Distinguished Women from the Creation to A.D. 1854*. New York: Harper & Brothers, Publishers, 1855.

Hart, John S. *Female Prose Writers of America*. Philadelphia: E. H. Butler, 1866.

Harris, S. F. 'The Theology of Dr Girardeau.' *Methodist Quarterly Review* 37, no. 1 (April 1893): pp. 29-45.

Hatfield, Edwin Francis. 'Mary Stanley Bunce Shindler.' In *The Poets of the Church: A Series of Biographical Sketches of Hymn-Writers*, pp. 549-51. New York: Anson D. F. Randolph & Company, 1884.

Hodge, Charles. '*Doctrine of the Reformed Church on the Lord's Supper.*' *The Biblical Repertory and the Princeton Review 20 (April 1848)*: pp. 227-77.

———. 'On the Sonship of Christ.' *The Biblical Repertory 5, no. 1* (1829): pp. 429-80.

———. 'Romish Baptism.' *The Biblical Repertory and Princeton Review* 17, no. 3 (July 1845): pp. 444-71.

——. *Systematic Theology*. 3 vols. Peabody, MA: Hendrickson Publishers, 2003.

Howe, George. 'History of Columbia Theological Seminary.' In *Memorial Volume of the Semi-Centennial of the Theological Seminary at Columbia, South Carolina*, pp. 131-56. Columbia, SC: Presbyterian Publishing House, 1884.

Howe, George. *History of the Presbyterian Church in South Carolina*. 2 vols. Columbia, SC: W. J. Duffie, 1883.

Hume, David. *The Natural History of Religion*, ed. H. E. Root. Stanford, CA: Stanford University Press, 1956.

Humphrey, Edward Porter. 'Our Theology in its Developments.' Philadelphia: Presbyterian Board of Publication, 1857.

Hyde, William and Howard L. Conard, eds. *Encyclopedia of the History of St. Louis*. 6 vols. St. Louis: The Southern History Company, 1899.

Johnson, Thomas Carey. *The Life and Letters of Benjamin Morgan Palmer*. Richmond, VA: Presbyterian Committee of Publication, 1906.

Jones, Charles Colcock. *The Religious Instruction of the Negroes in the United States*. Savannah, GA: Thomas Purse and Co., 1842.

King, William L. *The Newspaper Press of Charleston*. Charleston, SC: Lucas & Richardson, 1882.

Knowles, Richard Brinsley. *The Life of James Sheridan Knowles*. London: James McHenry, 1872.

Law, Thomas H. 'Dr Thornwell as a Preacher and a Teacher.' *Thornwell Centennial Addresses*, pp. 5-21. Spartanburg, SC: Band and White Printers, 1913.

Mackey, Albert Gallatin. *An Encyclopaedia of Freemasonry*. Philadelphia: L. H. Everts, 1894.

——. *A Lexicon of Freemasonry*. London: Charles Griffin and Company, 1860.

McPheeters, W. M. *Columbia Seminary, A Retrospect Involving a Responsibility*. Columbia, SC: R. L. Bryan, 1901.

*Memorial Volume of the Semi-centennial of the Theological Seminary at Columbia, South Carolina*. Columbia, SC: Presbyterian Publishing House, 1884.

Miller, Samuel, *Letters on Unitarianism Addressed to the Members of the First Presbyterian Church in the City of Baltimore*. Trenton, NJ: George Sherman, 1821.

*Minutes of the General Assembly of the Presbyterian Church in the U.S.A.* Vol. 7. Philadelphia: Geddes and Bailey, 1833.

Nevin, John Williamson. *The Mystical Presence: A Vindication of the Reformed or Calvinistic Doctrine of the Holy Eucharist*. Philadelphia: S. R. Fisher & Co., 1867.

Norton, Andrews. *A Statement of Reasons for Not Believing the Doctrines of the Trinitarians concerning the Nature of God and the Person of Christ*. Boston: Hilliard, Gray, and Co., 1833.

'Order of Services at the Centennial Celebration of Harvard University, on the 8th of September, 1836.' Cambridge, MA: Harvard University, 1836.

Owen, John, *An Exposition of the Epistle to the Hebrews with Preliminary Exercitations*. 7 vols. Edinburgh: Banner of Truth, 1991.

———. *The Works of John Owen*. 16 vols. Edited by William H. Goold. New York: Robert Carter & Brothers, 1850–1852.

Palmer, Benjamin Morgan, Jr. *A Weekly Publication Containing Sermons*. 2 vols. New Orleans: Clark & Hofeline, 1875–1876.

———. 'Baconianism and the Bible.' *Southern Presbyterian Review* 6, no. 2 (October 1852): pp. 250-252.

———. 'Benjamin Morgan Palmer, D. D.' In *Annals of the American Pulpit, Volume 9*, edited by William B. Sprague, p. 347. New York: Robert Carter and Brothers, 1859.

——. 'Christianity, The Only Religion for Man: A Discourse Delivered Before the Graduating Class of the University of North Carolina, June 4, 1855.' Raleigh, NC: The Carolina Cultivator, 1855.

——. 'Feeling After God.' In *The Treasury: A Magazine of Religious and Current Thought for Pastor and People*, 1885, p. 2.531.

——. *Formation of Character: 12 Lectures Delivered at First Presbyterian Church of New Orleans.* New Orleans: Religious Book Depository, 1889.

——. 'Life, Character and Genius of the Late Reverend James H. Thornwell.' *Southern Presbyterian Review* 15, no. 2 (October 1862): pp. 255-309.

——. *The Life and Letters of James Henley Thornwell D.D., LL.D: Ex-President of the South Carolina College, Late Professor of Theology in the Theological Seminary at Columbia, South Carolina.* Richmond, VA: Whittet & Shepperson, 1875.

——. 'Opening Address.' In *Memorial Volume of the Semi-Centennial of the Theological Seminary at Columbia, South Carolina,* pp. 3-8. Columbia, SC: Presbyterian Publishing House, 1884.

——. *Selected Writings of Benjamin Morgan Palmer: Articles Written for The Southwestern Presbyterian in the Years 1869–70.* Edinburgh: Banner of Truth, 2014.

——. *Sermons by Rev. B. M. Palmer, D.D., Delivered in 1ˢᵗ Presbyterian Church, New Orleans, during the months of January and February, 1883.* New Orleans: T. H. Thomason, 1883.

——. 'Slavery A Divine Trust: The Duty of the South to Preserve and Perpetuate the Institution as it Now Exists.' New York: George P. Nesbitt & Co., 1861.

——. *Theology of Prayer.* Richmond, VA: Presbyterian Committee of Publication, 1894.

——. *The Threefold Fellowship and the Threefold Assurance.* Richmond, VA: Presbyterian Committee of Publication, 1902.

Parker, Joel. *Lectures on Universalism.* New York: E. Loomis, 1830.

*Plan of Government of the Theological Seminary of the Synod of South Carolina, Georgia, Alabama, and Florida of the Presbyterian Church in the United States, Columbia, S.C. as Amended in 1896.* Newnan, GA: S. W. Murray, Printer, 1896.

Plumer, William Swan. *The Rock of Our Salvation: A Treatise Respecting The Natures, Person, Offices, Work, Sufferings, and Glory of Jesus Christ.* New York: American Tract Society, 1867.

Priestley, Joseph. *An History of Early Opinions Concerning Jesus Christ, Compiled from Original Writers Proving that the Christian Church Was at First Unitarian*, Vol. 1. Birmingham: Person and Rollason, 1786.

Reid, George. 'A Sermon delivered in the Second Presbyterian Church, Charleston, S.C. on the 17th September, 1820, Commemorative of the Life and Character of the Reverend Andrew Flinn, D. D., Late Pastor of Said Church.' Charleston, SC: J. Huff, 1820.

Rice, John H. 'A Review of "Memoirs of Dr Joseph Priestley and Observations of His Writings," by Thomas Cooper.' *The Virginia Evangelical and Literary Magazine* (February 1820): pp. 63-74.

Rutt, John Towill. *Life and Correspondence of Joseph Priestley.* London: R. Hunter, 1832.

Sanderson, Joseph, ed. *The Pulpit Treasure: An Evangelical Monthly for Pastors, Christian Workers and Families.* Vol. 2. New York: E. B. Treat, 1885.

Schaff, Philip. *History of the Christian Church.* Vol. 3, 3rd edition (Peabody, MA: Hendrickson Publishers, 2006).

Shedd, William G. T. *Dogmatic Theology.* Phillipsburg, NJ: P&R Publishing, 2003.

Shindler, Mary Dana. *A Southerner Among the Spirits: A Record of Investigations into the Spiritual Phenomena.* Memphis, TN: Southern Baptist Publication Society, 1877.

Shuttleworth, Philip Nicholas. *The Consistency of The Whole Scheme of Revelation with itself and with Human Reason*. New York: J&J Harper, 1832.

Sims, J. Marion. *The Story of My Life*. New York: D. Appleton and Company, 1884.

Singer, C. Gregg, *A Theological Interpretation of American History* (Nutley, NJ: Craig Press, 1964).

Smith, John Pye. *The Scripture Testimony to the Messiah*. 3 vols. London: Jackson and Walford, 1837.

Smyth, Thomas. *Autobiographical Notes, Letters, and Reflections of Thomas Smyth, D. D.* Edited by Louisa Cheves Stoney. Charleston, SC: Walker, Evans & Cogswell Co., 1914.

———. 'The Battle of Fort Sumter: Its Mystery and Miracle, God's Mastery and Mercy.' *Southern Presbyterian Review* 14 (October 1860): pp. 365-99.

———. 'The Bible and Not Reason, the Only Certain and Authoritative Source of Our Knowledge, Even of the Existence of God' [*alt.* 'The Knowledge of God's Existence Originally a Revealed Truth']. 7.3 (January 1854): pp. 325-47.

———. 'The Bible and Not Reason, the Only Authoritative Source and Standard of Our Knowledge of the Nature of God – What it Teaches Concerning the Unity of God' [alt. 'The Unity of God Unsearchable by Reason, and only known from Scripture']. *Southern Presbyterian Review* 7, no. 4 (April 1854): pp. 461-84.

———. *Calvin and His Enemies: A Memoir of the Life, Character and Principles of Calvin*. Philadelphia: Presbyterian Board of Publication, 1856.

———. *The Complete Works of Thomas Smyth*. Edited by J. W. Flinn. 10 vols. Columbia, SC: R. L. Bryan Company, 1905–1912.

———. 'The Distinctions in the Godhead Personal and not Nominal.' *Southern Presbyterian Review* 12, no. 2 (July 1859): pp. 289-309.

———. 'The Doctrine of the Trinity either the Offspring of Reason or of Primitive Revelation.' *Southern Presbyterian Review* 9, no. 2 (October 1855): pp. 246-49.

———. 'The Doctrine of the Trinity, Not Theoretical or Speculative, but Practical in its Nature and Fundamental in its Importance.' *Southern Presbyterian Review* 8, no. 2 (October 1854): pp. 153-81.

———. 'On Elohim as a Title of God, and as Implying a Plurality in the Godhead.' *Southern Presbyterian Review* 8, no. 4 (April 1855): pp. 545-59.

———. 'The Nature and Origin of the Pagan Doctrine of Triads, or a Trinity' [alt. 'The Trinity of Paganism']. *Southern Presbyterian Review* 8, no. 4 (April 1855): pp. 560-79.

———. 'The Necessity and Importance of Controversy.' *Southern Presbyterian Review* 7, no. 1 (July 1853): pp. 60-74.

———. 'Objections to the Doctrine of the Trinity from the Unity of God, as Taught in Scripture, Answered' [alt. 'Unity of God in Scripture Taught as to imply Plurality']. *Southern Presbyterian Review* 8, no. 3 (January 1855): pp. 305-28.

———. 'Presumptive Arguments for the Trinity.' *Southern Presbyterian Review* 9, no. 1 (July 1855): pp. 1-31.

———. 'The Primitive Revelation of a Divine and Incarnate Saviour Traced in the History and Rites of Bacchus.' *Southern Presbyterian Review* 3, no. 4 (April 1850): pp. 658-71.

———. 'The Province of Reason, Especially in Matters of Religion.' *Southern Presbyterian Review* 7, no. 2 (October 1853): pp. 274-92.

———. 'The Testimony of the Ancient Jews to the Trinity.' *Southern Presbyterian Review* 10, no. 1 (April 1857): pp. 94-105.

———. 'Testimony of the Early Fathers to the Doctrine of the Trinity.' *Southern Presbyterian Review* 9, no. 3 (January 1856): pp. 313-44.

———. 'Testimony of the Reformers to the Doctrine of the Trinity.' *Southern Presbyterian Review* 9, no. 4 (April 1856): pp. 473-91.

———. 'On the Trinity – The Objections and Unreasonableness, Contradiction, and the Human Origin of the Word Trinity' [*alt.* 'A Priori Objections to the Doctrine of the Trinity Considered']. *Southern Presbyterian Review* 8, no. 1 (July 1854): pp. 54-90.

———. 'The Trinity of the Godhead the Doctrine of the Scriptures.' *Southern Presbyterian Review* 11, no. 1 (April 1858): pp. 68-91.

———. 'The Trinity of the Godhead, the Doctrine of the Holy Scriptures, (Continued).' *Southern Presbyterian Review* 11, no. 2 (July 1858): pp. 175-93.

———. 'The Trinity of the Godhead the Doctrine of the Holy Scriptures.' *Southern Presbyterian Review* 14, no. 1 (April 1861): pp. 92-95.

———. 'The Trinity of the Godhead the Doctrine of the Scriptures.' *Southern Presbyterian Review* 14, no. 2 (July 1861): pp. 227-45.

———. *The Unity of the Human Races.* New York: George P. Putnam, 1850.

Thornwell, James Henley. 'A Student's Notes on Theological Lectures delivered by JHT,' part 4. Columbia Seminary Notebooks, Reformed Theological Seminary Library Archives, Jackson, MS.

———. *Collected Writings.* Edited by John B. Adger and John L. Girardeau. 4 vols. Richmond, VA: Presbyterian Committee of Publication, 1871.

———. 'Memoir of Dr Henry.' *Southern Quarterly Review* 3, no. 1 (April 1856): pp. 189-206.

———. 'Report on Slavery.' *Southern Presbyterian Review* 5, no. 3 (January 1852): pp. 379-94.

———. 'Slavery and the Religious Instruction of the Coloured Population.' *Southern Presbyterian Review* 4, no. 1 (July 1850): pp. 105-141.

Townsend, George. *Scriptural Communion with God*. 2 vols. London: Francis & John Rivington, 1849.

Turretin, Francis. *Institutes of Elenctic Theology*. Edited by James T. Dennison Jr. Translated by George Musgrave Giger. 2 vols. Phillipsburg, NJ: P&R Publishing, 1992.

Tustin, Septimus. 'Unpublished Letter from Mr Randolph of Roanoke.' *The Sailors Magazine and Naval Journal* 25, no. 1 (August 1853): pp. 177-79.

Twain, Mark. *Mark Twain's Notebooks & Journals, Volume 2 (1877–1883)*. Edited by Frederick Anderson, Lin Salamo and Bernard L. Stein. Berkley, CA: University of California Press, 1975.

Unitarian Book and Tract Society of Charleston, *Annual Reports Rendered by the Managers of the Charleston Unitarian Book and Tract Society, 1855*. Charleston, SC: Walker & Evans, 1855.

———. *The Twenty-Sixth Annual Report of the Managers of the Unitarian Book and Tract Society*. Charleston: Walker & Burke, 1847.

———. *Twenty-Ninth Report of the Managers of the Charleston Unitarian Book and Tract Society*. Charleston, SC: Walker and James, 1850.

———. *The Two Stand-Points, and the Contrast: A Discourse, Delivered in the Unitarian Church, Charleston SC, and also, an Appendix, Embracing Reports*. Charleston: Walker & Evans, 1854.

———. *What is the Worth of Doctrine? A Sermon Preached at the Anniversary of the Charleston Unitarian Book and Tract Society to which is added The Annual Report of the Directors*. Charleston, SC: Walker & Burke, 1848.

Unitarian Universalist Congregation of Columbia, SC, 'Early Scholarly History.' http://www.uucolumbia.dreamhosters.com/wp-content/uploads/2015/10/Early-Scholarly-History-of-UUFC.pdf.

———. 'Our UUCC History.' http://www.uucolumbia.dreamhosters.com/about-us/our-story/history/.

Vaughn, C. R. 'Theology of Prayer.' *The Union Seminary Magazine* 5 (1893–1894): pp. 296-98.

Warfield, Benjamin Breckinridge. *Calvin and Augustine.* Philadelphia: P&R Publishing, 1956.

Wauchope, George Armstrong. *Writers of South Carolina.* Columbia, SC: The State Co., 1910.

Webb, R. A. *Christian Salvation: Its Doctrine and Experience.* Richmond, VA: Presbyterian Committee of Publication, 1921.

———. 'Evolution Controversy.' *The Life Work of John L. Girardeau, D.D., LL.D.* Edited by George A. Blackburn. Columbia, SC: The State Company, 1916.

———. 'Palmer's Theology of Prayer.' *The Presbyterian Quarterly* 8 (1894): pp. 285-92.

———. *The Reformed Doctrine of Adoption.* Grand Rapids, MI: Eerdmans, 1947.

*Webster, Noah. An American Dictionary of the English Language, Volume 1. New York: S. Converse, 1828.*

*Westminster Confession of Faith.* Glasgow: Free Presbyterian Publications, 1994.

Whaling, Thornton. 'Dr Thornwell as a Theologian.' In *Thornwell Centennial Addresses*, pp. 22-30. Spartanburg, SC: Band and White Printers, 1913.

———. 'The Philosopher. In *The Life Work of John L. Girardeau, D.D., LL.D.,* pp. 285-303. Edited by George A. Blackburn. Columbia, SC: The State Company, 1916.

———. 'The Theologian.' In *The Life Work of John L. Girardeau, D.D., LL.D.,* pp. 304-40. Edited by George A. Blackburn. Columbia, SC: The State Company, 1916.

Wilson, Joseph R. 'Memorial Address.' In *Memorial Addresses Delivered Before the General Assembly of 1886 on the Occasion of the Quarter-Centennial of the Organization of the Southern Assembly in 1861.* Presbyterian Committee of Publication, 1886.

## Secondary Sources

Ahlstrom, Sydney E. *A Religious History of the American People.* New Haven, CT: Yale University Press, 1972.

———. 'Scottish Philosophy and American Theology.' *American Society of Church History* 24 (September 1955): pp. 257-72.

Ayres, Lewis. *Nicea and Its Legacy.* Oxford: Oxford University Press, 2004.

———. '*Nicea and Its Legacy*: An Introduction,' *Harvard Theological Review* 100 (2007): pp. 141-44.

Barnes, Michel René. 'De Régnon Reconsidered.' *Augustinian Studies* 26 (1995): pp. 51-79.

Beliles, Mark A. and Jerry Newcombe. *Doubting Thomas? The Religious Life and Legacy of Thomas Jefferson.* New York: Morgan James, 2014.

Berkhof, Louis. *Systematic Theology.* 2 vols. Grant Rapids, MI: Eerdmans, 1996.

Berry, Stephen R. *Sons of God, An Examination of the Doctrine of Adoption in the Thought of John Lafayette Girardeau.* St. Louis, MO: PCA Historical Center, 1997.

———. *The Southern Presbyterian Diaconate: A Thornwellian Principle Elaborated by John Lafayette Girardeau.* St. Louis, MO: PCA Historical Center, 1997.

Bishop, Charles C. 'The Pro-slavery Argument Reconsidered: James Henley Thornwell, Millennial Abolitionist.' *South Carolina Historical Magazine* 73 (January 1972): pp. 18-36.

Bonnefoy, Yves, ed. *Asian Mythologies.* Chicago: University of Chicago Press, 1993.

Bowers, J. D. *Joseph Priestley and English Unitarianism in America*. University Park, PA: The Pennsylvania State University Press, 2007.

Bozeman, Theodore Dwight. 'James Henley Thornwell: Ancient and Modern.' *Affirmation* 6, no. 2 (1993): pp. 50-71.

———. *Protestants in an Age of Science: The Baconian Ideal and Antebellum Religious Thought*. Chapel Hill: The University of North Carolina Press, 1977.

———. 'Science, Nature, and Society: A New Approach to James Henley Thornwell.' *Journal of Presbyterian History* 50, no. 3 (Fall 1972): pp. 306-25.

Bray, Gerald. *The Doctrine of God*. Leicester: InterVarsity Press, 1993.

———. 'Evangelicals Losing Their Way: The Doctrine of the Trinity.' In *The Compromised Church: The Present Evangelical Crisis*, pp. 53-65. Edited by John Armstrong. Wheaton, IL: Crossway, 1998.

Bruce, Philip Alexander. *History of the University of Virginia, 1819–1919: The Lengthened Shadow of One Man. 5 vols*. New York: The Macmillan Company, 1920.

Buzzard, Anthony. *The Doctrine of the Trinity: Christianity's Self-Inflicted Wound*. Morrow, GA: International Scholars Publications, 1998.

———. *Jesus Was Not a Trinitarian*. Morrow, GA: Restoration Fellowship, 2007.

———. Telephone Interview. 12 June 2015.

Buzzard, Barbara. 'A Review.' http://www.21stcr.org/multimedia/articles/mary_dana_book_review.html.

Calhoun, David B. *The Glory of the Lord Risen Upon It: First Presbyterian Church Columbia, South Carolina 1795–1995*. Columbia, SC: R. L. Bryan, 1994.

———. *Our Southern Zion: Old Columbia Seminary (1828–1927)*. Edinburgh: Banner of Truth, 2012.

———. *Pleading for a Reformation Vision: Life and Selected Writings of William Childs Robinson (1897–1982)*. Edinburgh: Banner of Truth, 2013.

———. 'William Childs Robinson.' In *Confessing Our Hope: Essays Celebrating the Life and Ministry of Morton H. Smith*. Edited by Joseph Pipa Jr. and C. N. Willborn. Taylors, SC: Greenville Presbyterian Theological Seminary, 2004.

Calhoun, Joanne. *The Circular Church: Three Centuries of Charleston History*. Charleston, SC: The History Press, 2008.

Clarke, Erskine. *Dwelling Place: A Plantation Epic*. New Haven: Yale University Press, 2005.

———. *Our Southern Zion: A History of Calvinism in the South Carolina Low Country, 1690–1990*. Tuscaloosa, AL: University of Alabama Press, 1996.

———. 'Southern Nationalism and Columbia Theological Seminary.' *American Presbyterians* 66, no. 2 (Summer 1988): pp. 123-133.

———. *To Count Our Days: A History of Columbia Theological Seminary*. Columbia, SC: University of South Carolina Press, 2019.

———. *Wrestlin' Jacob: A Portrait of Religion in Antebellum Georgia and the Carolina Low Country*. Tuscaloosa, AL: University of Alabama Press, 2000.

Conser, Walter H., Jr. *God and the Natural World: Religion and Science in Antebellum America*. Columbia, SC: University of South Carolina Press, 1993.

Cooke, George Willis. *Unitarianism in America: A History of Its Origin and Development*. Boston: American Unitarian Association, 1902.

Crisp, Oliver. 'John Girardeau: Libertarian Calvinist?' *Journal of Reformed Theology* 8, no. 3 (2014): pp. 284-300.

Davis, Stephen T. *Christian Philosophical Theology.* Oxford: Oxford University Press, 2006.

Douglas, J. D., ed. *The New International Dictionary of the Christian Church.* Grand Rapids, MI: Zondervan, 1978.

Eglinton, James. *Trinity and Organism: Towards a New Reading of Herman Bavinck's Organic Motif.* London: T&T Clark International, 2012.

Eliade, Mircea, ed. *The Encyclopedia of Religion.* Vol. 5. New York: Macmillan Publishing Company, 1987.

Ellis, Brannon. *Calvin, Classical Trinitarianism, and the Aseity of the Son.* Oxford: Oxford University Press, 2012.

Eliot, Alexander. *The Timeless Myths: How Ancient Legends Influence the World Around Us.* New York: Continuum Publishing Company, 1996.

Evans, William Borden. *Imputation and Impartation: Union with Christ in American Reformed Theology.* Eugene, OR: Wipf and Stock, 2009.

Farmer, James Oscar, Jr. *The Metaphysical Confederacy: James Henley Thornwell and the Synthesis of Southern Values.* Macon, GA: Mercer University Press, 1986.

Fairbairn, Donald. *Life in the Trinity: An Introduction to Theology with the Help of the Church Fathers.* Downers Grove, IL: IVP Academic, 2009.

Ferguson, Sinclair. 'Reformed Doctrine of Sonship.' In *Pulpit and People: Essays in Honour of William Still,* pp. 81-88. Edited by Nigel M. De S. Cameron and Sinclair B. Ferguson. Edinburgh: Rutherford House, 1986.

Ferguson, Sinclair B., David F. Wright, and J. I. Packer, eds. *New Dictionary of Theology.* Downers Grove, IL: InterVarsity Press, 1988.

Ford, Lacy K., Jr. *Origins of Southern Radicalism: The South Carolina Upcountry 1800–1860*. Oxford: Oxford University Press, 1988.

Fortson, Donald, III. *The Presbyterian Creed: A Confessional Tradition in America, 1729–1870*. Eugene, OR: Wipf and Stock, 2009.

Foster, Mary Preston. *Charleston: A Historic Walking Tour*. Charleston, SC: Arcadia Publishing, 2005.

Fox-Genovese, Elizabeth and Eugene D. Genovese. *The Mind of the Master Class: History and Faith in the Southern Slaveholders' Worldview*. New York: Cambridge University Press, 2005.

Frank, Lisa Tendrich. *Women in the American Civil War*. Vol. 1. Santa Barbara, CA: ABC-CLIO, Inc., 2008.

Freehling, William W. 'James Henley Thornwell's Mysterious Antislavery Moment.' *The Journal of Southern History* 57, no. 3 (August 1991): pp. 383-406.

Garber, Paul Leslie. 'A Centennial Appraisal of James Henley Thornwell.' In *A Miscellany of American Christianity*, pp. 95-137. Edited by Stuart C. Henry. Durham, NC: Duke University Press, 1963.

———. 'James Henley Thornwell: Presbyterian Defender of the Old South.' *Union Seminary Review* 54, no. 2 (February 1943): pp. 93-116.

Genovese, Eugene D. *The Southern Front: History and Politics in the Cultural War*. Columbia, MO: University of Missouri Press, 1995.

Goodwin, Thomas and Benjamin Palmer. *What Happens When I Pray?* and *Profiting from Prayer: An abridgement and rewrite of the 'Theology of Prayer' by B. M. Palmer (1818–1902), together with an abridged rewrite of 'The Return of Prayers' by Thomas Goodwin (1600–1680)*. Prepared by N. R. Needham and David Harman. London: Grace Publications Trust, 1997.

Green, Erwin Luther. *A History of the University of South Carolina*. Columbia, SC: The State Company, 1916.

Greenwood, Andrea and Mark W. Harris. *An Introduction to the Unitarian and Universalist Traditions*. Cambridge: Cambridge University Press, 2011.

Grenz, Stanley J. *Rediscovering the Triune God: The Trinity in Contemporary Theology*. Minneapolis: Fortress Press, 2004.

Gunton, Colin. *Father, Son and Holy Spirit: Essays Toward a Fully Trinitarian Theology*. Edited by Colin E. Gunton. London: T&T Clark, 2003.

———. *The One, the Three and the Many: God, Creation and the Culture of Modernity*. Oxford: Clarendon Press, 1993.

———. *The Promise of Trinitarian Theology*. 2nd ed. Edinburgh: T&T Clark, 1997.

Hastings, James, ed. *Encyclopaedia of Religion and Ethics*. Edinburgh: T&T Clark, 1922.

Hill, Samuel S., ed. *Encyclopedia of Religion in the South*. Macon, GA: Mercer University Press, 1984.

Himes, Charles F. *Life and Times of Judge Thomas Cooper*. Carlisle, PA: Himes Estate, 1918.

Holifield, E. Brooks. *The Gentlemen Theologians: American Theology in Southern Culture*. Durham, NC: Duke University Press, 1978.

———. 'Mercersburg, Princeton, and the South: The Sacramental Controversy in the Nineteenth Century.' *Journal of Presbyterian History* 54 (1976): pp. 238-57.

Hollis, Daniel W. 'Thornwell and the Status Quo.' In *University of South Carolina*. 2 vols. Columbia, SC: University of South Carolina Press, 1951–1956.

Holmes, Stephen R. *The Quest for the Trinity: The Doctrine of God in Scripture, History and Modernity*. Downers Grove, IL: InterVarsity Press, 2012.

Hoole, William Stanley. 'The Gilmans and the Southern Rose.' *North Carolina Historical Review* 11 (1934): pp. 116-28.

Horton, Michael S. *Covenant and Salvation: Union with Christ.* Louisville: Westminster John Knox, 2007.

Hovenkamp, Herbert. *Science and Religion in America: 1800–1860.* Philadelphia: University of Pennsylvania Press, 1978.

Howe, Daniel W. 'A Massachusetts Yankee in Senator Calhoun's Court: Samuel Gilman in South Carolina.' *The New England Quarterly* 44, no. 2 (1975): pp. 197-220.

Hughes, Richard T. 'A Civic Theology for the South: The Case of Benjamin M. Palmer.' *Journal of Church and State* 25 (1983): pp. 447-67.

Jenkins, Thomas E. *The Character of God: Recovering the Lost Literary Power of American Protestantism.* Oxford: Oxford University Press, 1997.

Jenson, Robert W. *Systematic Theology.* Vol. 1, *The Triune God.* Oxford: Oxford University Press, 1997.

Juergensmeyer, Mark and Wade Clark Roof, eds. *Encyclopedia of Global Religion.* Vol. 1. Santa Barbara, CA: University of California, 2012.

Johnson, Steven. *The Invention of Air: A Story of Science, Faith, Revolution, and the Birth of America.* New York: Riverhead Books, 2008.

Kay, Brian. *Trinitarian Spirituality: John Owen and the Doctrine of God in Western Devotion.* Milton Keynes, UK: Paternoster, 2007.

Kelly, Douglas F. 'Adoption: An Underdeveloped Heritage of the Westminster Standards.' *The Reformed Theological Review* 52, no. 3 (Sept.–Dec. 1993): pp. 110-20.

———. *If God Already Knows, Why Pray?* Fearn, Scotland: Christian Focus Publications, 1996.

———. 'Prayer and Union with Christ.' *Scottish Bulletin of Evangelical Theology* 8 (1990): pp. 109-27.

———. *Preachers with Power: Four Stalwarts of the South.* Edinburgh: Banner of Truth, 1992.

———. 'Robert Lewis Dabney.' In *Reformed Theology in America: A History of Its Modern Development*, edited by David F. Wells, pp. 211-236. Grand Rapids, MI: Baker Books, 1997.

———. *Systematic Theology.* Vol. 1, *Grounded in Holy Scripture and Understood in the Light of the Church; The God Who Is: The Holy Trinity.* Fearn, Scotland: Mentor, 2008.

———. *Systematic Theology.* Vol. 2, *Grounded in Holy Scripture and Understood in the Light of the Church; The Beauty of Christ: A Trinitarian Vision.* Fearn, Scotland: Mentor, 2014.

Kelly, J. N. D., *Early Christian Doctrines: Revised Edition* (New York: Harper Collins Publishers, 1978).

LaMotte, Louis C. *Colored Light: The Story of the Influence of Columbia Theological Seminary 1828–1936.* Richmond, VA: Presbyterian Committee of Publication, 1937.

Leftow, Brian. 'Modes without Modalism.' In *Persons: Human and Divine*, pp. 357-75. Edited by Peter van Inwagen and Dean Zimmerman. Oxford: Oxford University Press, 2007.

Leith, John H. 'James Henley Thornwell and the Shaping of the Reformed Tradition in the South.' In *Probing the Reformed Tradition*, pp. 424-47. Edited by Elsie Anne McKee and Brian G. Armstrong. Louisville: John Knox Press, 1989.

Leithart, Peter J. *Traces of the Trinity: Signs of God in Creation and Human Experience.* Grand Rapids, MI: Brazos Press, 2015.

Letham, Robert. *The Holy Trinity In Scripture, History, Theology, and Worship.* Phillipsburg, NJ: P&R Publishing, 2004.

———. *Through Western Eyes, Eastern Orthodoxy: A Reformed Perspective.* Fearn, Scotland: Mentor, 2007.

Lyall, Francis. 'Grotius, Hugo (1583–1645).' In *New Dictionary of Theology*. Edited by Sinclair B. Ferguson, David F. Wright and J. I. Packer. Leicester: InterVarsity Press, 1988.

Macleod, John. *Scottish Theology in Relation to Church History*. Edinburgh: Publication Committee of the Free Church of Scotland, 1943.

Macaulay, John Allen. *Unitarianism in the Antebellum South*. Tuscaloosa, AL: University of Alabama, 2001.

Maclear, J. F. 'Thomas Smyth, Frederick Douglass, and the Belfast Antislavery Campaign.' *The South Carolina Historical Magazine* 80, no. 4 (October 1979): pp. 286-97.

Maddex, Jack P. 'The Collected Writings of James Henley Thornwell, D.D., LL.D.' *American Presbyterians* 66, no. 4 (1988): pp. 264-68.

———. 'From Theocracy to Spirituality: The Southern Presbyterian Reversal on Church and State.' *Journal of Presbyterian History* (Winter 1976): pp. 438-57.

Malone, Dumas. *The Public Life of Thomas Cooper*. New Haven, CT: Yale University Press, 1926.

Marsden, George M. 'Scotland and Philadelphia: Common Sense Philosophy from Jefferson to Westminster.' *Reformed Theological Journal* 29 (1979): pp. 8-12.

Matheson, Donald S. *History of First Presbyterian Church, Cheraw, S.C.* 1943.

McGrath, Alister. 'The Doctrine of the Trinity: An Evangelical Reflection.' In *God the Holy Trinity: Reflections on Christian Faith and Practice*, pp. 17-35. Edited by Timothy George. Grand Rapids, MI: Baker Academic, 2006.

Munoz, Vincent Phillip. *God and the Founders: Madison, Washington, and Jefferson*. Cambridge: Cambridge University Press, 2009.

Needham, N. R. *2000 Years of Christ's Power, Part One: The Age of the Early Church Fathers*. London: Grace Publications Trust, 1997.

————. *2000 Years of Christ's Power, Part Three: Renaissance and Reformation*. London: Grace Publications Trust, 2004.

————. 'Christ Ascended for Us – "Jesus' Ascended Humanity and Ours."' *Evangel* 25.2 (Summer 2007): pp. 42-47.

Newbigin, Lesslie. *The Open Secret*. Grand Rapids, MI: Eerdmans, 1995.

O'Brien, Michael. *Conjectures of Order: Intellectual Life and the American South, 1810–1860*. 2 vols. Chapel Hill, NC: University of North Carolina Press, 2004.

O'Connor, Thomas H. *The Athens of America: Boston 1825–1845*. Boston, MA: University of Massachusetts Press, 2006.

Old, Hughes Oliphant. *The Reading and Preaching of Scriptures in the Worship of the Christian Church*. Vol. 6, *The Modern Age*. Grand Rapids, MI: Eerdmans, 2007.

'Overture 43: Pursuing Racial Reconciliation and the Advance of the Gospel.' *44th General Assembly of the Presbyterian Church of America*. http://www.pcahistory.org/ga/actions/44thGA_2016_Actions.pdf

Packer, J. I. 'A Puritan Perspective: Trinitarian Godliness according to John Owen.' In *God the Holy Trinity*, edited by Timothy George. Grand Rapids, MI: Baker Academic, 2006.

Pannenberg, Wolfhart. *Systematic Theology, Volume 1*. Grand Rapids, MI: Eerdmans, 1991.

Parry, Robin. *Worshiping Trinity: Coming Back to the Heart of Worship*. Eugene, OR: Cascade Books, 2012.

Pasquarello, Michael. *Christian Preaching: A Trinitarian Theology of Proclamation*. Grand Rapids, MI: Baker, 2006.

Pauw, Amy Plantinga. *The Supreme Harmony of All: The Trinitarian Theology of Jonathan Edwards*. Grand Rapids, MI: Eerdmans, 2002.

Philips, J. Davison. *Time of Blessing, Time of Hope: Columbia Theological Seminary, 1976–1986*. Decatur, GA: Columbia Theological Seminary, 1994.

Plantinga, Cornelius. 'Social Trinity and Tritheism.' In *Trinity, Incarnation, and Atonement: Philosophical and Theological Essays*, pp. 21-47. Edited by Ronald J. Feenstra and Cornelius Plantinga. Notre Dame, IN: University of Notre Dame Press, 1990.

Powell, William S., ed. *Dictionary of North Carolina Biography: Volume 2 D–G*. Chapel Hill, NC: The University of North Carolina Press, 1986.

Porter, Barbara Nevling, ed. *One God or Many? Concepts of Divinity in the Ancient World*. Bethesda, MD: CDL Press, 2000.

Prince, Harold B. *A Presbyterian Bibliography*. Metuchen, NJ: The Scarecrow Press, 1983.

Quicke, Michael. *Preaching as Worship: An Integrative Approach to Formation in Your Church*. Grand Rapids, MI: Baker, 2011.

———. 'Trinity.' In *The New Interpreter's Handbook of Preaching*. Nashville, TN: Abingdon, 2008.

Rankin, W. Duncan. *James Henley Thornwell and the Westminster Confession of Faith*. Greenville, SC: A Press, 1986.

Rankin, W. Duncan et al. *An Index to the Southern Presbyterian Review*. Jackson, MS: Reformed Theological Seminary, 1995.

Reeves, Michael. *Delighting in the Trinity: An Introduction to the Christian Faith*. Downers Grove, IL: IVP Academic, 2012.

'Report on Race Relations.' *213th Meeting of the General Synod of the Associate Reformed Presbyterian Church*. http://theaquilareport.com/arp-synod-approves-report-on-race-relations/.

Richards, J. McDowell, ed. *Soli Deo Gloria, New Testament Studies in Honor of William Childs Robinson*. Richmond, VA: John Knox Press, 1968.

Richards, J. McDowell. *As I Remember It: Columbia Seminary 1932–1971*. Decatur, GA: CTS Press, 1985.

Robinson, William C. *Columbia Theological Seminary and the Southern Presbyterian Church, 1831–1931: A Study in Church History, Presbyterian Polity, Missionary Enterprise, and Religious Thought*. Decatur, GA: Dennis Lindsey Printing Company, 1931.

Sanders, Fred. *The Deep Things of God: How the Trinity Changes Everything*. Wheaton, IL: Crossway, 2010.

————. 'The Trinity.' In *Mapping Modern Theology: A Thematic and Historical Introduction*, pp. 21-45. Edited by Kelly M. Kapic and Bruce L. McCormack. Grand Rapids, MI: Baker Academic, 2012.

Schmidt, George P. *The Old Time College President*. New York: Columbia University Press, 1930.

Schneider, Herbert A. *A History of American Philosophy*. New York: Columbia University Press, 1946.

Schweitzer, William M. *God Is a Communicative Being: Divine Communicativeness and Harmony in the Theology of Jonathan Edwards*. London: T&T Clark, 2012.

Shuster, Marguerite. 'Preaching the Trinity: A Preliminary Investigation.' In *The Trinity: An Interdisciplinary Symposium on the Trinity*, edited by Stephen Davis. Oxford: Oxford University Press, 1999.

Sloan, Douglas. *The Scottish Enlightenment and the American College Ideal*. New York: Teachers College Press, 1971.

Smith, Christian and Melinda Lundquist Denton. *Soul Searching: The Religious and Spiritual Lives of American Teenagers*. Oxford: Oxford University Press, 2005.

Smith, Morton H. Preface to *Election and Reprobation*, by James Henley Thornwell. Jackson, MS: Presbyterian Reformation Society, 1961.

———. *Studies in Southern Presbyterian Theology*. Phillipsburg, NJ: P&R Publishing, 1962.

Smith, Shelton H. *In His Image, But . . . Racism in Southern Religion, 1780–1910*. Durham, NC: Duke University Press, 1972.

———. 'The Church and the Social Order in the Old South as Interpreted by James H. Thornwell.' *Church History* 7, no. 2 (June 1938): pp. 115-24.

Spettel, Sara and Mark Donald White, 'The Portrayal of J. Marion Sims' Controversial Surgical Legacy.' *The Journal of Urology* 185 (June 2011): pp. 2424-27.

Studebaker, Steven M. *Jonathan Edwards' Social Augustinian Trinitarianism in Historical and Contemporary Perspectives*. Piscataway, NJ: Gorgias Press, 2008.

Sundquist, Linda A. *The Poetess of Song: The Life of Mary Shindler*. Livermore, CA: Wingspan Press, 2006.

———. Telephone Interview. 17 June 2015

Ter Haar, Berand J. *Ritual & Mythology of the Chinese Triads: Creating an Identity*. Leiden: Brill, 1998.

Thompson, Ernest Trice. *Presbyterians in the South*. 3 vols. Richmond: John Knox Press, 1963–1973.

Tindall, George Brown and David E. Shi. *America: A Narrative History*. 4th ed. New York: W. W. Norton & Company, 1996.

Torrance, James B. *Worship, Community & The Triune God of Grace*. Downers Grove, IL: InterVarsity Press, 1996.

Torrance, Thomas F. *The Christian Doctrine of God, One Being Three Persons*. Edinburgh: T&T Clark, 1996.

———. *The Ground and Grammar of Theology*. Charlottesville, VA: The University Press of Virginia, 1980.

———. *The Trinitarian Faith*. Edinburgh: T&T Clark, 1995.

Turner, Arlin. *George W. Cable: A Biography*. Durham, NC: Duke University Press, 1956.

Vandervelde, L. G. *The Presbyterian Church in the Federal Union, 1860–1869*. Cambridge, MA: 1932.

Ware, Bruce A. *Father, Son, & Holy Spirit: Relationships, Roles & Relevance*. Wheaton, IL: Crossway Books, 2005.

Waugh, Barry. 'A Guide to the *Complete Works of Rev. Thomas Smyth, D.D.*' http://pcahistory.org/findingaids/smyth/Waugh_2012_SmythGuide.pdf.

Wells, John Miller. *Southern Presbyterian Worthies*. Richmond, VA: Presbyterian Committee of Publication, 1936.

Westerkamp, Marilyn J. 'James Henley Thornwell, Pro Slavery Spokesman Within a Calvinist Faith.' *South Carolina Historical Magazine* 87, no. 1 (January 1986): pp. 49-64.

White, Henry Alexander. *Southern Presbyterian Leaders*. New York: The Neale Publishing Company, 1911.

White, James R. *The Forgotten Trinity: Recovering the Heart of Christian Belief*. Minneapolis, MN: Bethany House Publishers, 1998.

Wills, Gary. *Inventing America: Jefferson's Declaration of Independence*. Garden City, NY: Doubleday & Co., 1978.

Woolley, Paul. 'A Study in Church History.' *Evangelical Quarterly* (January 1932): pp. 84-89.

## Dissertations and Theses

Bozeman, Theodore Dwight. 'Baconianism and the Bible: The Baconian Ideal in Ante-Bellum American Presbyterian Thought.' PhD diss., Duke University, 1974.

Bradenburg, Walter Perry. 'The Place of James Henley Thornwell in the History of Education in South Carolina.' MA thesis, University of South Carolina, 1939.

Clarke, Erskine. 'Thomas Smyth: Moderate of the Old South.' ThD diss., Union Theological Seminary (VA), 2001.

Doescher, Kirsten Lynn Alworth. 'A Home for a Seminary: The Columbia Theological Seminary and the Hall's House.' MA thesis, University of South Carolina, 2001.

Dubose, Curtis W. 'A Critical Analysis of the Theology Behind James Henley Thornwell's Support of the Institution of Slavery in the Old South.' ThM thesis, Reformed Theological Seminary, 1999.

Duncan, Christopher M. 'Benjamin Morgan Palmer: Southern Presbyterian Divine.' PhD diss., Auburn University, 2008.

Duncan, J. Ligon, III. 'Common Sense and American Presbyterianism: An Evaluation of the Impact of Scottish Realism on Princeton and the South.' MTh thesis, Covenant Theological Seminary, 1987.

Eubank, Wayne Carter. 'Benjamin Morgan Palmer, A Southern Divine.' PhD diss., Louisiana State University, 1943.

Garber, Paul Leslie. 'The Religious Thought of James Henley Thornwell.' PhD diss., Duke University, 1939.

Garth, David Kinney. 'The Influence of Scottish Common Sense Philosophy on the Theology of James Henley Thornwell and Robert Lewis Dabney.' PhD diss., Union Theological Seminary, 1979.

Hickey, Doralyn J. 'Benjamin Morgan Palmer: Churchman of the Old South.' PhD diss., Duke University, 1962.

Jordan, Edward Thomas. 'The Ministry of the Holy Spirit in the Preparation and Delivery of Sermons: As Evidenced by Four Representative Southern Presbyterian Exemplars' DMin thesis, Gordon-Conwell Theological Seminary, 2008.

Kolman, Elma Leona. 'The History of the Presbyterian Church in New Orleans (1817–1860),' MA thesis, Tulane University, 1939.

Loring, Eduard N. 'Charles C. Jones: Missionary to Plantation Slaves, 1831–1847.' PhD diss., Vanderbilt University, 1976.

McCormick, Lawrence Ray. 'James Henley Thornwell and the Theological Justification of Slavery: A Study in the Development of Proslavery Ideology.' PhD diss., University of Southern California, 1992.

Sheppard, Craig A. 'The Compatibility of the Doctrine of Election with the Free Offer of the Gospel in James Henley Thornwell.' ThM thesis, Reformed Theological Seminary, 1997.

———. 'A Theological Evaluation and Comparison of the Atonement and Justification in the Writings of James Henley Thornwell (1812–1862) and John Lafayette Girardeau (1825–1898).' PhD diss., University of Wales, 2008.

Trumper, Tim J. R. 'An Historical Study of Adoption in the Calvinistic Tradition.' PhD diss., University of Edinburgh, 2001.

Vance, John Lloyd. 'The Ecclesiology of James Henley Thornwell: An Old South Presbyterian Theologian.' PhD diss., Drew University, 1990.

Watkin, Robert N., Jr. 'The Forming of the Southern Presbyterian Minister: From Calvin to the American Civil War.' PhD diss., Vanderbilt University, 1969.

Willborn, C. N. 'John L. Girardeau (1825–98), Pastor to Slaves and Theologian of Causes: A Historical Account of the Life and Contributions of an Often Neglected Southern Presbyterian Minister and Theologian.' PhD diss., Westminster Theological Seminary, 2003.

Wingard, Brian T. '"As the Lord Puts Words in Her Mouth": The Supremacy of Scripture in the Ecclesiology of James Henley Thornwell and Its Influence Upon the Presbyterian Churches of the South.' PhD diss., Westminster Theological Seminary, 1992.

# Christian Focus Publications

Our mission statement –

STAYING FAITHFUL

In dependence upon God we seek to impact the world through literature faithful to His infallible Word, the Bible. Our aim is to ensure that the Lord Jesus Christ is presented as the only hope to obtain forgiveness of sin, live a useful life and look forward to heaven with Him.

Our books are published in four imprints:

## CHRISTIAN FOCUS

Popular works including biographies, commentaries, basic doctrine and Christian living.

## CHRISTIAN HERITAGE

Books representing some of the best material from the rich heritage of the church.

## MENTOR

Books written at a level suitable for Bible College and seminary students, pastors, and other serious readers. The imprint includes commentaries, doctrinal studies, examination of current issues and church history.

## CF4•K

Children's books for quality Bible teaching and for all age groups: Sunday school curriculum, puzzle and activity books; personal and family devotional titles, biographies and inspirational stories – because you are never too young to know Jesus!

Christian Focus Publications Ltd,
Geanies House, Fearn, Ross-shire,
IV20 1TW, Scotland, United Kingdom.
www.christianfocus.com